COGAT®
GRADE 1 AND 2

Test Prep *with*
Two Practice Tests

Level 7 & Level 8

Savant Test Prep™

www.SavantPrep.com

Please leave a review for this book!

Thank you for purchasing this resource.

Please take a moment to leave a
review on the website where you purchased this.

TABLE OF CONTENTS

INTRODUCTION

COGAT® GENERAL INFORMATION

- COGAT® stands for Cognitive Abilities Test®.
- The test measures students' reasoning skills and problem-solving skills.
- It provides educators with an overall assessment of students' academic strengths and weaknesses.
- The COGAT® is commonly used as a screener for gifted and talented programs.
    - Gifted and Talented (G&T) selection sometimes requires a teacher recommendation as well.
- The test is usually administered in a group setting.
- A teacher (or other school associate) administers the test, reading the directions.
- Please check with your school/testing site regarding its testing procedures, as these may differ.

COGAT® LEVEL 7 AND LEVEL 8 FORMAT

- Students in first grade take the COGAT® Level 7. Students in second grade take the COGAT® Level 8.
- The first grade test has 136 questions. The second grade test has 154 questions.
- The test is divided into 3 main parts, each called a "Battery." Each Battery has three question types.
- See the chart below for the number of questions for 1st grade (1st) and 2nd grade (2nd).

VERBAL BATTERY	NON-VERBAL BATTERY	QUANTITATIVE BATTERY
1st: Picture Analogies: 16 Questions 2nd: Picture Analogies: 18 Questions	1st: Figure Analogies: 16 Questions 2nd: Figure Analogies: 18 Questions	1st: Number Puzzles: 12 Questions 2nd: Number Puzzles: 14 Questions
1st: Picture Classification: 16 Questions 2nd: Picture Classification: 18 Questions	1st: Figure Classification: 16 Questions 2nd: Figure Classification: 18 Questions	1st: Number Series: 16 Questions 2nd: Number Series: 18 Questions
1st: Sentence Completion: 16 Questions 2nd: Sentence Completion: 18 Questions	1st: Paper Folding: 12 Questions 2nd: Paper Folding: 14 Questions	1st: Number Analogies: 16 Questions 2nd: Number Analogies: 18 Questions

- Often, schools administer one Battery per day, allowing approximately 45 minutes per Battery.
- Students have around 15 minutes to complete each question type (for example, students would have around 15 minutes to complete Picture Analogies).
- See the following pages for examples and explanations of each question type.

COGAT® SCORING

- Students receive points for correct answers. Points are not deducted for incorrect answers. (Therefore, students should at least guess versus leaving a question blank.)
- In general, schools have a "cut-off" COGAT® score, which they consider together with additional criteria, for gifted & talented acceptance. This varies by school.
- This score is usually at least 98%. (However, some schools accept scores that are 95% or even 85%.)
- A score of 98% means that your child scored as well as, or better than, 98% of those in his/her testing group.
- COGAT® scores are available for the entire test and can be broken down by Battery.
- Depending on the school/program, such a "cut-off" score may only be required on one or two of the Batteries (and not on the test overall).
- It is essential to check with your school/program for their acceptance procedures.
- The COGAT® Practice Tests in this book can not yield these percentiles because they have not been given to a large enough group of students to produce an accurate comparison/calculation.)

HOW TO USE THIS BOOK

1. Go over the Question Examples together with your child. These begin on the next page.

2. Do Practice Test 1 (Workbook Format).
    - Do these questions with your child, especially if this is your child's first exposure to COGAT®-prep questions. These questions have a "workbook format," meaning they are meant to be done together.
    - Do not assign a time limit.
    - Talk about what the question is asking your child to do.
    - Questions progress in difficulty. (The first few questions are quite simple.)
    - Go over the answers using the Answer Key.
    - For questions missed, go over the answers again, discussing what makes the correct answer better than the other choices.

3. Do Practice Test 2.
    - If your child progressed easily through Practice Test 1, see how well they can do without your help.
    - If your child needed assistance with much of Practice Test 1, then continue to assist your child.
    - If you wish to assign a time limit, assign around 15 minutes per question type.
    - Go over the answers using the Answer Key.
    - For questions missed, go over the answers again, discussing what makes the correct answer better than the other choices.

4. **Need more practice?**

    - **Get 300+ new questions per book.**   • **Check out Savant Test Prep™ books on Amazon®.**

TEST-TAKING TIPS

- Ensure your child listens carefully to the directions, especially in the Sentence Completion section.
- Make sure (s)he does not rush through questions. (There is no prize for finishing first!) Tell your child to look carefully at the question. Then, tell your child to look at each answer choice before marking his/her answer.
    - If you notice your child continuing to rush through the questions, tell him/her to point to each part of the question. Then, point to each answer choice.
- If (s)he does not know the answer, then use the process of elimination. Cross out any answer choices which are clearly incorrect, then choose from those remaining.
- This tip/suggestion is entirely at your discretion. You may wish to offer some sort of special motivation to encourage your child to do his/her best. An extra incentive of, for example, an art set, a building block set, or a special outing can go a long way in motivating young learners!
- The night before testing, make sure your child gets enough sleep, without interruptions. (Think about the difference in **your** brain function with a good night's sleep vs. without. The same goes for your child's.)
- The morning before the test, ensure your child eats a healthy breakfast with protein and complex carbs. Do not let them eat sugar, chocolate, etc.
- If you can choose the time your child will take the test (for example, if (s)he will take the test individually, instead of at school with a group), opt for a morning testing session, when your child will be most alert.

QUESTION EXAMPLES

- Here is an overview of the COGAT® question types.
- This section has <u>examples</u> to introduce your child to test concepts.
    - Do these together with your child.
- Below the questions are explanations for parents.

1. PICTURE ANALOGIES (VERBAL BATTERY)

• **Directions (read to child):** The pictures in the top boxes go together in some way. Look at the bottom boxes. One box is empty. Look at the row of pictures next to the boxes. These are the answer choices. Which one of these choices goes with the picture in the bottom box like the pictures in the top boxes go together?

• **Explanation (for parents):** Your child must figure out how the images in the top set of boxes are related and belong together. Then, (s)he must figure out which answer choice would go with the bottom left image so that the bottom set would have the same analogous relationship as the top set. (The small arrows demonstrate that the images go together.)

• **Strategy 1:** Define a "rule" to describe how the top set belongs together. Then, take this "rule" and use it with the bottom picture. Look at the answer choices, and figure out which answer would make the bottom set follow your "rule."

• **Using the above question as an example, say to your child:**
In this question, we see a spider and a web. A spider's home is its web. A rule would be, "what is in the first box has its home in the second box." On the bottom we see a bird. Let's try the answer choices with our rule. A bird's home is not a flower, bench, or another bird. A nest is correct because it's a bird's home.

• **Strategy 2:** Try to come up with a sentence to describe how the top set belongs together. Then, use this sentence with the bottom picture. Look at the answer choices, and figure out which answer would make the sentence work with this bottom set. With both strategies, if more than one answer choice works, then you need a more specific rule/sentence.

• The examples on the next page outline some of the logic used in analogy questions. While the COGAT® uses pictures (not words) at this level in verbal analogies, this will still help familiarize your child with analogy logic.

• **Directions (read to child):** I am going to read you a question. The words go together in some way. One word is missing. Next, I will read you the answer choices. Let's figure out which one is the missing word. (Parent note: the answer and logic are below the question.)

Question	Answer Choices			
1. Spider -is to- Web as Bird -is to- ? *Answer - Nest (Animal: Animal's Home)*	Flower	Bench	Nest	Bird
2. Acorns -are to- Squirrel as Seeds -are to- ? *Answer - Bird (Animal: Animal's Food)*	Grass	Bird	Fish	Snake
3. Calf -is to- Cow as Cub -is to- ? *Answer - Tiger (Animal Baby: Animal Adult)*	Tiger	Horse	Goose	Bull
4. Lion -is to- Fur as Snake -is to- ? *Answer - Scales (Animal: Animal's Covering)*	Lizard	Hair	Fangs	Scales
5. Happy -is to- Sad as Wet -is to- ? *Answer - Dry (Opposites)*	Damp	Clean	Water	Dry
6. Tiger -is to- Cheetah as Butterfly -is to- ? *Answer - Moth (Similar: Similar (Flying Insects))*	Bird	Bat	Moth	Jaguar
7. Flower -is to- Bouquet as Kernel -is to- ? *Answer - Corn Cob (Part: Whole)*	Snack	Plant	Corn Cob	Crop
8. Ship -is to- Port as Car -is to- ? *Answer - Garage (Object: Location)*	Truck	Garage	Marina	Wheel
9. Pencil -is to- Paper as Paint -is to- ? *Answer - Wall (Object: Object Used With)*	Wall	Color	Red	Light
10. Lumber -is to- Fence as Paper -is to- ? *Answer - Book (Object: Product That Object Is Put Together To Make)*	Log	Branch	Tree	Book
11. Cheese -is to- Refrigerator as Ice -is to- ? *Answer - Freezer (Object: Item Used to Store/Hold Object)*	Snow	Toaster	Freezer	Cube
12. Box -is to- Cube as Globe -is to- ? *Answer - Sphere (Object: Similar Shape)*	Prism	Sphere	Oval	Pentagon
13. Straw -is to- Juice as Spoon -is to- ? *Answer - Cereal (Utensil: Object Utensil Is Used With)*	Cereal	Salad	Steak	Sandwich
14. Egg -is to- Chicken as Milk -is to- ? *Answer - Cow (Food/Drink: Source of Food/Drink)*	Chick	Cheese	Rooster	Cow
15. Ambulance -is to- Paramedic as Tractor -is to- ? *Answer - Farmer (Vehicle: User)*	Doctor	Teacher	Scientist	Farmer
16. Doctor -is to- Stethoscope as Carpenter -is to- ? *Answer - Hammer (Worker Who Uses Object: Object)*	Boot	Builder	Cabinet	Hammer

2. PICTURE CLASSIFICATION (VERBAL BATTERY)

• **Directions (read to child):** The top row shows three pictures that are alike in some way. Look at the bottom row. There are four pictures. Which picture in the bottom row goes best with the pictures in the top row?

• **Explanation (for parents):** Together with your child, try to figure out a "rule" describing how the top pictures are alike and belong together. Then, apply the "rule" to each answer choice to determine which one follows it. If your child finds that more than one choice follows the rule, then a more specific rule is needed.

• **Using the above question as an example, say to your child:** In the top row, we see a ladybug, a party hat, and a dog. What do these have in common? It may be hard to see at first. Let's have another look. Each of these has spots. This is how they are alike. The only answer choice that has spots is the cheetah.

• **Tip:** You can help your child improve classification using items you see in everyday life or in books.

• The classification examples on the next page outline some of the logic used in classification questions. While the COGAT® uses pictures (not words) at this level in verbal analogies, this will still help familiarize your child with classification logic.

Good job! Let's do some more!

Caleb

• **Directions (read to child):** I am going to read you a group of words. The words go together in some way. Let's figure out how the words go together. Then, I will read you another group of words. Let's figure out which one from this group goes best with the words in the first group.

(Parent note: the answer and logic are below the question.)

Question				Answer Choices			
Question				Answer Choices			

1. Cave   Hive   Web | Spider   Nest   Vet   Bat
Answer - Nest (Animal Homes)

2. Butterfly   Ant   Bee | Worm   Horse   Bird   Dragonfly
Answer - Dragonfly (Animal Types (Insects))

3. Forest   Jungle   Desert | Tree   Valley   Rainforest   City
Answer - Rainforest (Habitats)

4. Lemon   Grape   Apple | Strawberry   Farm   Sweet   Lettuce
Answer - Strawberry (Kinds of Food (Fruit))

5. Scientist   Nurse   Detective | Superhero   Teenager   Pilot   Fairy
Answer - Pilot (Jobs)

6. Sock   Skate   Boot | Slipper   Cap   Mitten   Toe
Answer - Slipper (Objects Worn On Feet)

7. Hot Air Balloon   Jet   Helicopter | Ship   Airport   Bird   Airplane
Answer - Airplane (Vehicles for Air Travel)

8. Ruler   Measuring Tape   Scale | Thermometer   TV   Pen   Number
Answer - Thermometer (Object Use (Used to Measure))

9. Pillow   Blanket   Mattress | Towel   Chair   Sheet   Table
Answer - Sheet (Object Location (Found on Beds))

10. Fire   Sun   Stove | Cookie   Toaster   Beach   Camp
Answer - Toaster (Object Characteristics (Provide Heat))

11. Planet   Ball   Globe | Country   Goal   Bubble   Racetrack
Answer - Bubble (Object Shape (Spherical))

3. SENTENCE COMPLETION (VERBAL BATTERY)

• **Directions (read to child):** Listen to the question, then choose the best answer.

Which one of these shows a pair?

• **Explanation (for parents):** Unlike Picture Analogies and Picture Classification, Sentence Completion questions have different directions. The above example is a very simple one. (The answer is C.) The questions in this book's two practice tests will be more challenging. Make sure your child listens carefully to these questions. Test administrators will not repeat the questions.

• If listening is challenging for your child - tell him/her to repeat the directions back to you. Remind your child to listen to the entire question. (Some children will stop listening if they think they already know the answer.) Tell him/her to pay special attention to "negative" words like "not" or "no." (The two practice tests include questions like this.)

4. FIGURE ANALOGIES (NON-VERBAL BATTERY)

• **Directions (read to child):** The pictures in the top boxes go together in some way. Look at the bottom boxes. One box is empty. Look at the row of pictures next to the boxes. These are the answer choices. Which one of these choices goes with the picture in the bottom box like the pictures in the top box go together?

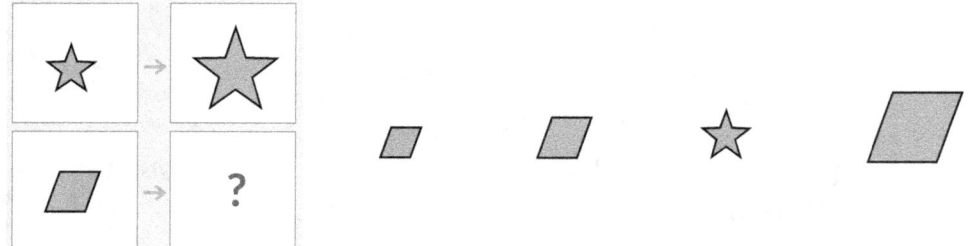

• **Using this question as an example, say to your child:** In the top left box, we see 1 star. In the top right box, we also see a star, but it has gotten bigger. Let's come up with a rule to describe how the picture has changed from left to right. From left to right, the shape gets bigger. On the bottom is a parallelogram. Let's look at the answer choices and see if any fit our rule. The first choice does not - the shape is smaller. The second choice does not - the shape is the same size. The third choice does not - it is a different shape. The last choice does - it is the same shape as the bottom box, but it is bigger.

• **Explanation (for parents):** In the directions, the word "picture" means a "figure" consisting of one or more shapes/lines/etc. Your child must figure out how the images in the top set of boxes are related and belong together. Then, (s)he must figure out which answer choice would go with the bottom left image so that the bottom set would have the same analogous relationship as the top set. (The small arrows demonstrate that the images go together.) Try to define a "rule" to describe how the top set belongs together. Make your "rule" describe a "change" that occurs from the top left box to the top right box. Next, take this "rule" describing the change, and apply it to the bottom picture. Then, look at the answer choices to determine which one would make the bottom set also follow your "rule." If more than one answer choice fits the rule, then the rule needs to be more specific.

- The images below outline "changes" in Figure Analogy questions (how the figures change in the analogy).

- In basic Figure Analogy questions, like the example, there is one "change" -or- a change that is quite obvious.

- In the below images #1-9, there is one change.

- More advanced questions, like #10-12 below, have two changes (or changes that are not as obvious).

Directions for the below images:
- See if your child can figure out how the first picture "changes" to the second picture below.
- The questions' "change" (the logic) is at the bottom of the page.

1.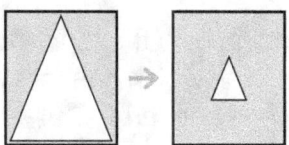

2.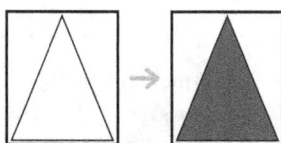

3.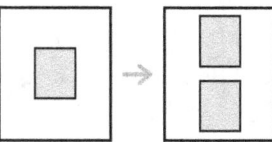

4.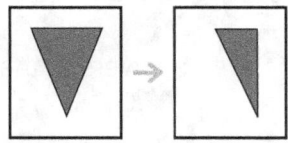

5.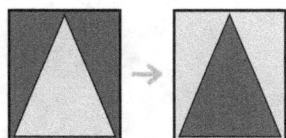

6.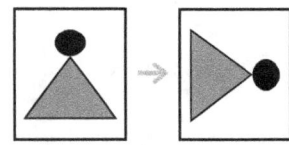

7.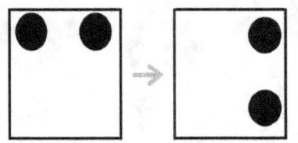

8.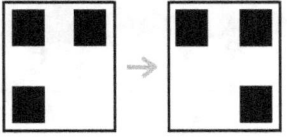

9.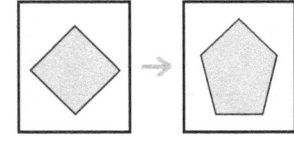

10.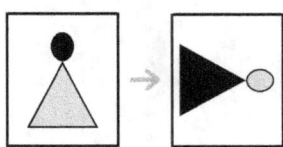

11.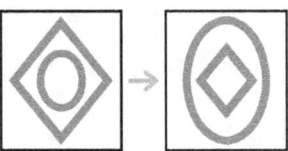

12.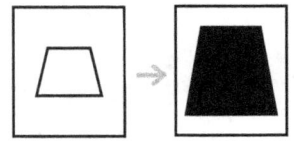

---

1. Size (gets smaller)
2. Color (white to dark gray)
3. Quantity (plus 1)
4. Whole to Half
5. Color Reversal
6. Rotation (clockwise, 90°)

7. Rotation (clockwise, 90°)
8. Rotation -or- Mirror Image/"Flip"
9. Number of Shape Sides (shape with +1 side)
10. Two Changes: Rotation (clockwise, 90°)
   and Color Reversal
11. Two Changes: Shape Position and Size
12. Two Changes: Shape Size and Color

5. FIGURE CLASSIFICATION (NON-VERBAL BATTERY)

• **Directions (read to child):** The top row shows three pictures that are alike in some way. Look at the bottom row. There are four pictures. Which picture in the bottom row goes best with the pictures in the top row?

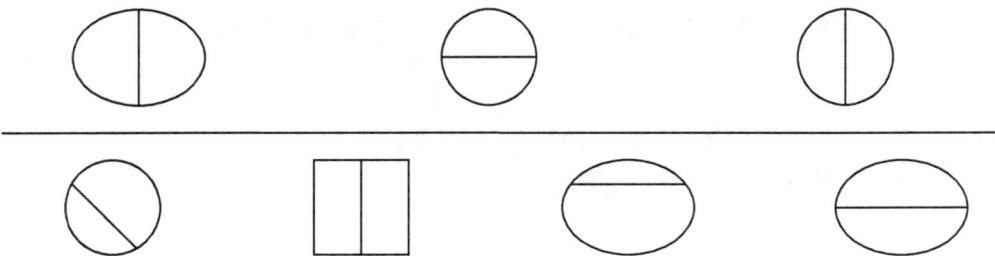

• **Explanation (for parents):** Together with your child, try to figure out a "rule" describing how the top pictures are alike and belong together. Then, apply the "rule" to each answer choice to determine which one follows it. If your child finds that more than one choice follows the rule, then a more specific rule is needed.

• **Using the above question as an example, say to your child:** Here we see 1 oval divided in half, 1 circle divided in half, and 1 circle divided in half. What is a rule that describes how they are alike? They are all round and divided in half. In the bottom row, which choice follows this rule? Choice 1 and 3 are round and divided, but it is not divided in half. Choice 2 is divided in half, but it is not round. Choice 4 is round and divided in half.

• The following examples include basic logic used in Figure Classification questions, with answers at the end.

• **Directions (read to child):** The top row shows three pictures that are alike in some way. Look at the bottom row. There are four pictures. Which picture in the bottom row goes best with the pictures in the top row?

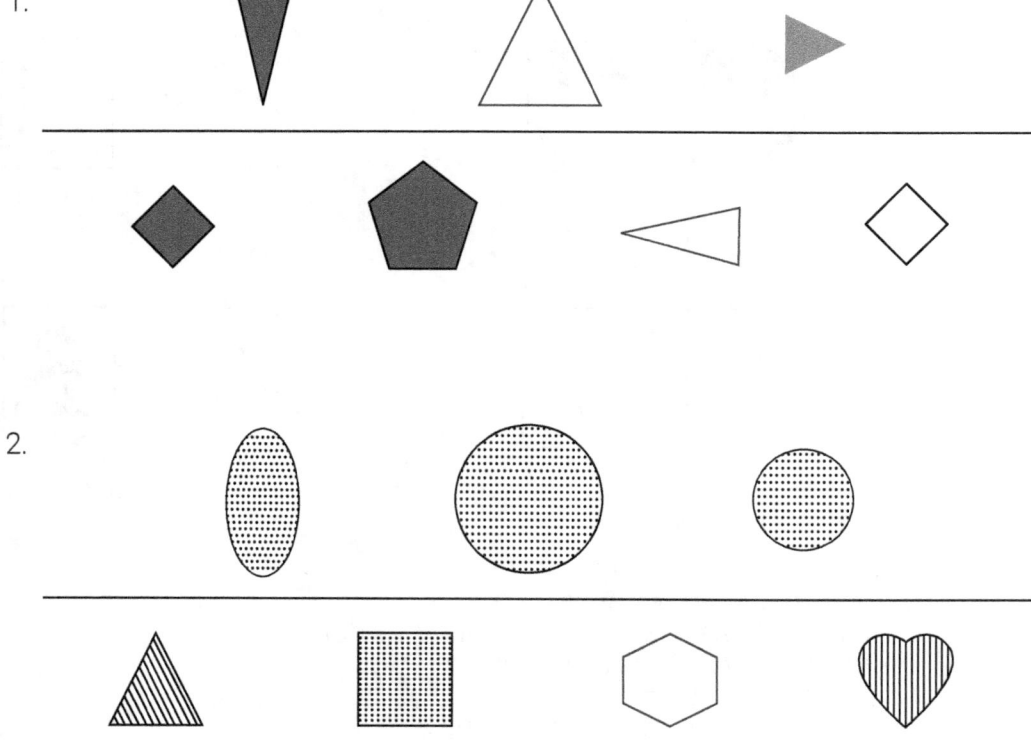

• **Note:** These are <u>more challenging</u>. If your child needs help, ask them the question next to the number.

3. Which way is it pointing?

4. What is the design inside?

5. How much is black? How much is white?

6. How many sides?

1-Choice 3: triangles   2-Choice 2: filled with dots   3-Choice 3: arrows point right
4-Choice 2: the designs are gray, wavy lines, gray   5-Choice 2: half is white, half is black
6-Choice 4: the shapes have 5 sides

7. How many shapes of each kind are together next to each other?

   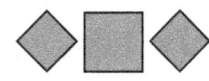

8. What kind of small shapes are there?

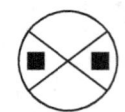  

9. What kinds of shape are gray or white? How many?

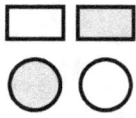 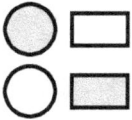 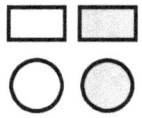

 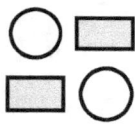 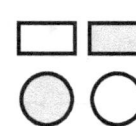 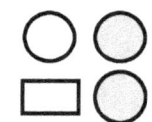

10. How many shapes are in each group?

  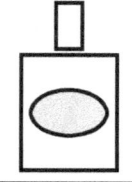

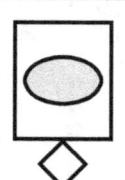 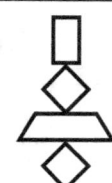 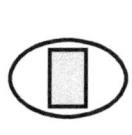 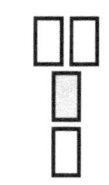

7-Choice 3: there are 2 identical shapes next to a shape that's a different kind of shape
8-Choice 4: the 2 small black shapes are the same
9-Choice 3: the 2 gray shapes are 1 rectangle and 1 circle   10-Choice 1: there are 3 shapes in the group

14

6. PAPER FOLDING (NON-VERBAL BATTERY)

• **Directions (read to child):** The top row of pictures shows a sheet of paper. The paper was folded, then something was cut out. Which picture in the bottom row shows how the paper would look after it's unfolded?

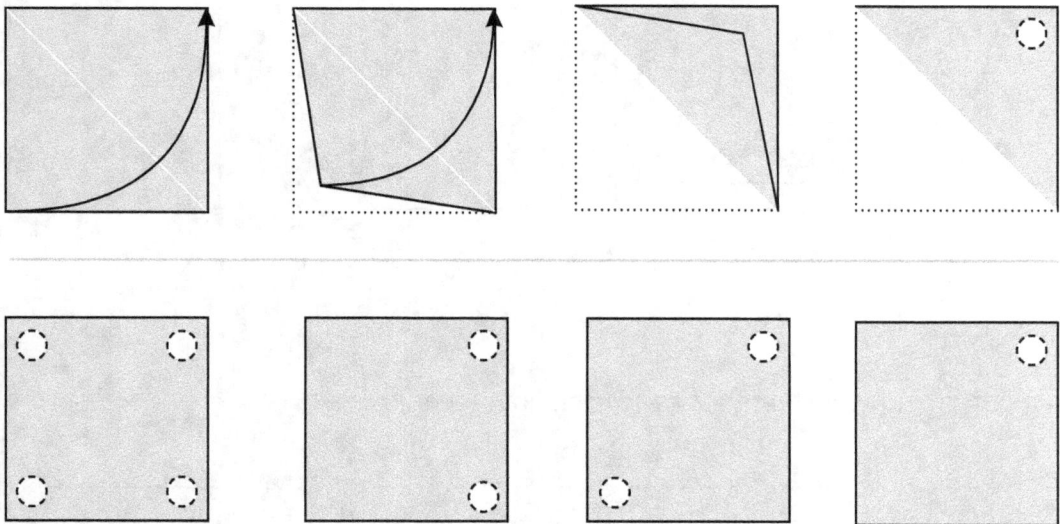

• **Explanation (read to child):** The first choice has too many holes. In the second choice, the holes are not in the correct position. The third choice has the correct number of holes and in the correct position. The last choice only shows the hole on top.

• **Tip:** If Paper Folding is challenging for your child, demonstrate using real paper and scissors. (It is common for kids to initially struggle with Paper Folding. It is not an activity most children have much experience with.)

• Show your child the following examples. Demonstrate using real paper, if needed.

Paper Folding Steps   Result

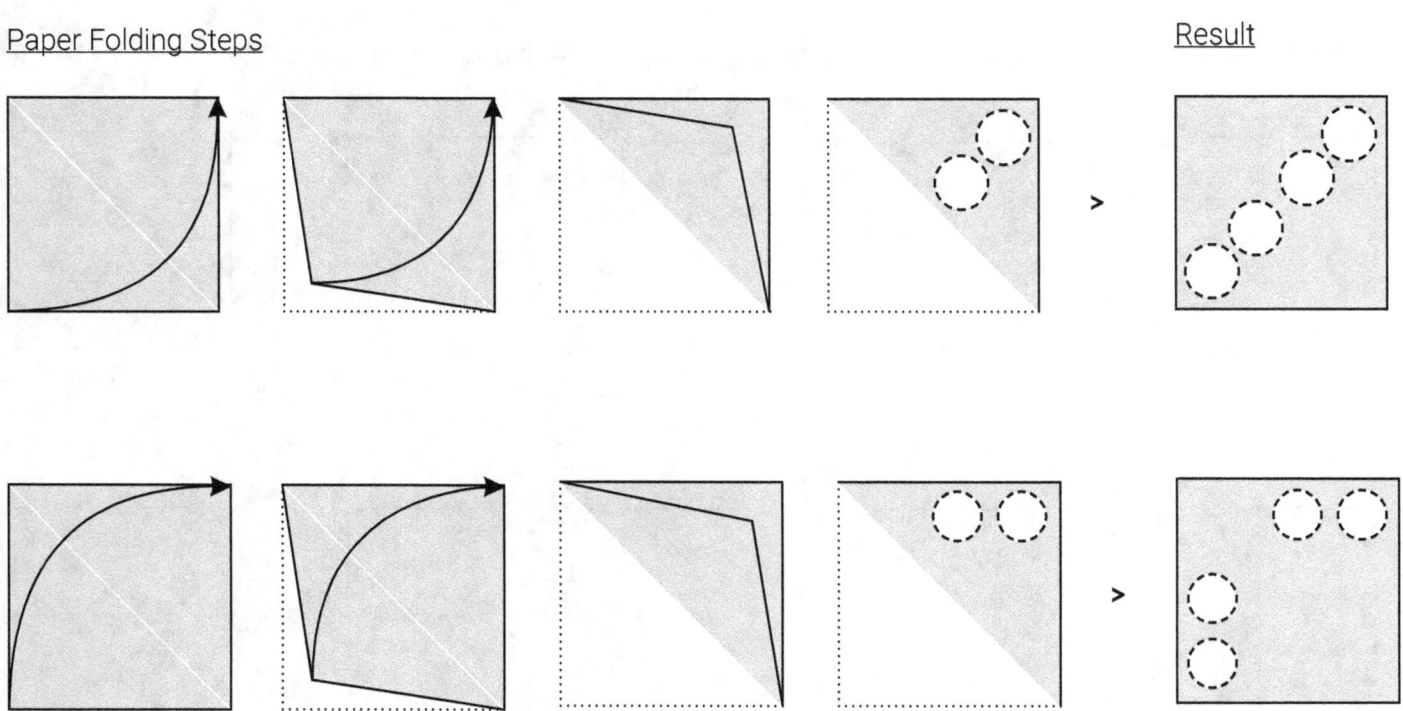

(In the question at the top of the page, the third choice is correct.)

In the example below, point out to your child that when the paper is unfolded the triangles point toward each other.

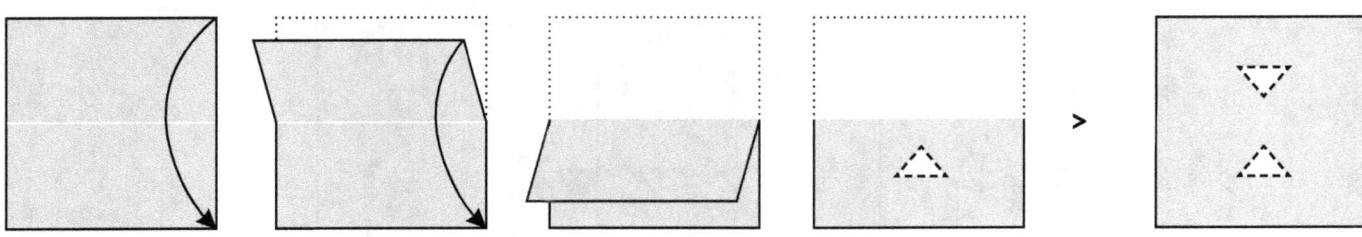

In the example below, point out to your child that the shape is cut into the fold line.

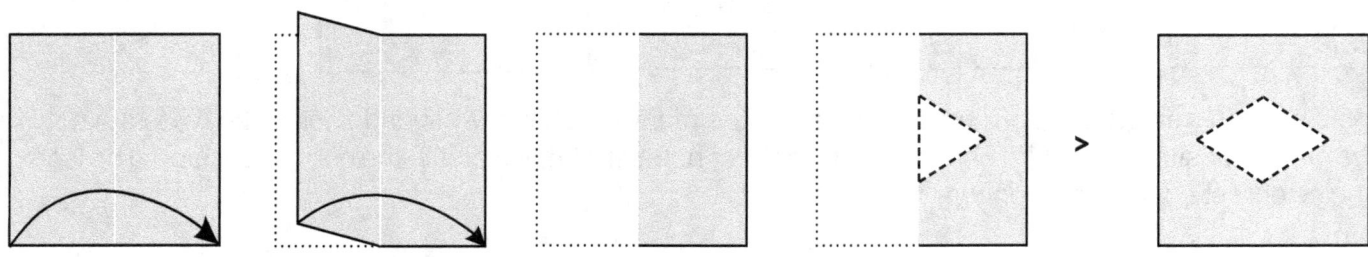

In the examples below, point out to your child how the paper is folded, and then folded again.

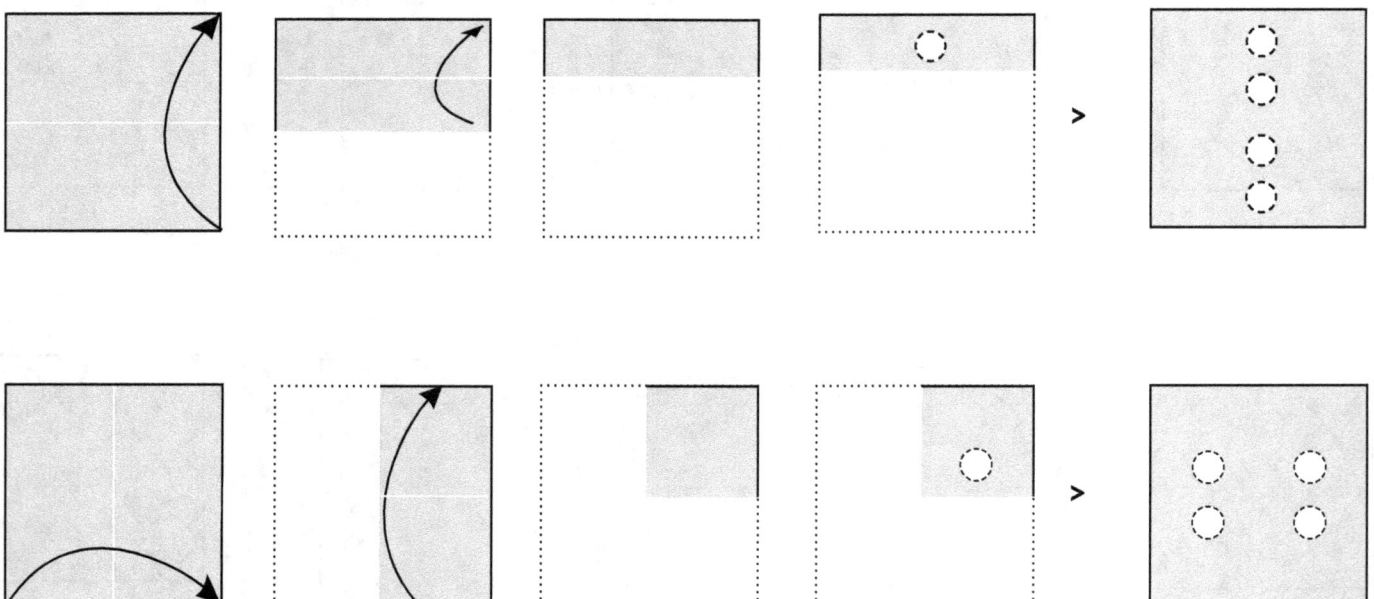

7. NUMBER ANALOGIES (QUANTITATIVE BATTERY)

• **Directions (read to child):** The pictures in the top boxes go together in some way. Look at the bottom boxes. One box is empty. Look at the row of answer choices next to the boxes. Which one of these choices goes with the picture in the bottom box like the pictures in the top box go together?

• **Explanation (read to child):** In the left box, there are 7 objects (stars). In the right box, there are 2 objects. From left to right, we see that 5 objects have been taken away. So, the rule here is "5 are taken away" or "-5." In the bottom left box, there are 9 objects. If our rule is "5 are taken away," if you have 9 and you take away 5, you get 4. The third answer choice is correct.

•**Tip:** Some analogies involve addition and subtraction, while others require children to do more complex calculations: dividing in half, doubling, or tripling. If your child first tries to add or subtract, but no answer choice matches the "rule," then try to double or triple (if the number increases from left to right) or try to halve (if the number decreases from left to right).

• Show your child the example below.

• **Explanation (read to child):** In the top left box, there are 2 stars. In the top right box, there is 1 star. Let's try the rule "take away 1." In the bottom left box, there are 4 stars. If our rule is "take away 1," then the answer should be 3 stars. However, there isn't an answer choice with 3 stars. Let's look again at the top boxes. If you divide 2 in half, you get 1. Let's try the rule "divide in half." If you take the 4 stars in the bottom left box and divide them in half, you get 2. The choice with two stars is correct.

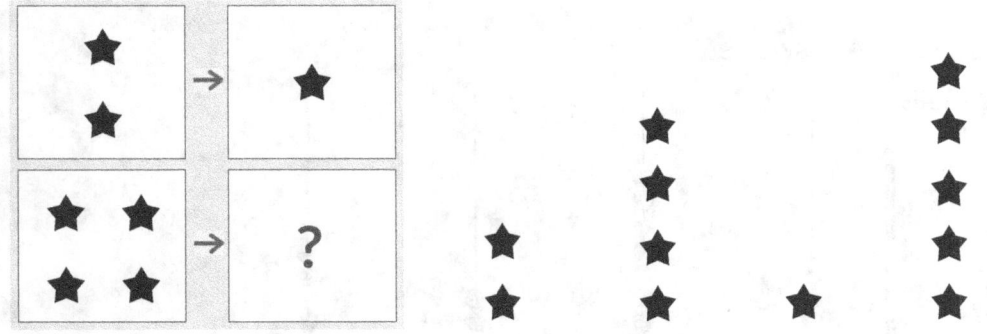

8. NUMBER SERIES (QUANTITATIVE BATTERY)

• **Directions (read to child):** Which rod should go in the place of the missing rod to finish the pattern?

• **Explanation for #1 (read to child):** Before the missing rod, the other rods have made a pattern that we need to figure out. Then, we will complete the pattern with the correct answer choice. From left to right, we see that the pattern is: 1 - 2 - 1 - 2 - 1. After 1, comes 2. This means that the missing rod needs 2 beads.

• Make sure your child accurately counts the number of beads. In the examples below, there are numbers under the rods indicating the number of beads. The practice test questions do not have these numbers.

• After you do #1, go over questions #2 - #7 together. The pattern and the answer are already given.

1.

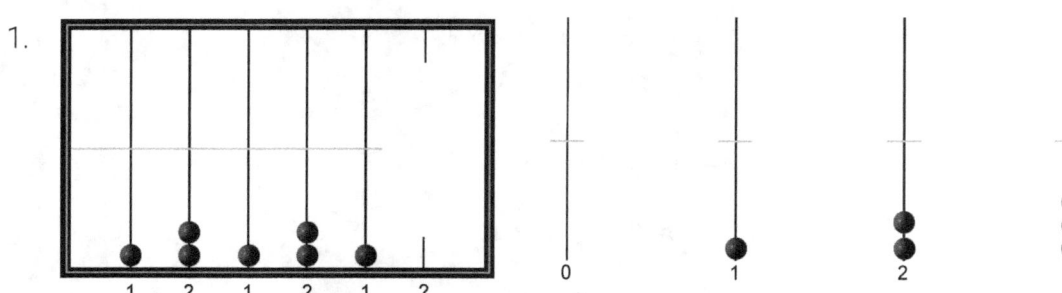

Pattern: the number of beads decreases by 1. The answer is 1.

2.

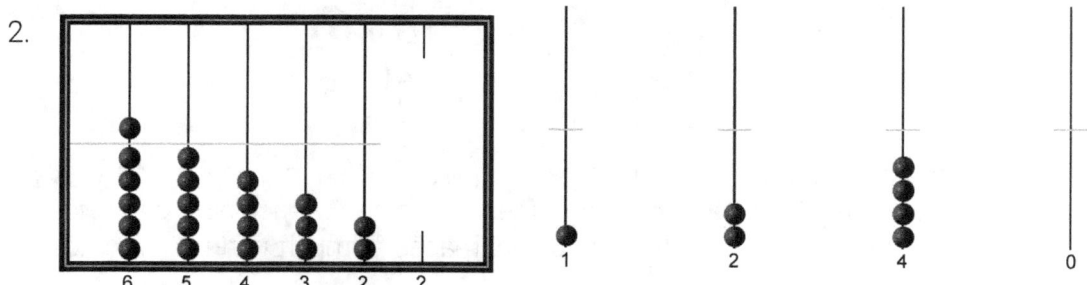

Pattern: every other rod increases by 1. And, the alternate rods equal 0. The answer is 0.

3.

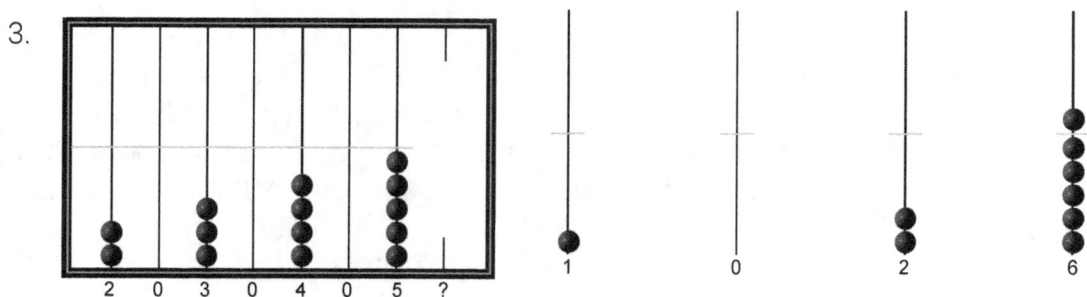

Pattern: the rods repeat 7 - 5 - 3. The answer is 7.

4.

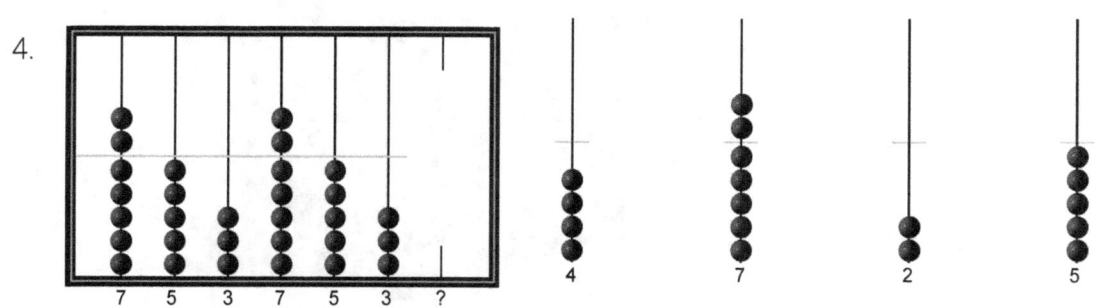

This one may be challenging. Every other rod increases by one (1 - 2 - 3 - 4). Then, every other rod (the alternate rods), increases by one (4 - 5 - 6 - 7). With the alternating rods increasing 1, 2, 3, 4, this means that the next rod will be 5.

5.

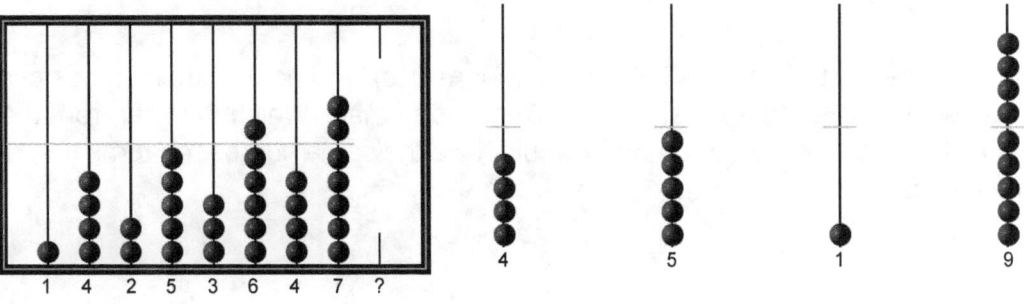

This one may be challenging also. Every other rod decreases by one (5 - 4 - 3). Then, every other rod (the alternate rods), increases by one (1 - 2 - 3). With the alternating rods decreasing 5, 4, 3, this means that the next rod will be 2.

6.

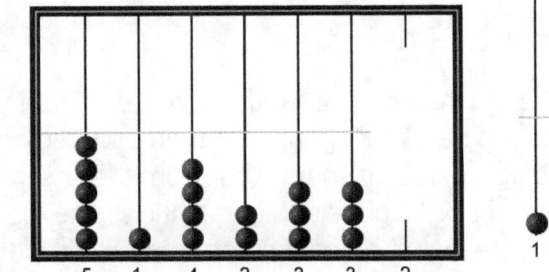  

Pattern: the rods decrease with the pattern 6 - 4 - 2 - 0, then increase with the reverse pattern 2 - 4 - 6.

7.

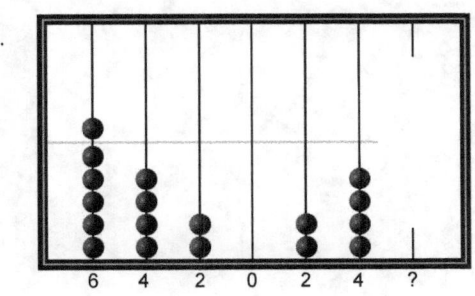  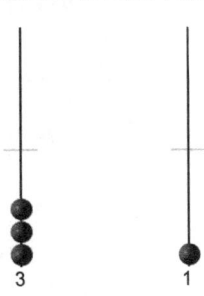

9. NUMBER PUZZLES, TRAIN FORMAT (QUANTITATIVE BATTERY)

• **Directions (read to child):** Which train car should you choose so that the top train is carrying the same number of items as the bottom train?

• **Explanation (read to child):** The top train carries four items (four hearts). The bottom train carries two items. Next to the train car with two hearts is a train car with a question mark. Which train car from the answer choices should be put here so that the bottom train would have the same number of items (hearts) as the top train? It would be the choice with 2 hearts (choice B).

• **Explanation for the below question (read to child):** Look at the top train and count the number of items in the train. The top train has 5 items (5 triangles). Look at the bottom train and count the number of items. The bottom train has 6 items. Like the earlier questions, we need to figure out which train car from the answer choices would be put in the place of the train car with a question mark. Like the earlier questions, the top train and the bottom train must carry the same number of items. For the top train and the bottom train to do this, one triangle must be taken away from the bottom train. In the answer choices, if an item has an "X" on it, this means that it would be taken away from the train. We need to take away one triangle, so we need to choose the train car with one "X" on top of the item. The last choice shows this.

20

10. NUMBER PUZZLES, EQUATION FORMAT (QUANTITATIVE BATTERY)

• **Directions (read to child):** Which number would be in place of the question mark so that both of the sides of this equal sign are the same?

• **Explanation:** This section is straightforward. Make sure your child pays attention to the plus and minus signs.

4	=	11	+	3	-	?

9   10   11   4

Ten is the answer.

Parents, read the below with your child.

Watch out!

This book is filled with tricky questions. Can you answer them?

Of course you can!

Pay close attention to each question and try your best.

We'll be here to help you along the way!

COGAT® PRACTICE TEST 1 (WORKBOOK FORMAT)

PICTURE ANALOGIES

What goes in the empty box?

Sara

Directions (read to child): The pictures in the top boxes go together in some way. One box on the bottom is empty. Look at the row of pictures next to the boxes. These are the answer choices. Which one of these goes with the picture in the bottom box like the pictures in the top boxes go together?

Explanation (for parents): A more detailed explanation and example questions are on p. 6-7. If you have not already, look these over. Following is an excerpt.

Your child must figure out how the images in the top set of boxes are related and belong together. Then, (s)he must figure out which answer choice would go with the bottom left image so that the bottom set would have the same analogous relationship as the top set. (The small arrows demonstrate that the images go together.)

Example (read this to child): Look at the boxes on top. In the first box, we see a fish. In the second box, we see a fishbowl. (Together, try to come up with a "rule" describing how they are alike and go together.) A fish can live in a fishbowl. The object in the second box is the home of the animal in the first box. Let's look in the bottom box. We see a bird. Now, let's look at the answer choices. Which one goes with the picture of a bird in the same way that the pictures in the top row go together? The bird cage (choice C). A bird can live in a bird cage.

Parent note: A common mistake for kids would be picking an answer that simply "has to do with" the first box. There is more than one answer choice that "has to do with" a bird. A parrot, an egg, and a feather all have to do with the bird in the bottom box. However, they do not follow the rule.

1.

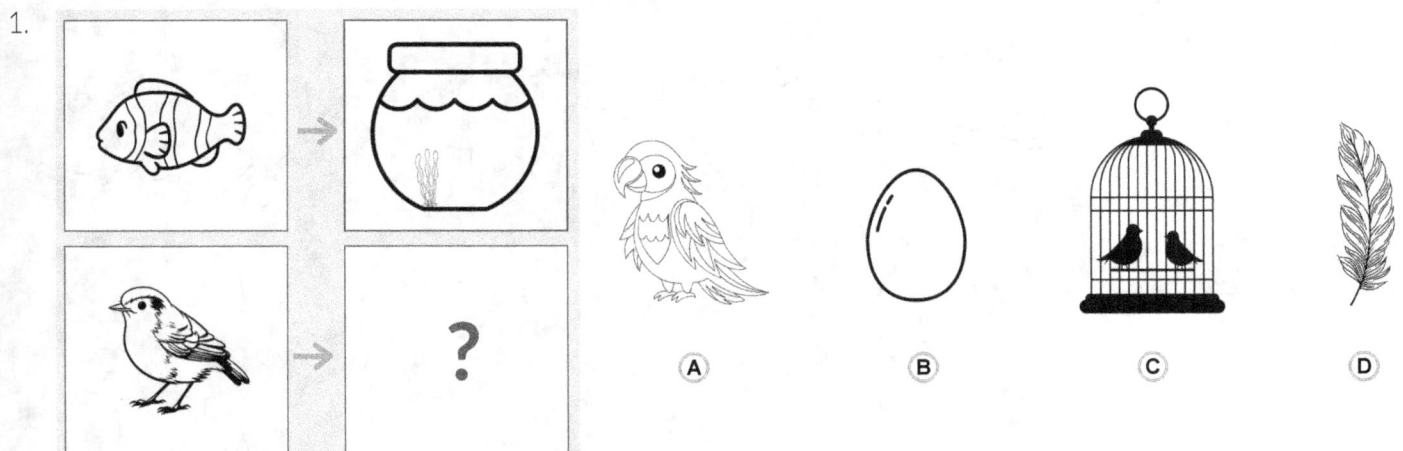

2.

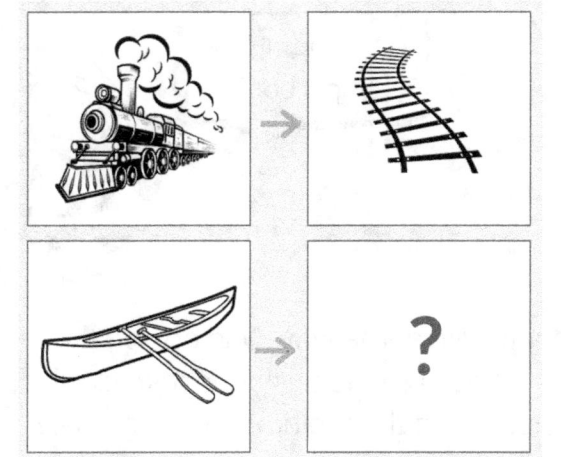

Ⓐ

Ⓑ

Ⓒ

Ⓓ

3.

Ⓐ

Ⓑ

Ⓒ

Ⓓ

4.

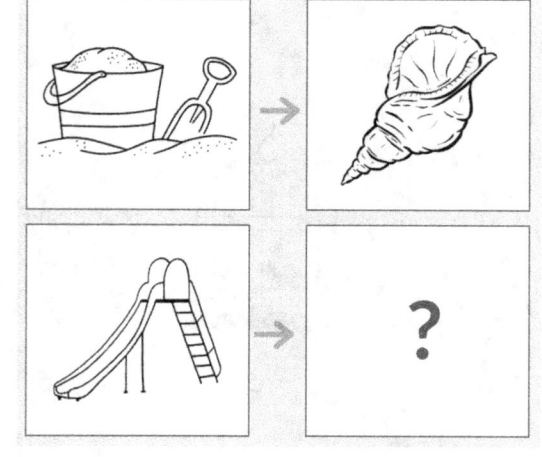

Ⓐ

Ⓑ

Ⓒ

Ⓓ

5.

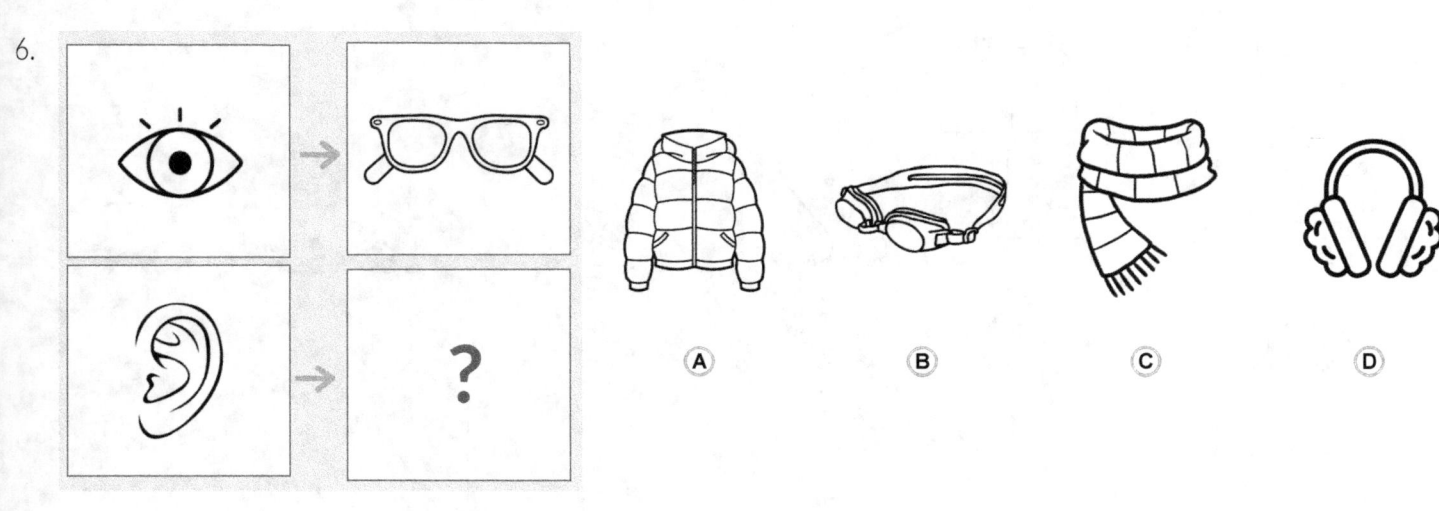

A B C D

6.

A B C D

7.

A B C D

8.

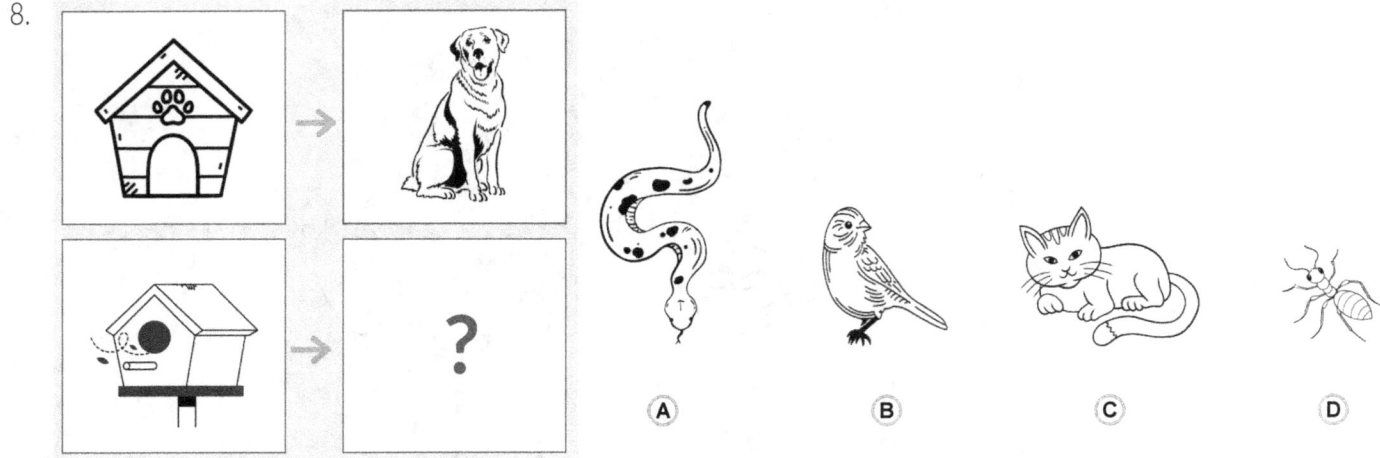

9.

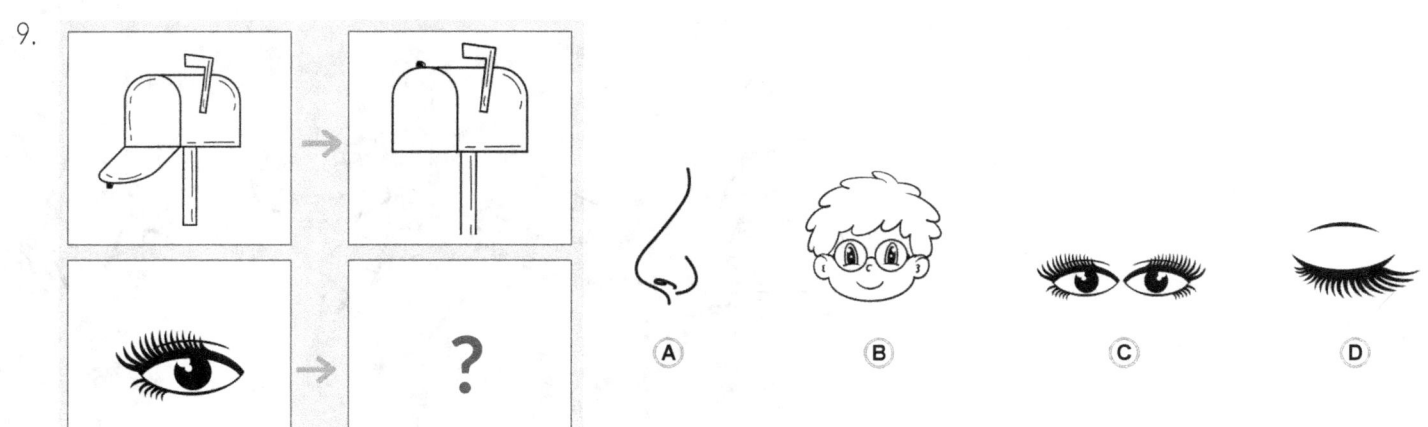

10.

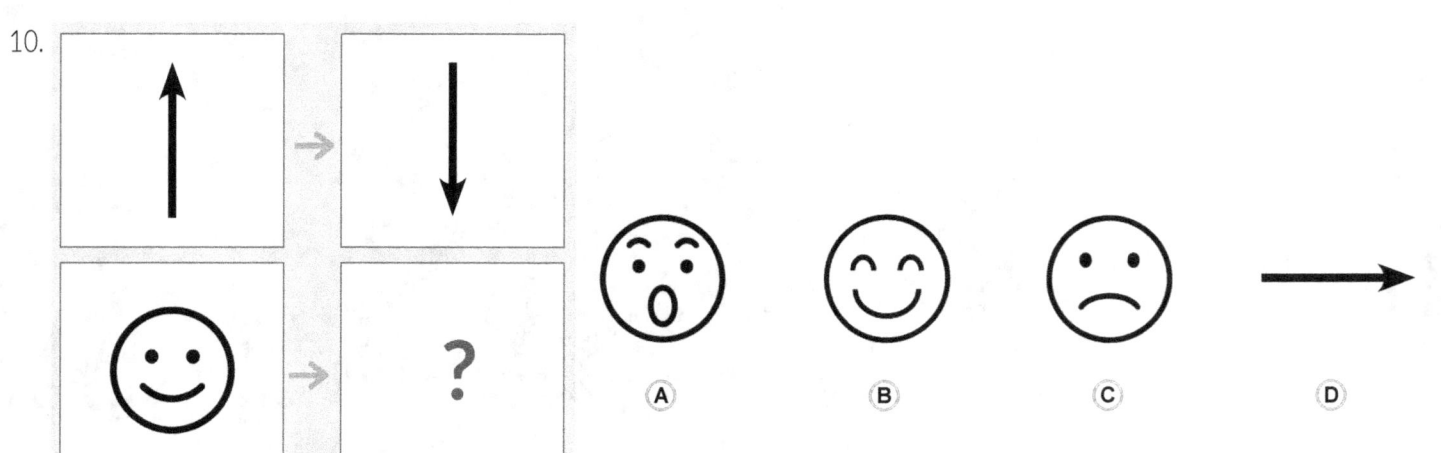

11.

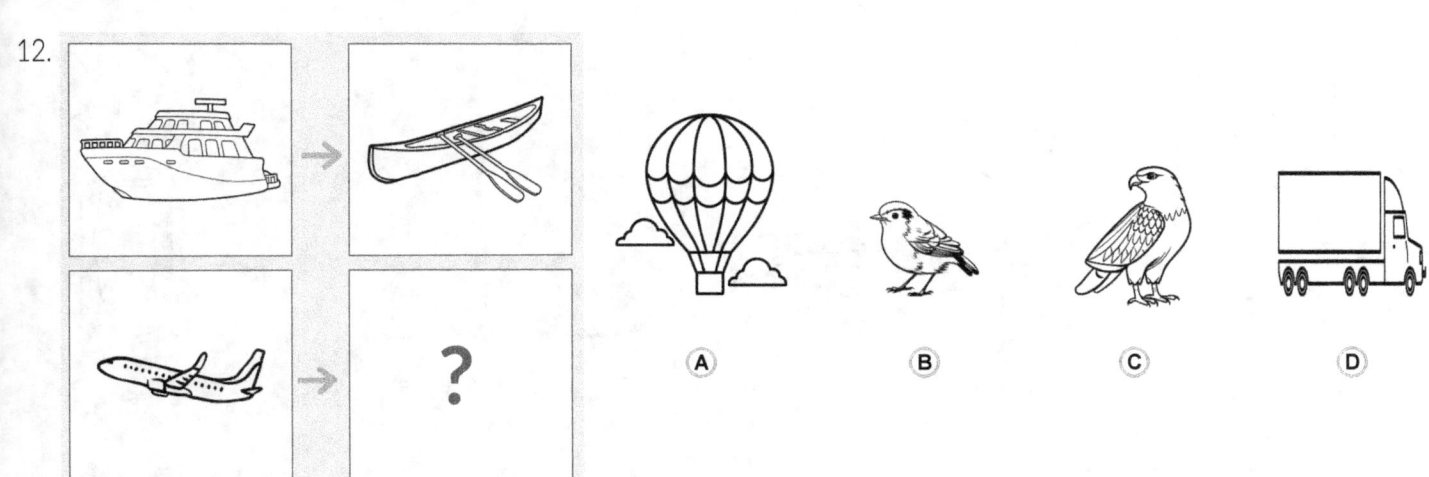

12.

13.

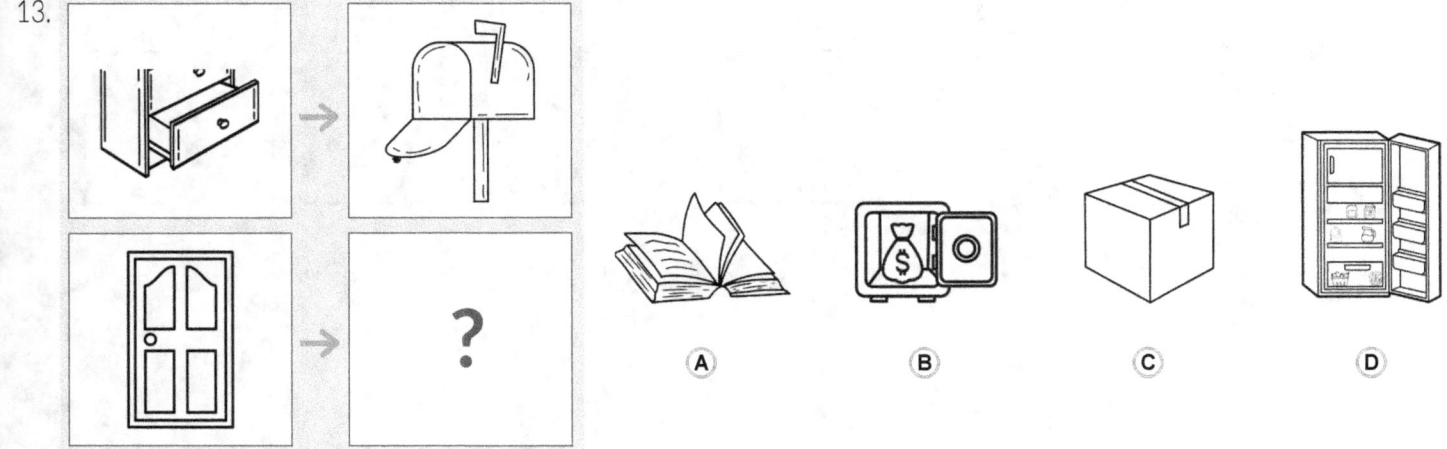

14.

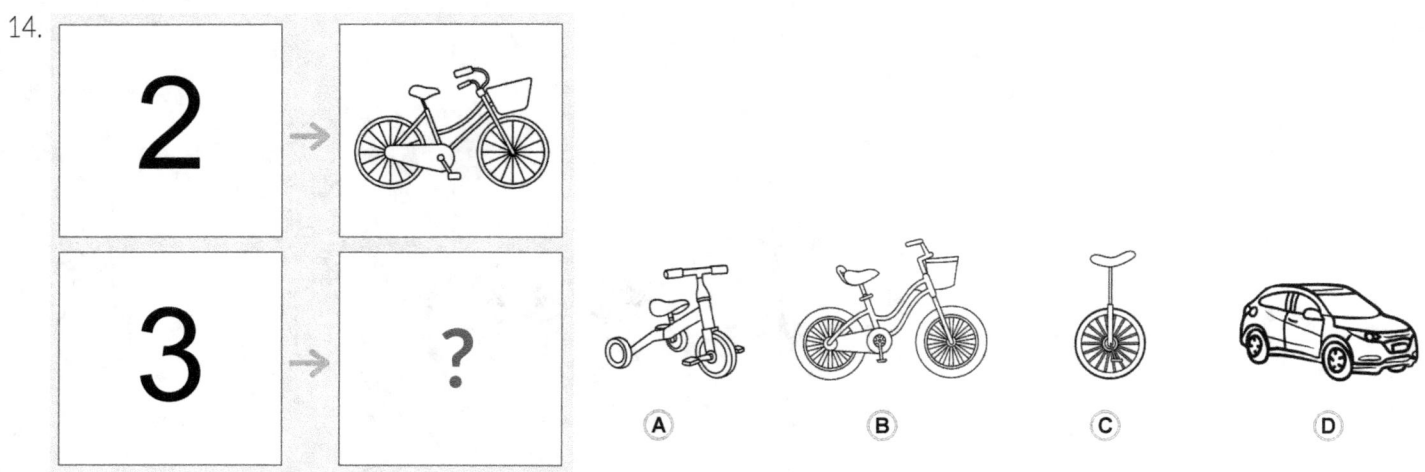

15.

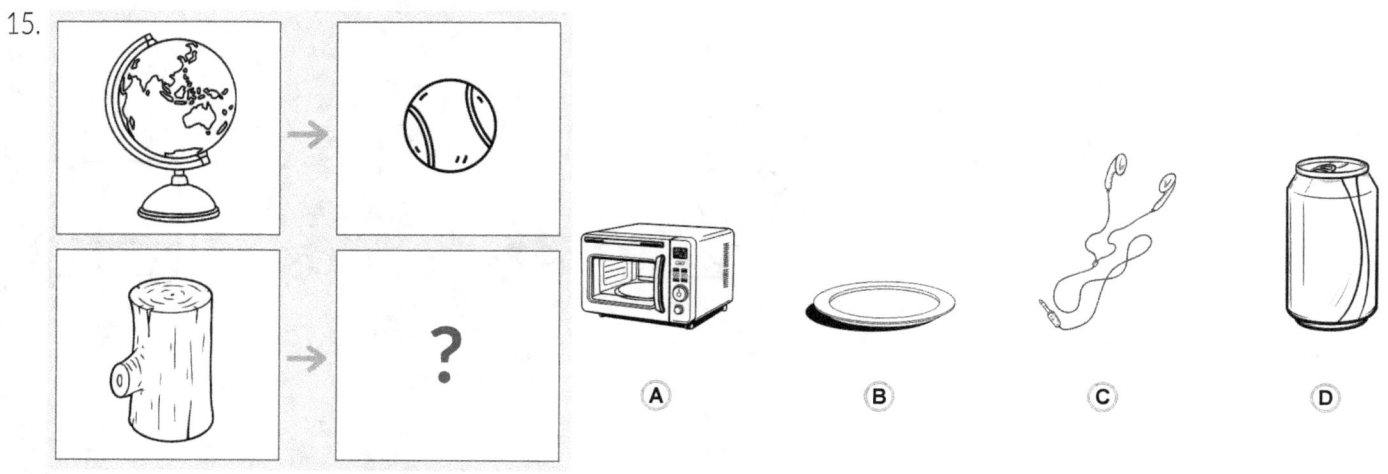

16.

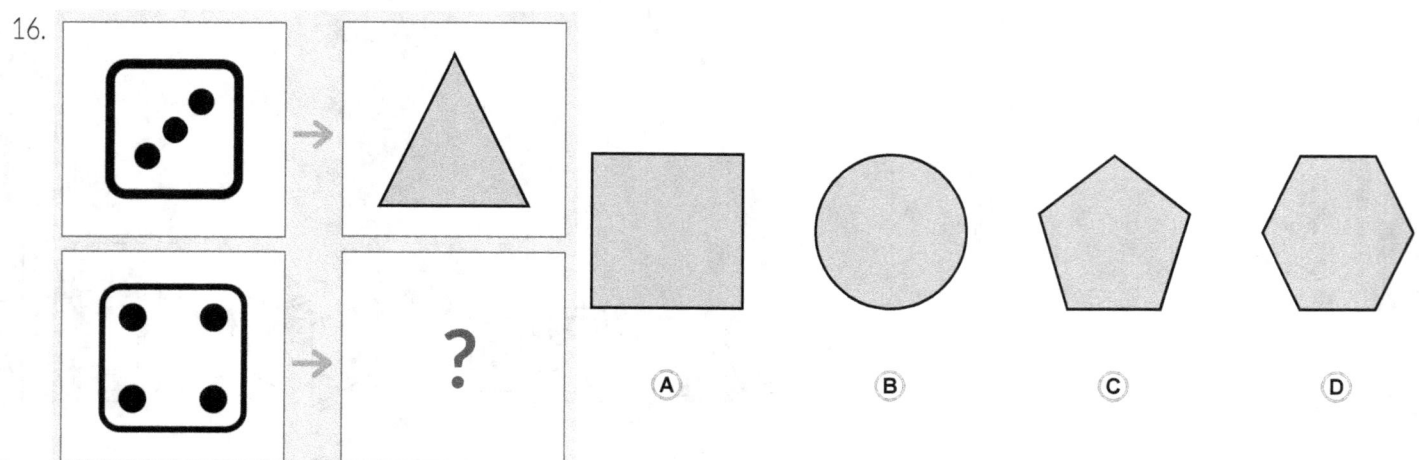

PICTURE CLASSIFICATION

Which one goes best?

Kai

Directions (read to child):

The top row shows three pictures that are alike in some way. Look at the bottom row. There are four pictures. Which picture in the bottom row goes best with the pictures in the top row?

Explanation (for parents):

A more detailed explanation and another Picture Classification example question is on p.8. If you have not already, look over p.8. Following is an excerpt. Together with your child, try to figure out a "rule" describing how the top pictures are alike and belong together. Then, apply the "rule" to each answer choice to determine which one follows it. If your child finds that more than one choice follows the rule, then a more specific rule is needed.

Example (read to child):

Let's look at the pictures on the top row. We see a hammer, wrench, and an ax. Let's come up with a "rule" to describe how these are each alike or how they belong together.

These are all tools. Now, let's look at the bottom row. Let's find the answer choice on the bottom that follows this same rule of things that are tools. Look carefully at each choice.

Which one of these goes best with the top row? Which one of them is a tool? The drill. (Choice C.)

1.

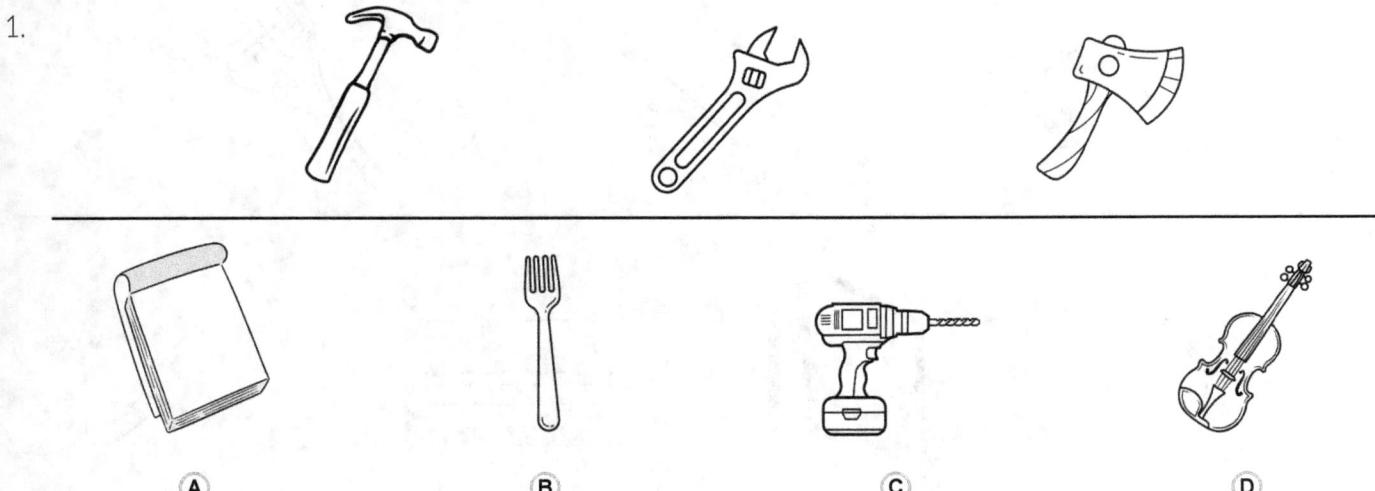

A   B   C   D

2.

Ⓐ   Ⓑ   Ⓒ   Ⓓ

3.

Ⓐ   Ⓑ   Ⓒ   Ⓓ

4.

Ⓐ   Ⓑ   Ⓒ   Ⓓ

5.

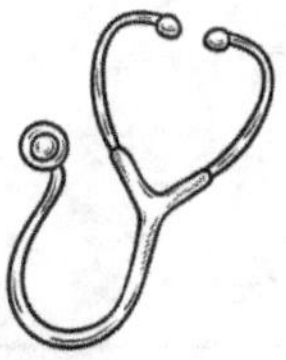

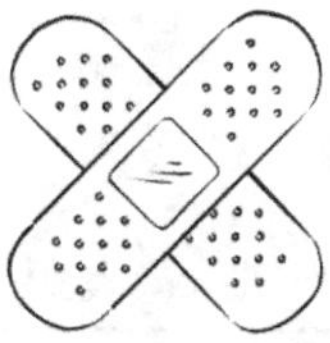

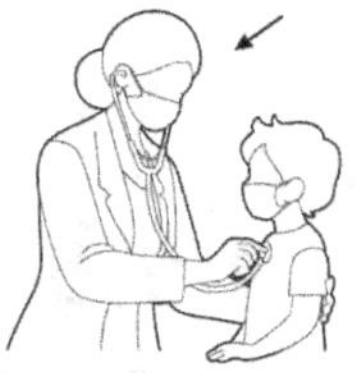

A	B	C	D

6.

A	B	C	D

7.

A	B	C	D

8.

Ⓐ   Ⓑ   Ⓒ   Ⓓ

9.

 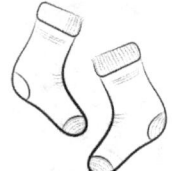 

Ⓐ   Ⓑ   Ⓒ   Ⓓ

10.

Ⓐ   Ⓑ   Ⓒ   Ⓓ

11.

 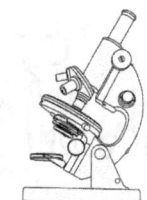 

Ⓐ

Ⓑ

Ⓒ

Ⓓ

12.

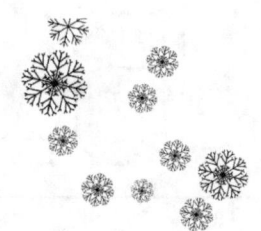  

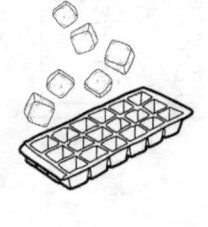
Ⓐ

Ⓑ

Ⓒ

Ⓓ

13.

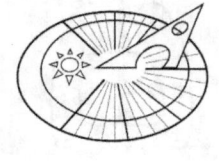
Ⓐ

Ⓑ

Ⓒ

Ⓓ

14.

Ⓐ Ⓑ Ⓒ Ⓓ

15.

  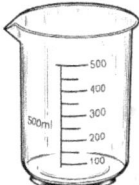

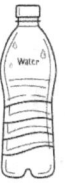  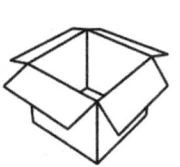 

Ⓐ Ⓑ Ⓒ Ⓓ

16.

  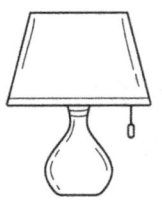 

Ⓐ Ⓑ Ⓒ Ⓓ

SENTENCE COMPLETION

Listen closely!

Maya

Directions (read to child): Listen to the question, then choose the best answer. I can only read the question one time.

Additional information (for parents): Read the questions in this section to your child.

As explained earlier in the Introduction on p.10, test administrators will read these questions only one time.

Therefore, it is imperative that your child practice careful listening skills, so that you will not need to repeat the questions.

1. Which picture group has an animal that can fly in the air?

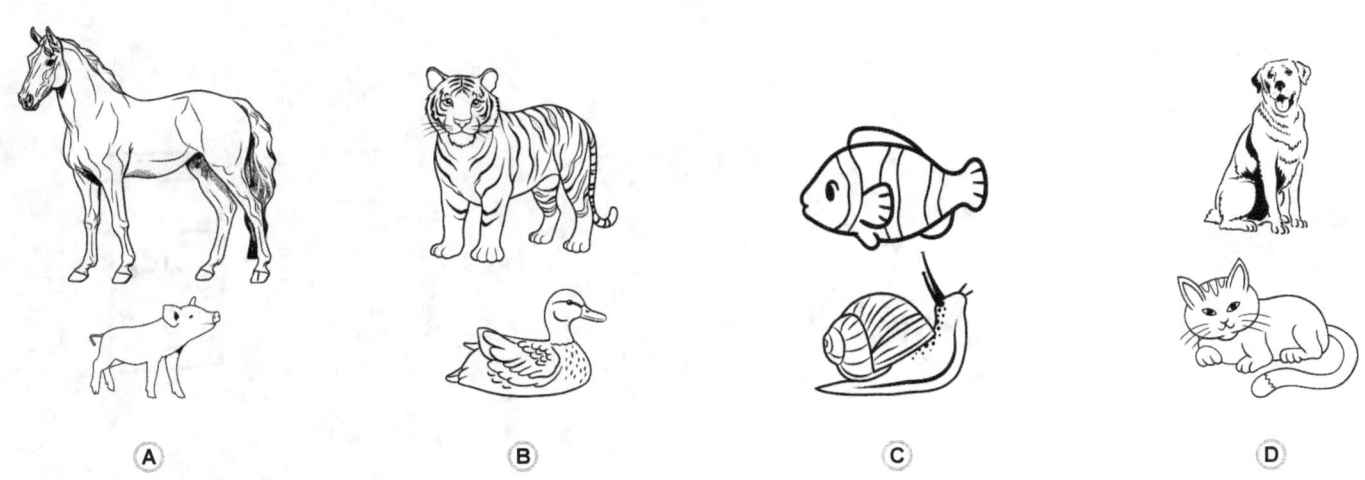

Ⓐ   Ⓑ   Ⓒ   Ⓓ

2. Which picture shows one kind of vegetable and one kind of fruit?

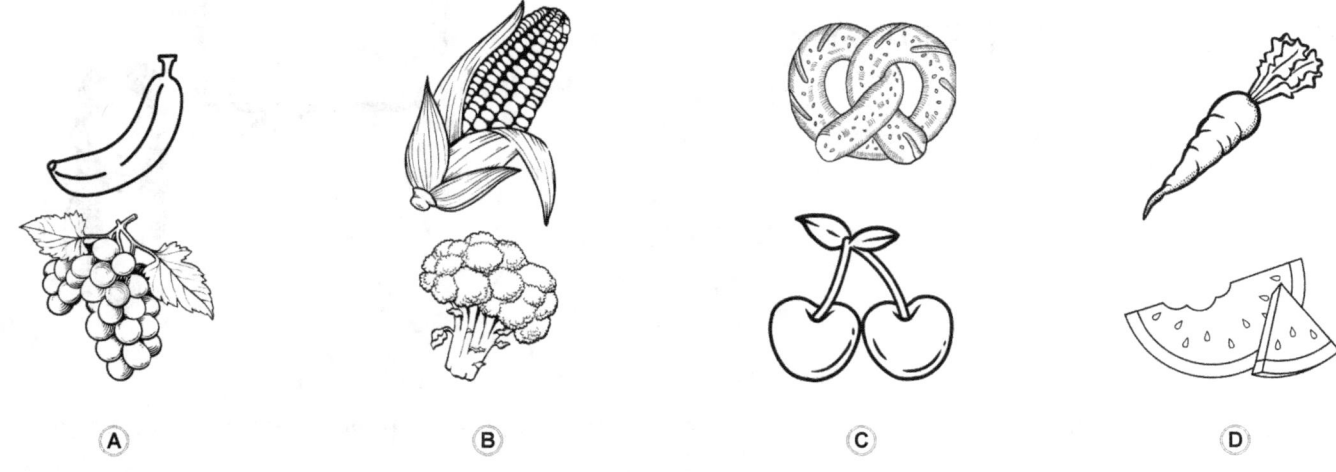

A   B   C   D

3. Your friend's favorite animal lives in the water. Which picture shows your friend's favorite animal?

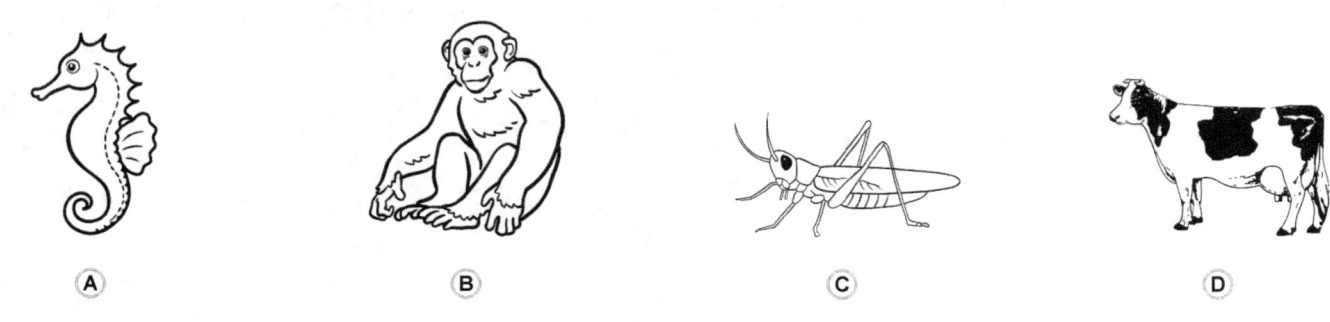

A   B   C   D

4. If you needed to water your garden, which one would you use?

A   B   C   D

5. If you needed to hold together two pieces of paper, which one would you not use?

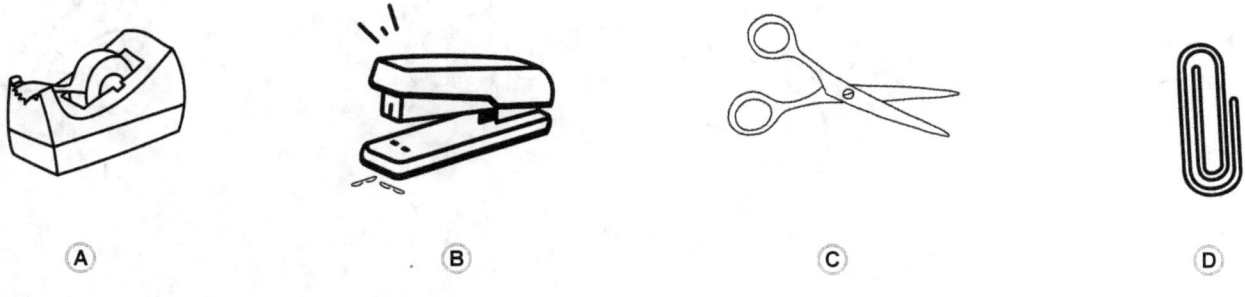

6. Which picture shows two musical instruments?

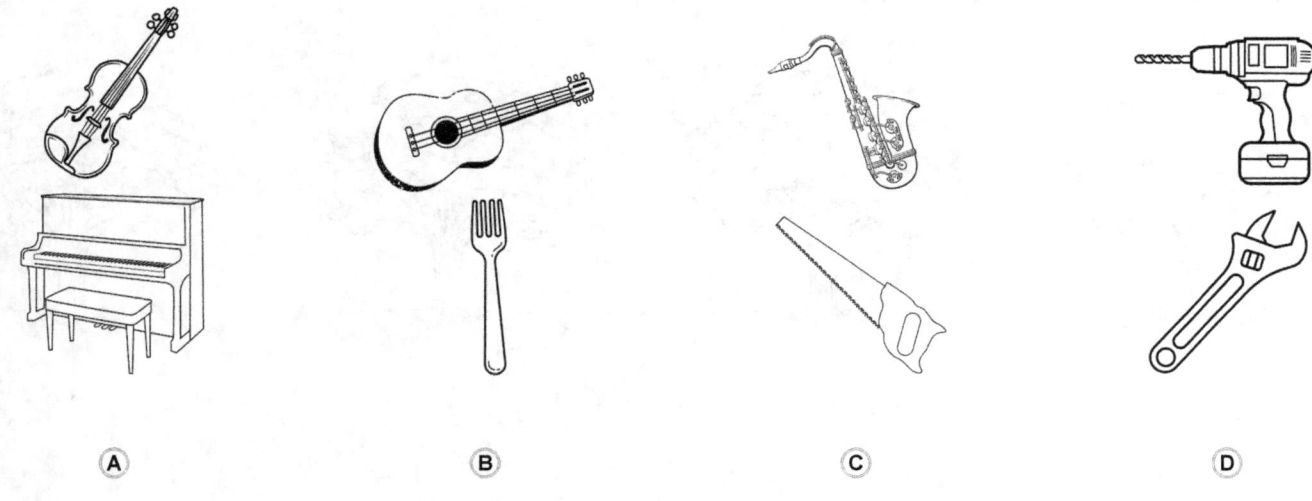

7. Which picture shows two things that come in pairs?

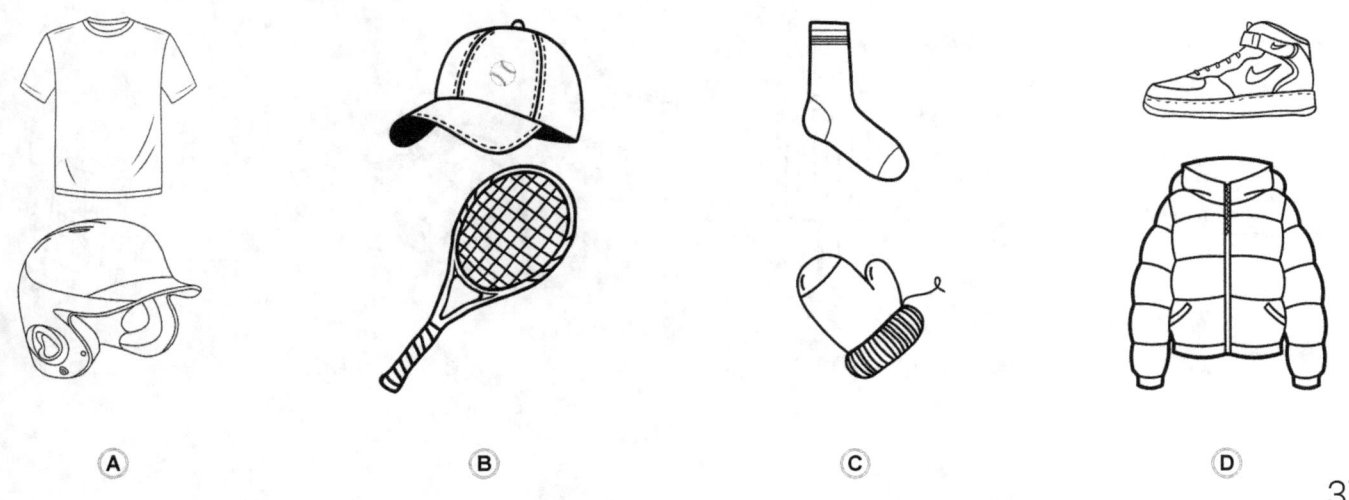

8. Which one of these plants can be used to make bread?

   A   B   C   D

9. Which picture shows two birds under a tree?

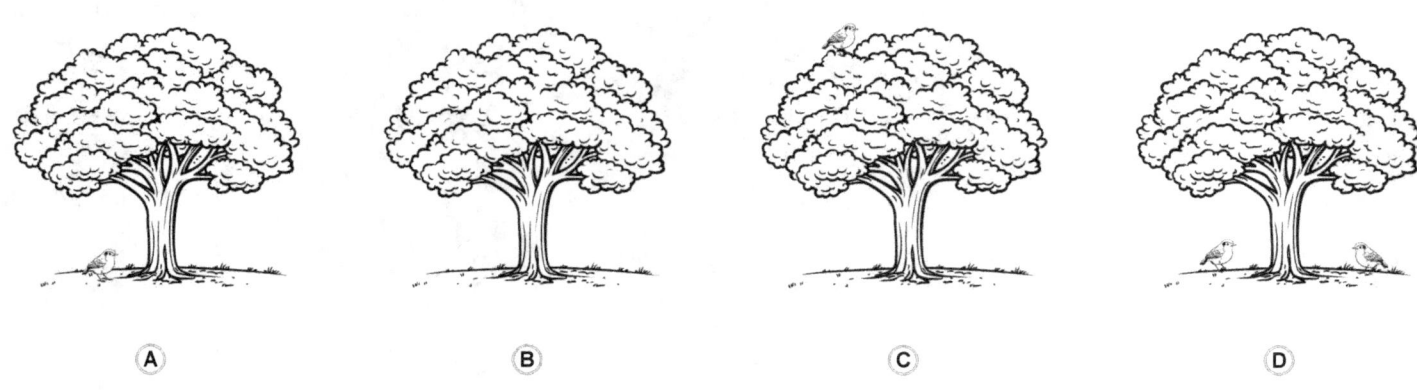

   A   B   C   D

10. You are going to a party. Which one item would you most likely be able to share with all of the guests?

   A   B   C   D

11. You are in your grandma's garden. Which of these would you most likely see?

A   B   C   D

12. Which picture is <u>not</u> related to bees or cows?

A   B   C

13. Your friend has a sweater made of wool. Wool comes from which animal?

A   B   C   D

14. A farmer is picking corn from his garden. Which body part would he __not__ use to do this?

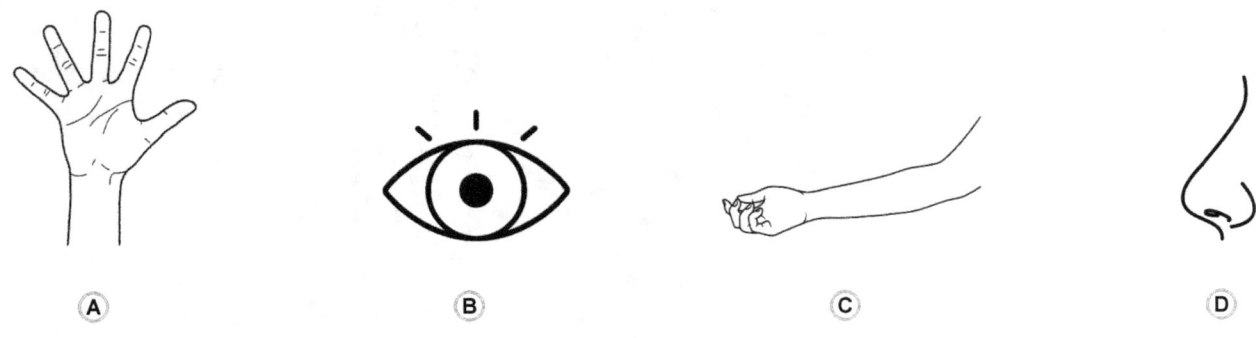

A   B   C   D

15. If you needed to see something that was far away, which one would be best to use?

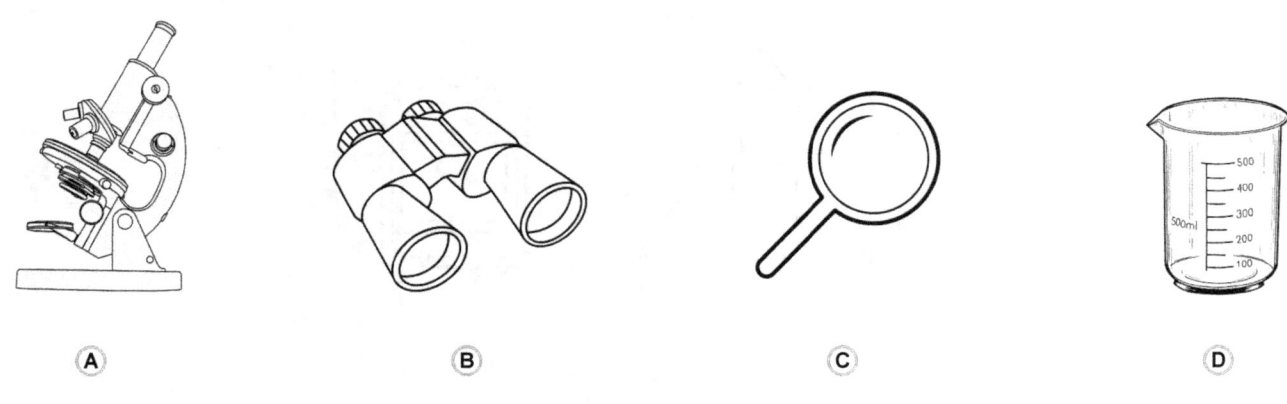

A   B   C   D

16. Which picture has the most 3-D shapes?

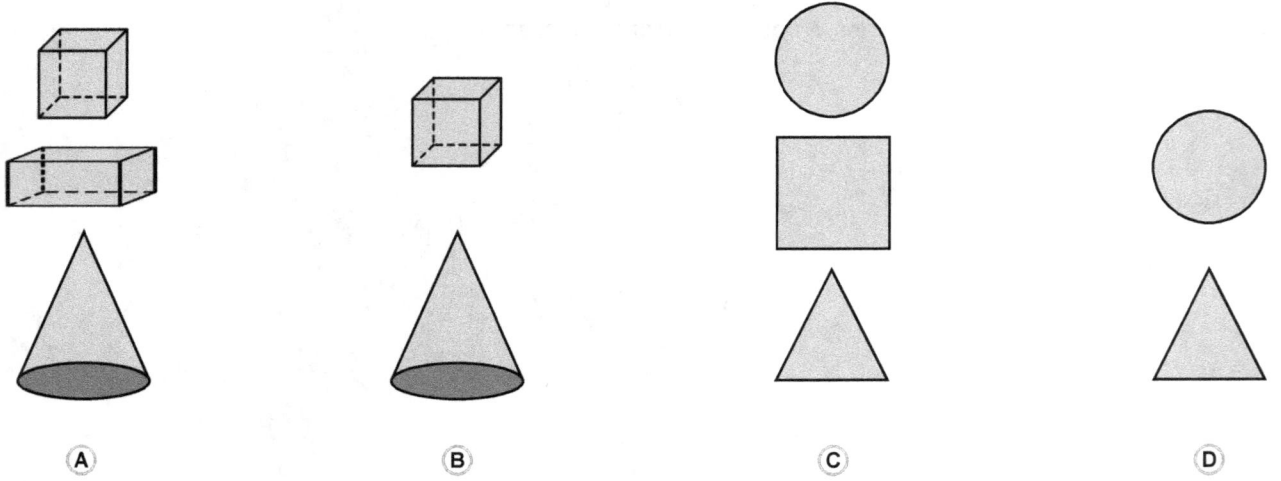

A   B   C   D

FIGURE ANALOGIES

"What goes in the empty box?" Sara asks.

Sara

Directions (read to child): The pictures in the top boxes go together in some way. Look at the bottom boxes. One box is empty. Look at the row of pictures next to the boxes. These are the answer choices. Which one of these choices goes with the picture in the bottom box like the pictures in the top boxes go together?

Explanation (for parents): A more detailed explanation and a Figure Analogies example question is on p.10. Look over p.10-11 if needed. Try to define a "rule" to describe how the top set belongs together. With Figure Analogies, this "rule" could describe a "change" that occurs from the top left box to the top right box. Next, take this "rule" describing the change, and apply it to the bottom picture.

Example (read this to child): In the first box, we see a gray square. In the second box, we see a square, but this time the top has lines and the bottom is gray. Our rule is that the same shape from the first box is in the second box, but in the second box the top has lines and the bottom is gray.

Let's look in the bottom box. We see another gray shape. Which answer choice follows our rule? Find the choice that shows the same shape as the first box, but the top has lines and the bottom is gray. Choice B is the right answer.

1.

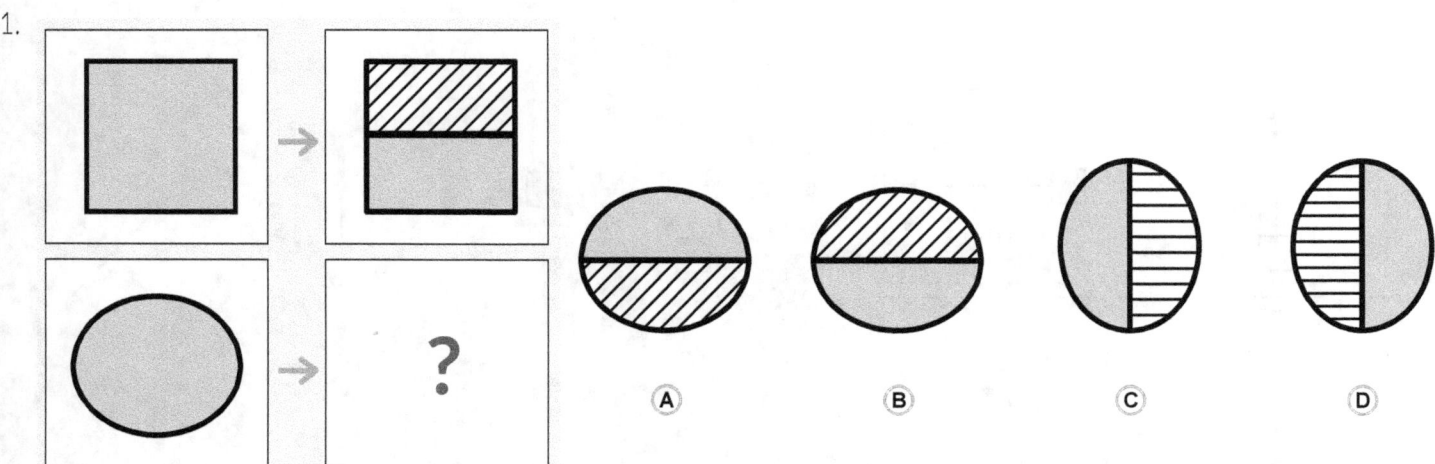

2.

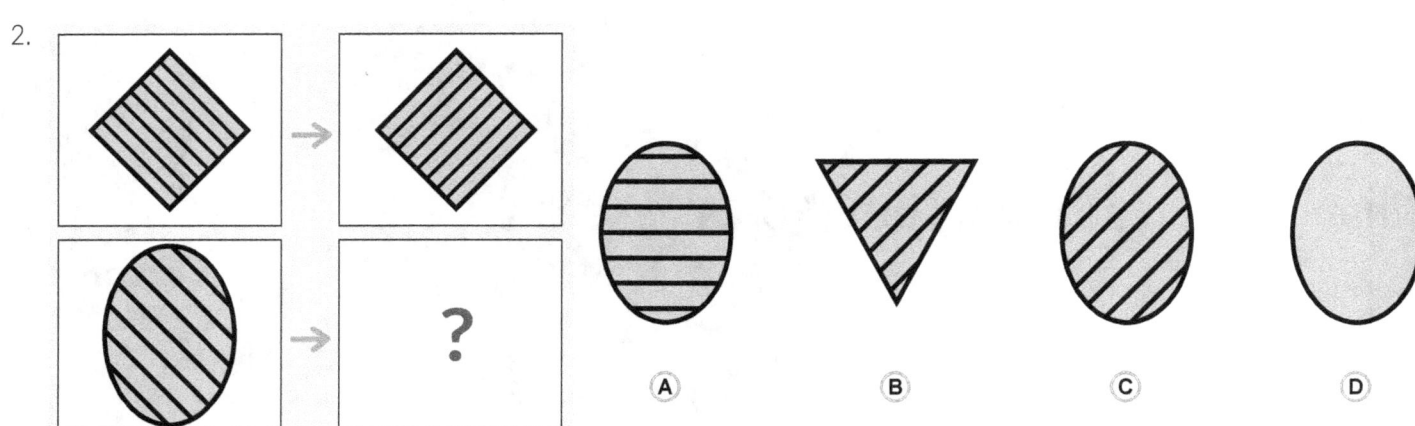

3.

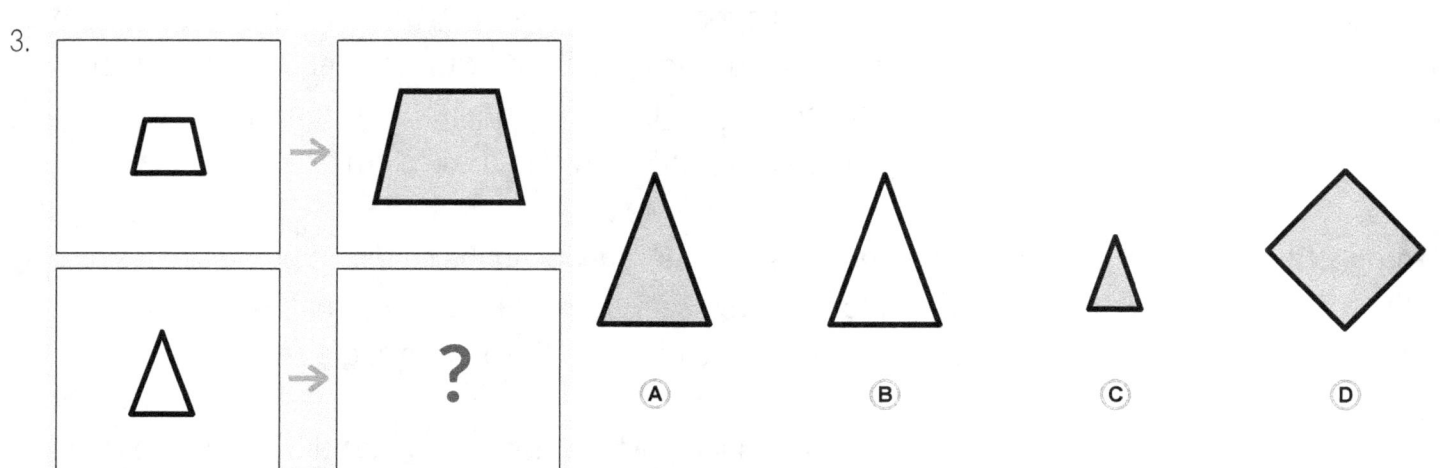

4.

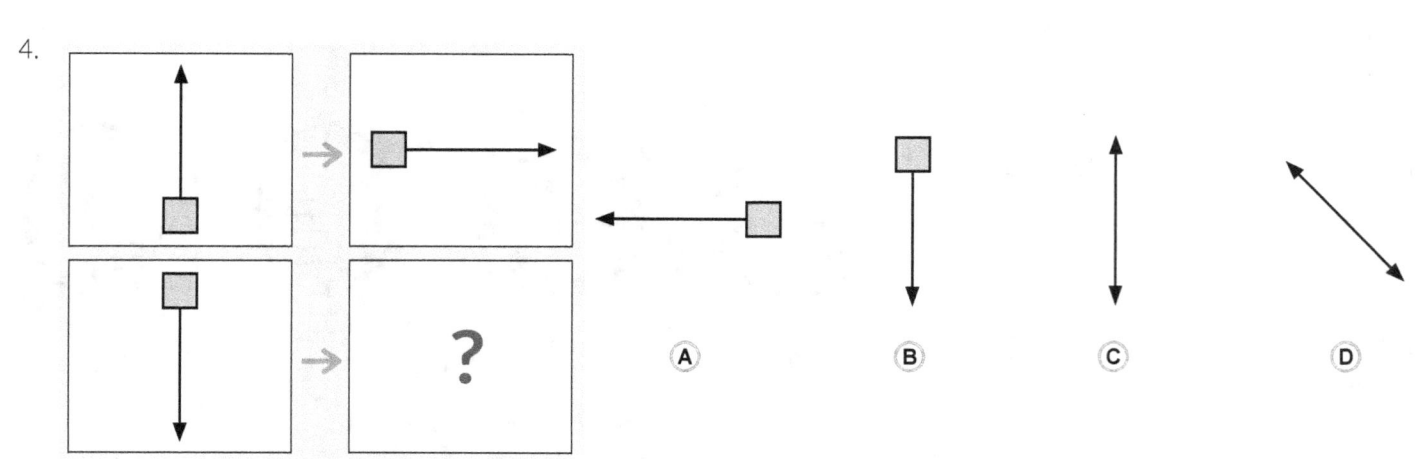

42

5.

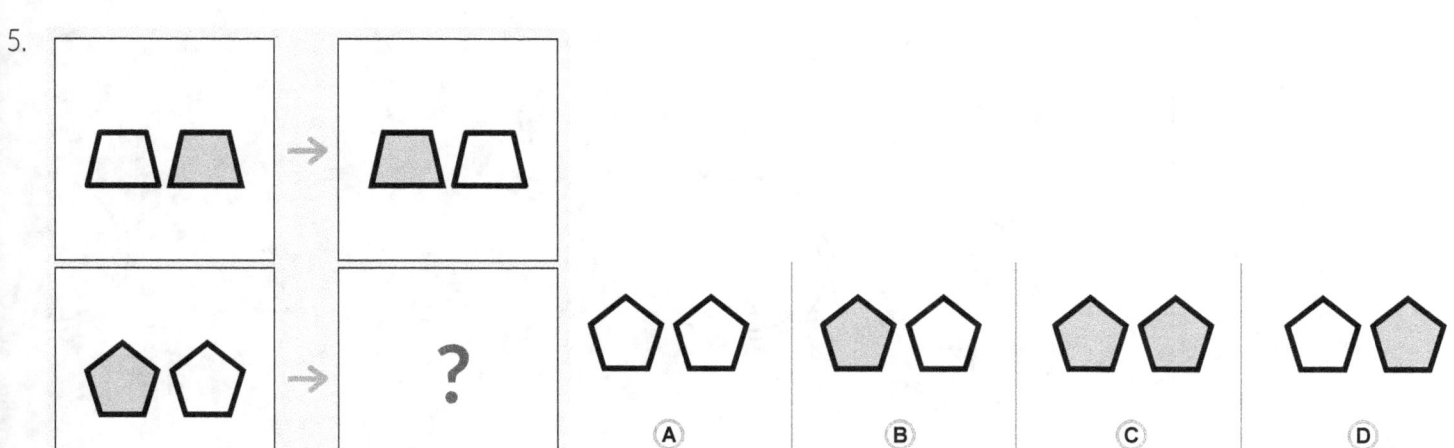

6.

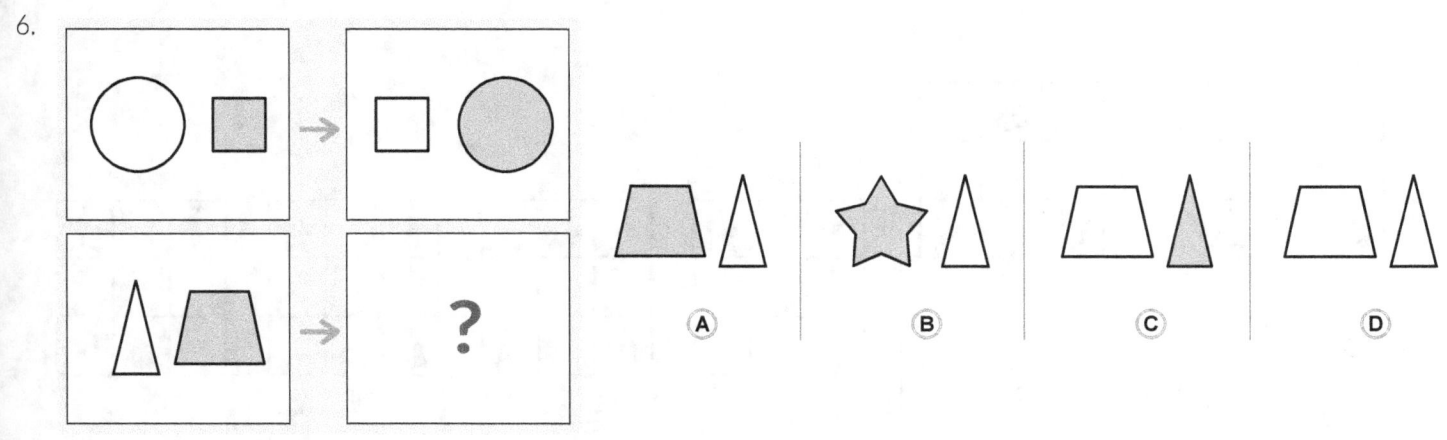

7.

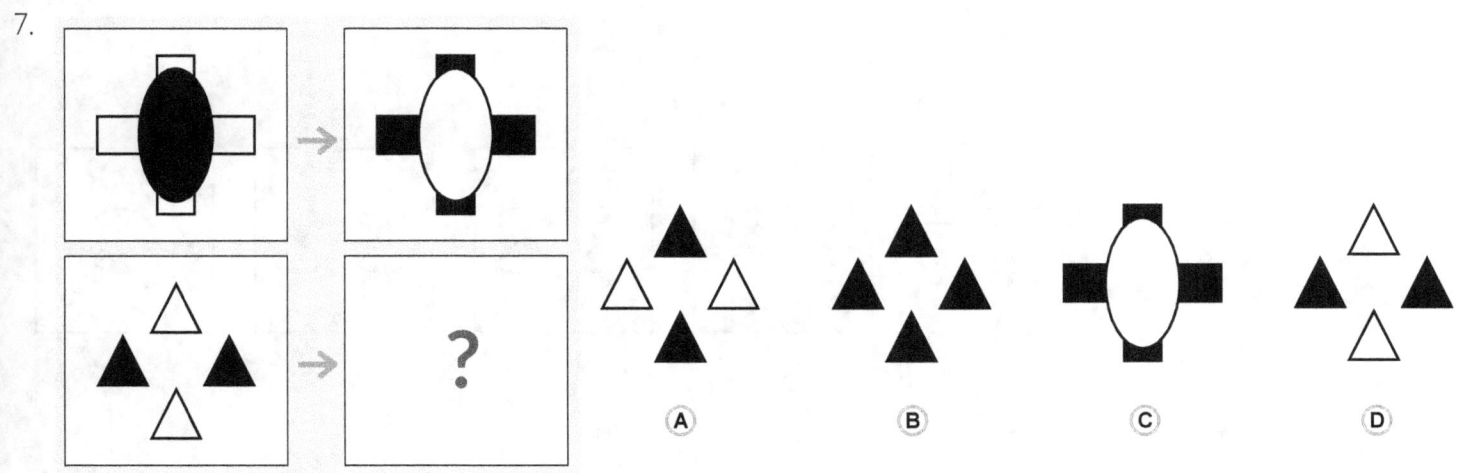

8.

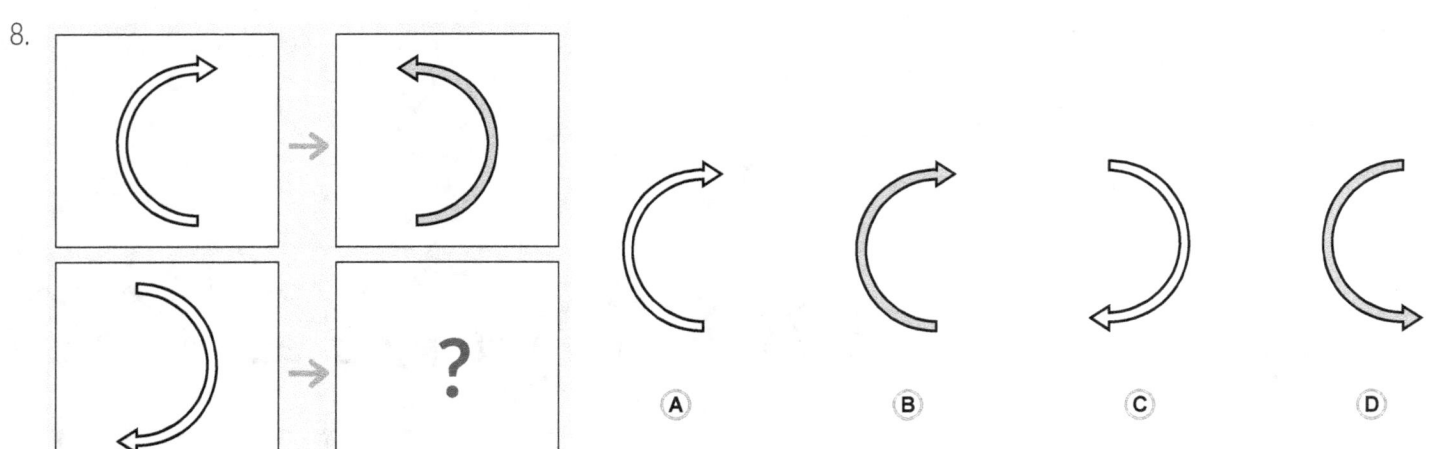

9.

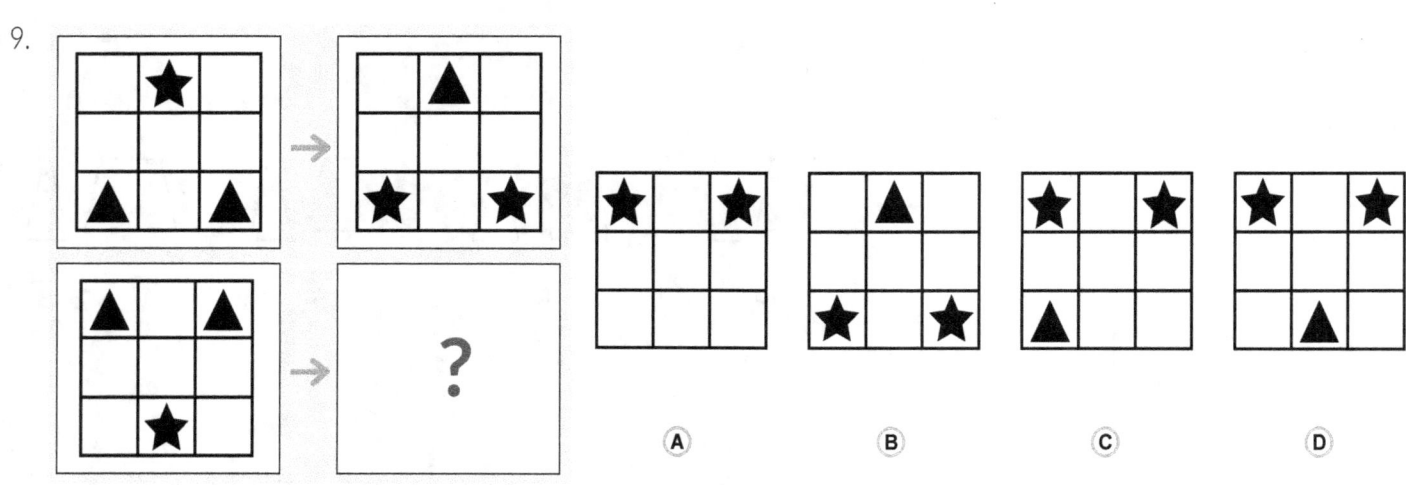

10.

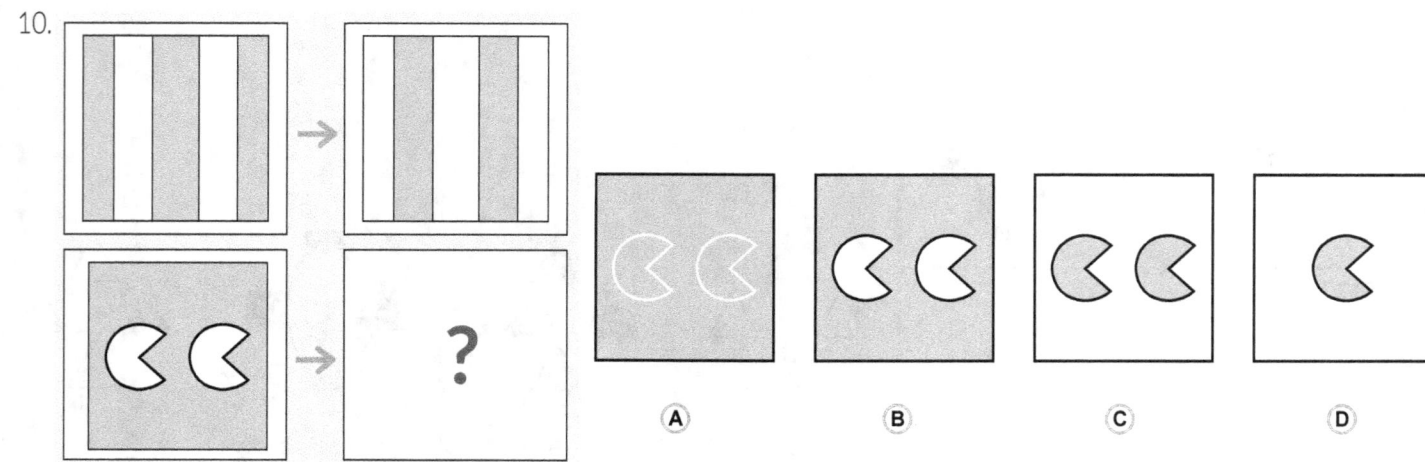

11.

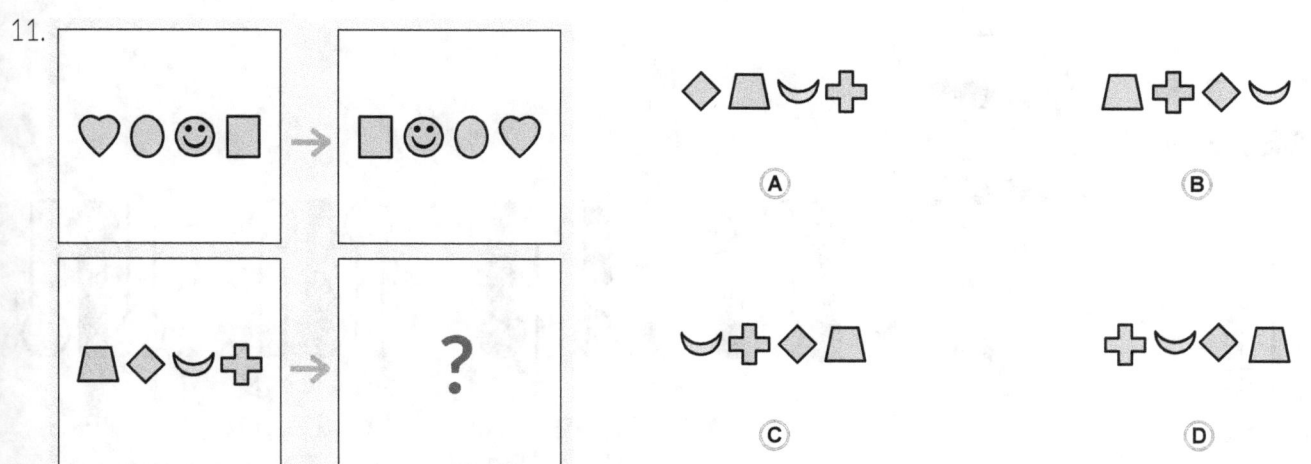

12.

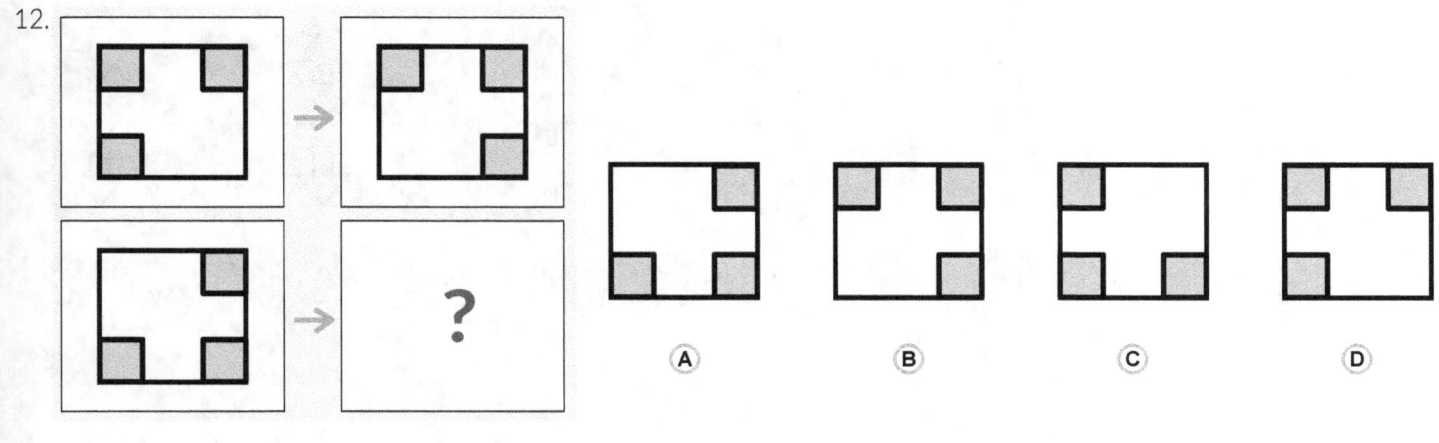

13.

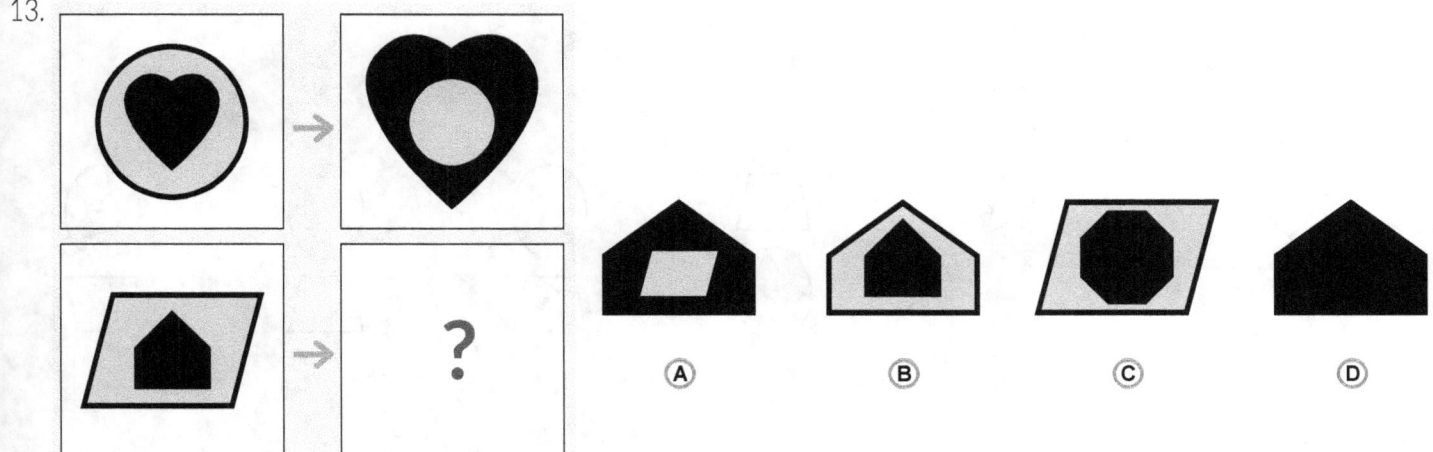

14.

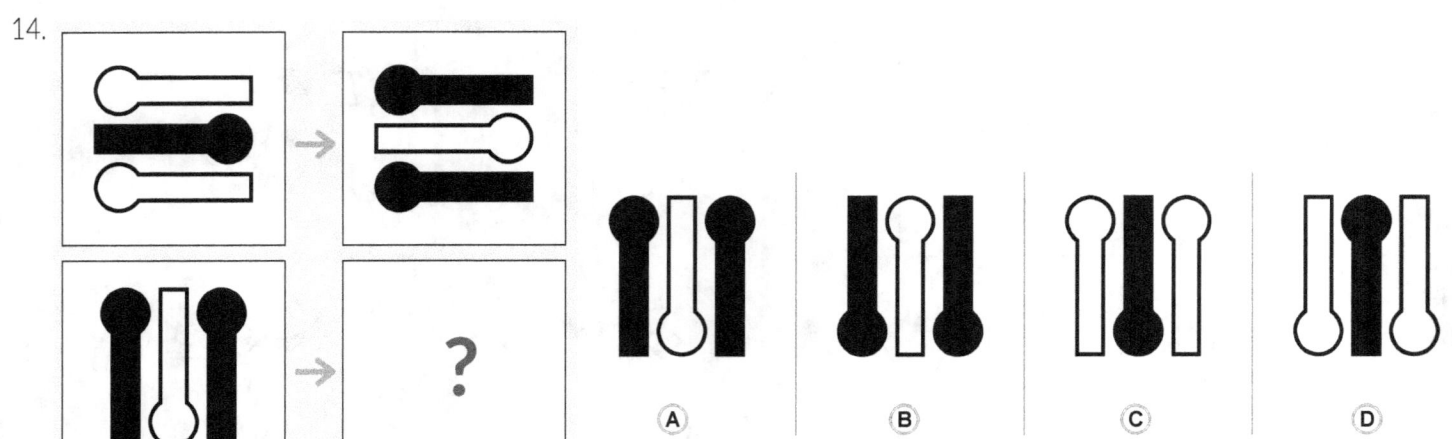

15.

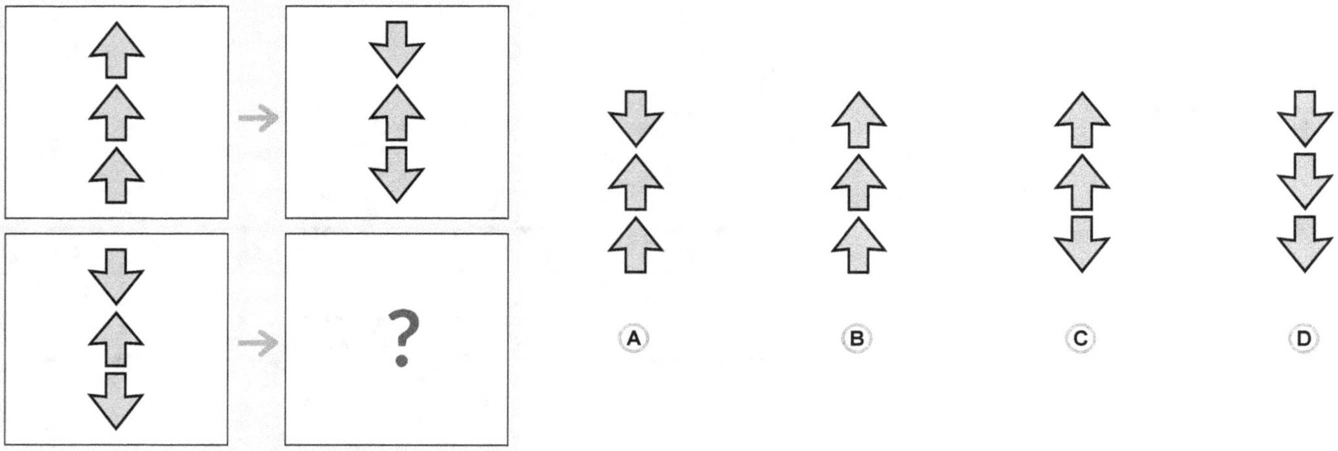

16.

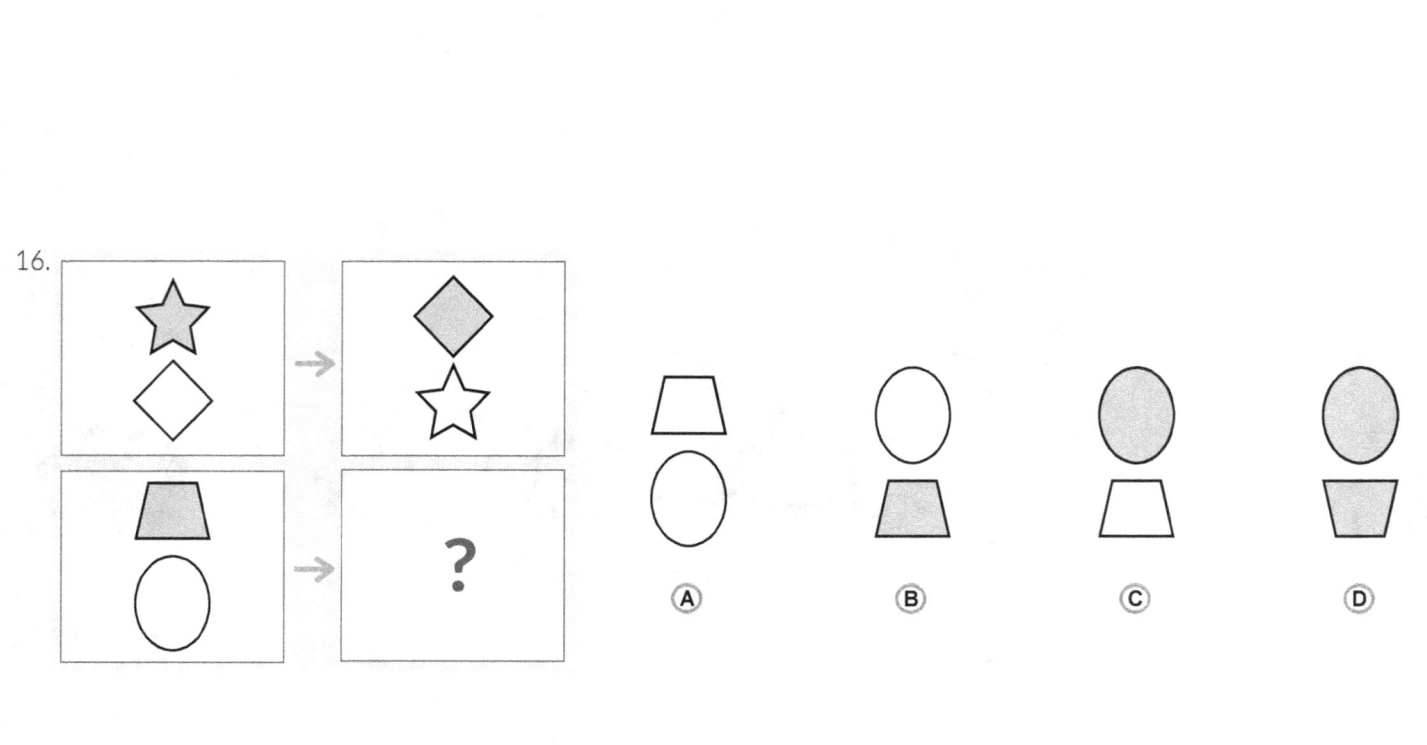

FIGURE CLASSIFICATION

Kai

"What picture on the bottom goes best with those on top?" Kai asks.

Directions (read to child): The top row shows three pictures that are alike in some way. Look at the bottom row. There are four pictures. Which picture in the bottom row goes best with the pictures in the top row?

Explanation (for parents): A more detailed explanation of Figure Classification questions is on p.12. Look over p.12 if needed. Following is an excerpt.

Together with your child, try to figure out a "rule" describing how the top pictures are alike and belong together. Then, apply the "rule" to each answer choice to determine which one follows it.

If your child finds that more than one choice follows the rule, then a more specific rule is needed.

Look at the 3 shapes on top. They are all the same shape with a diagonal line going the same way. The line starts in the lower left corner and goes to the upper right corner. Next, look carefully at each choice on the bottom row. Which one follows the rule? Choice D follows the rule.

1.

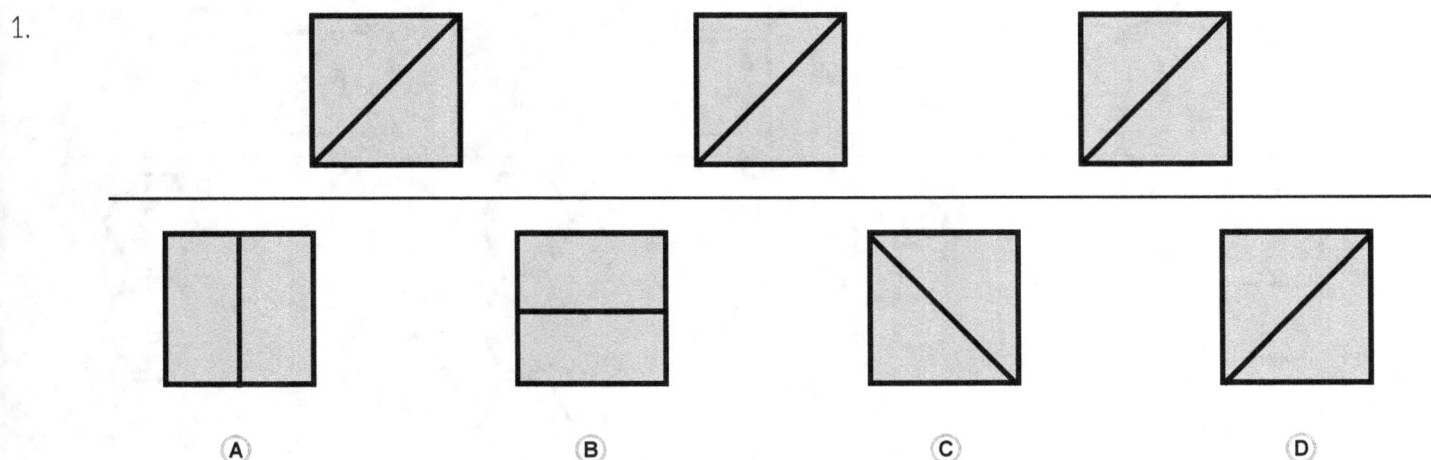

2.

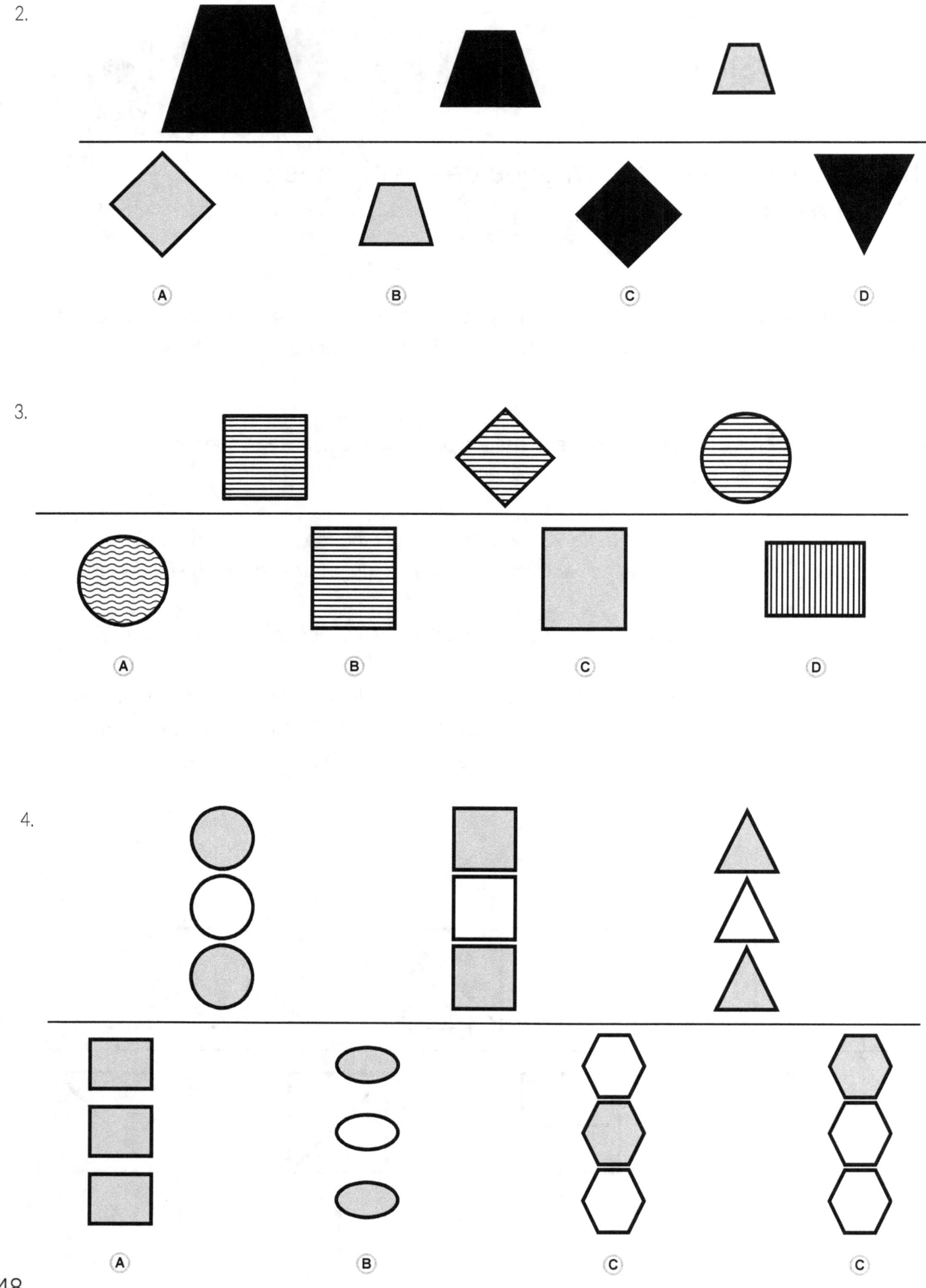

A   B   C   D

3.

A   B   C   D

4.

A   B   C   C

48

5.

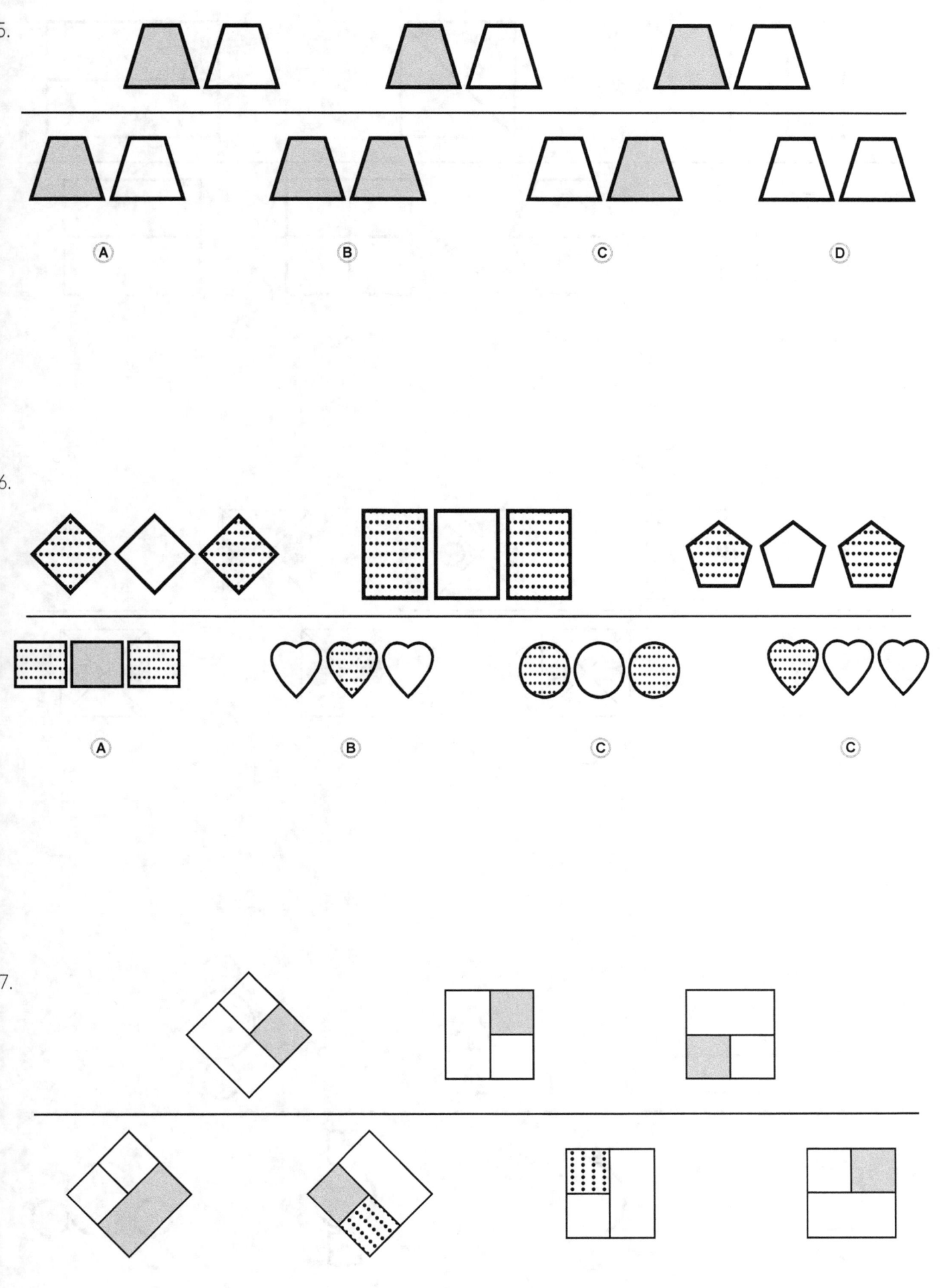

A B C D

6.

A B C C

7.

A B C D

49

8.

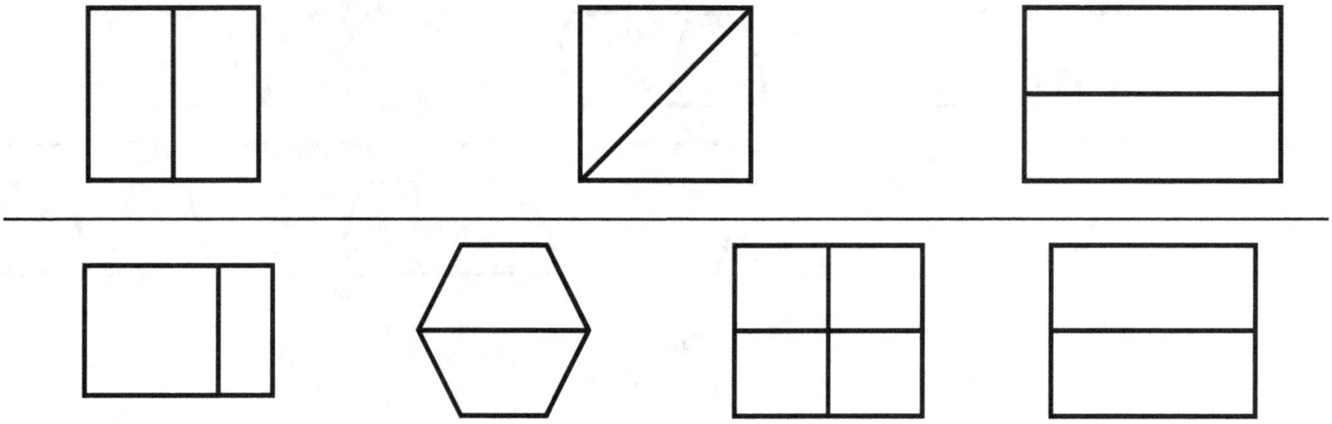

A B C D

9.

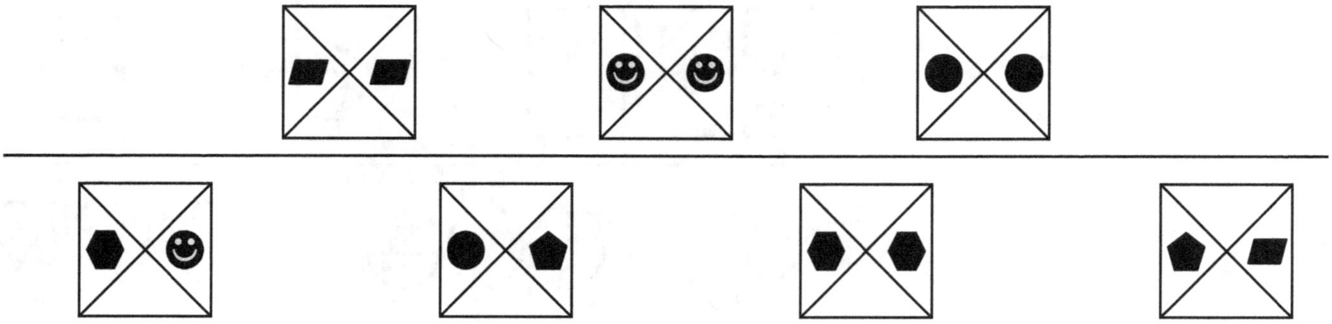

A B C D

10.

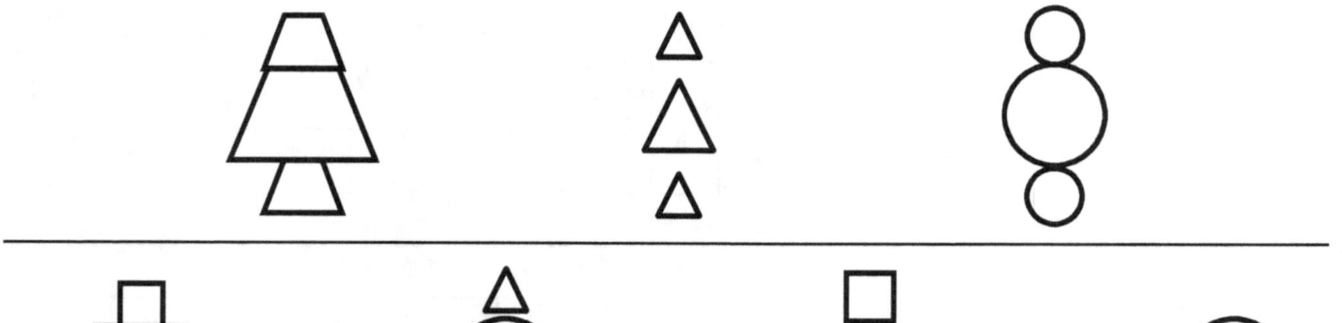

A B C D

11.

(A)   (B)   (C)   (D)

12.

A   B   C   D

13.

(A)   (B)   (C)   (D)

14.

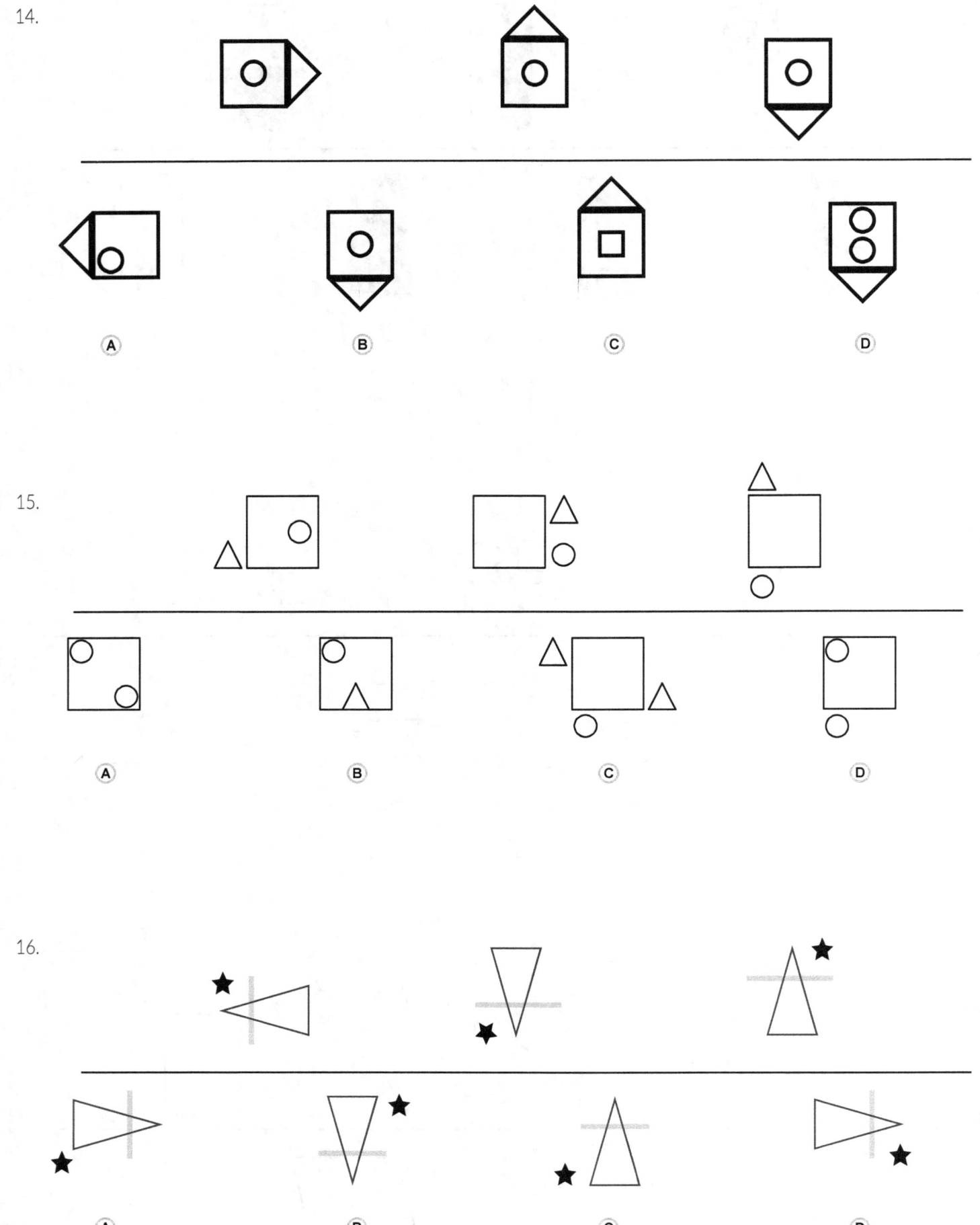

15.

16.

17.

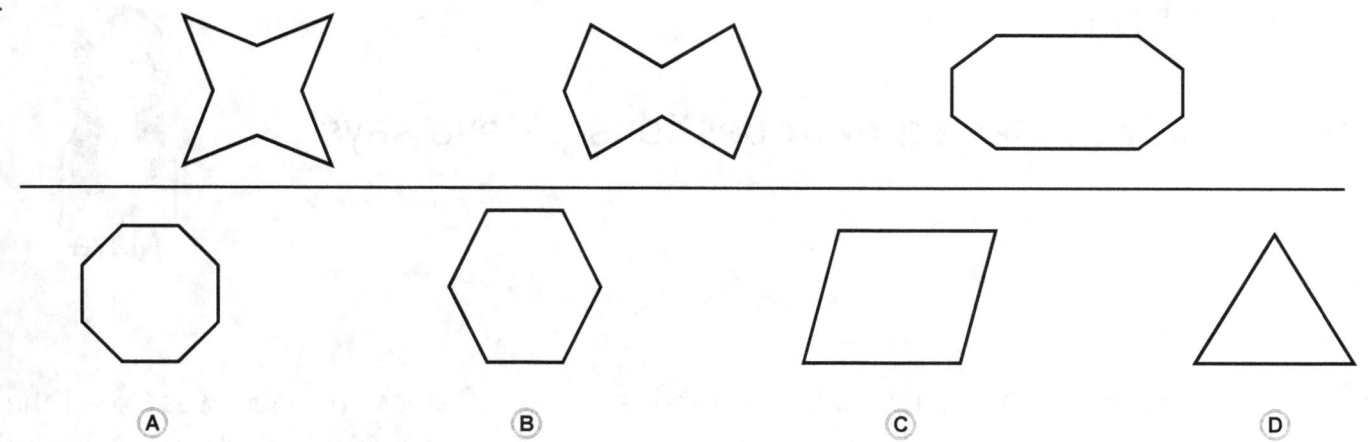

(A)   (B)   (C)   (D)

Keep up the good work!

Noah

PAPER FOLDING

"Look closely at these tricky questions!" Maya says.

Maya

Directions (read to child): The top row of pictures shows a sheet of paper. The paper was folded, then something was cut out. Which picture in the bottom row shows how the paper would look after it's unfolded?

Additional information (for parents): As explained earlier on p.15, children may initially be "stumped" by Paper Folding. If your child needs help, then try demonstrating with real paper and a hole puncher. Be sure to point out the number of holes made and their position after opening the paper.

1.

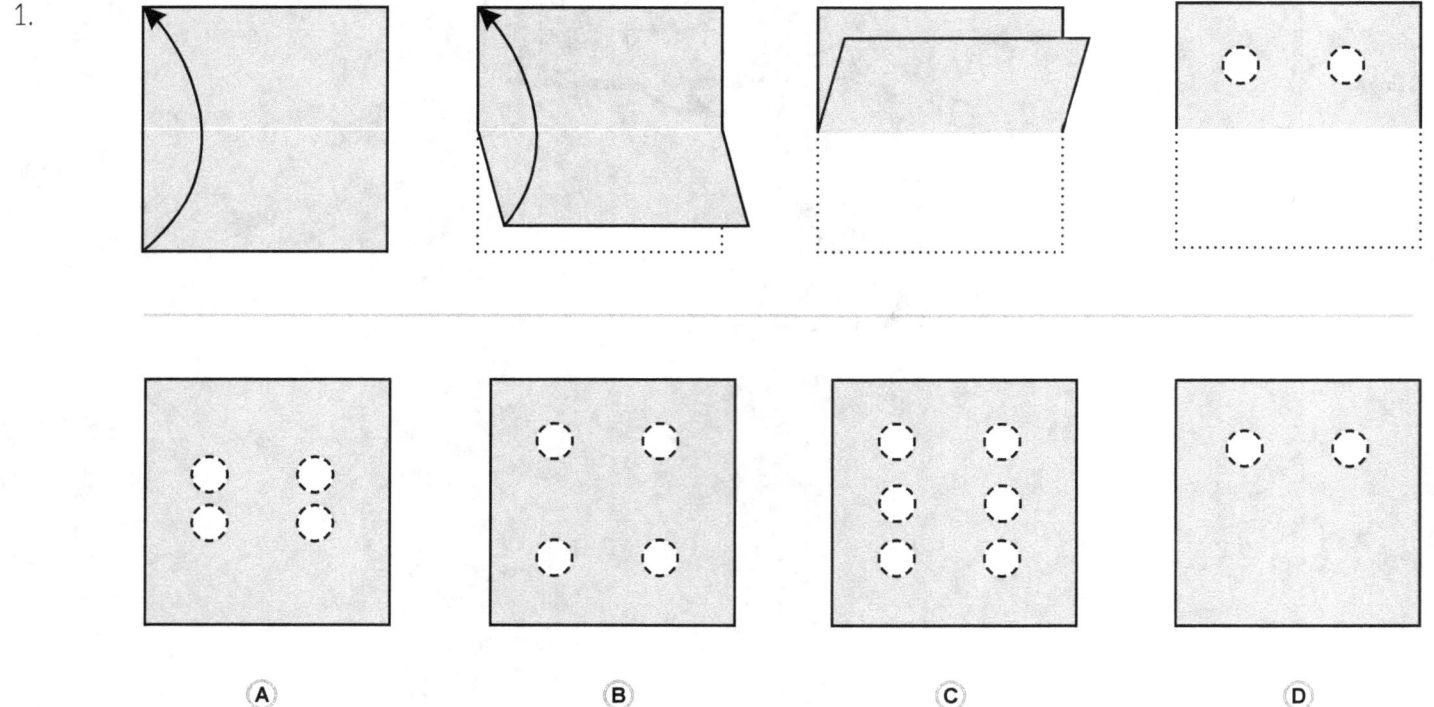

2.

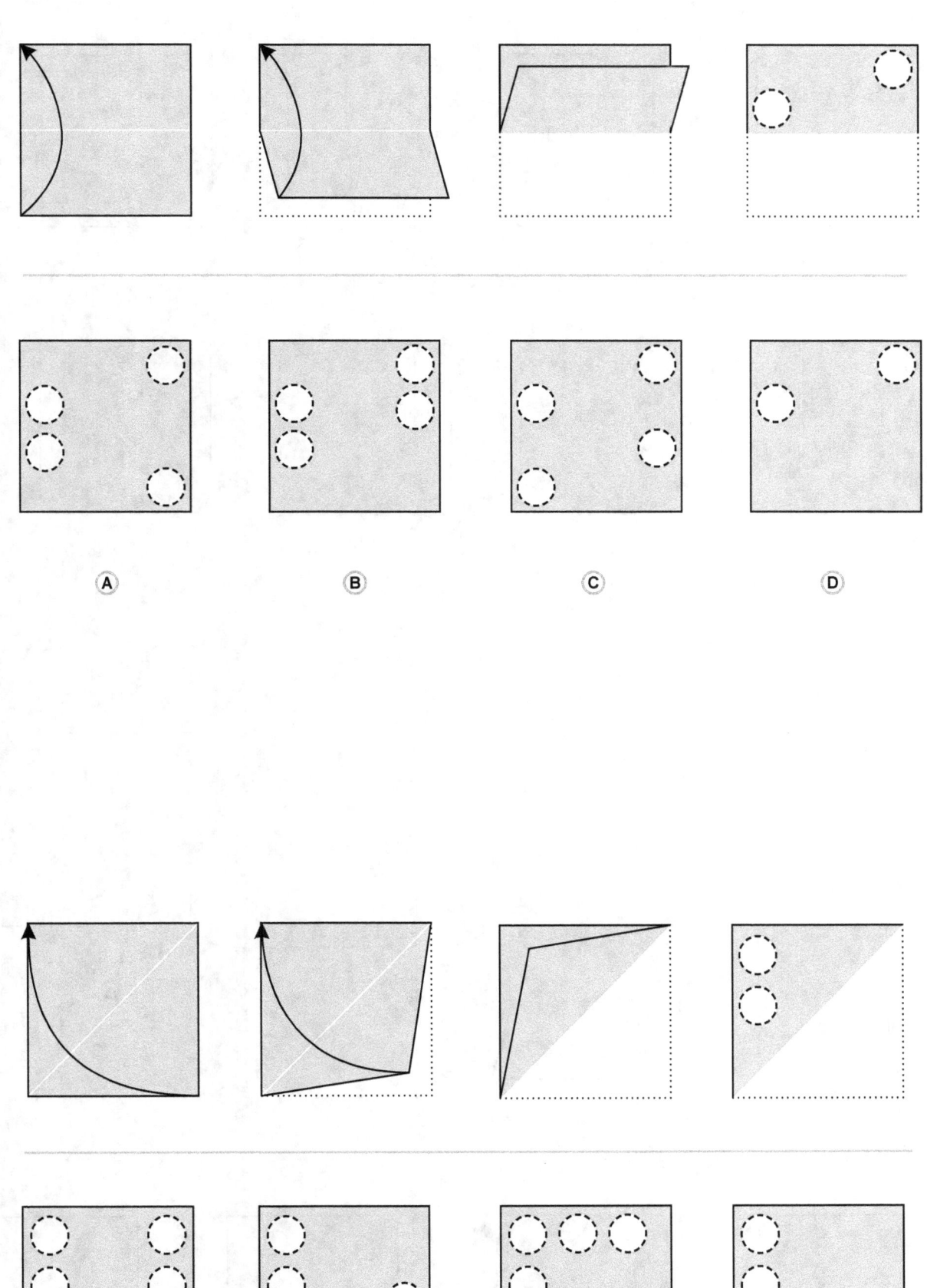

A

B

C

D

3.

A

B

C

D

55

4.

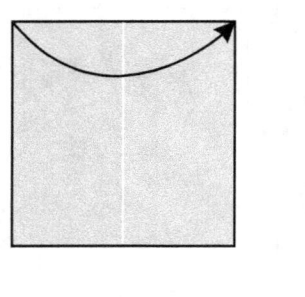 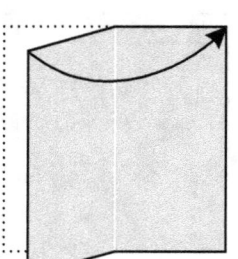 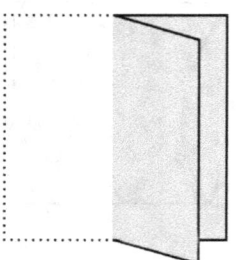 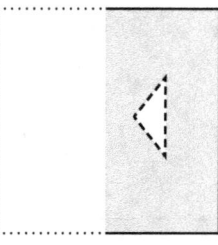

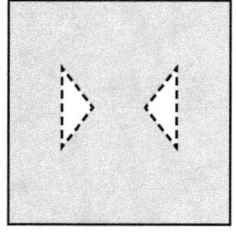 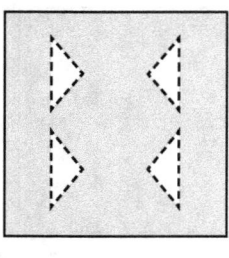 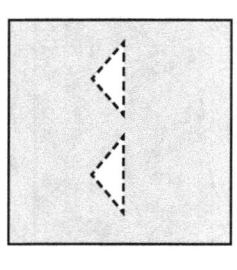

(A)　　　　　　　(B)　　　　　　　(C)　　　　　　　(D)

5.

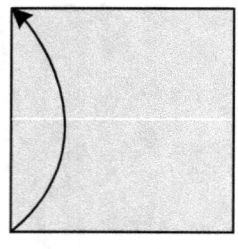 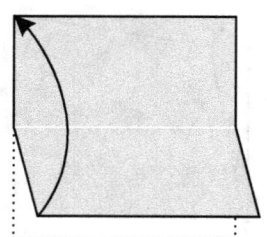 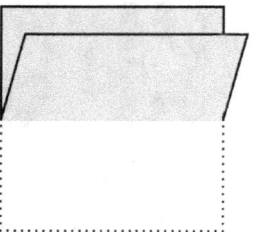 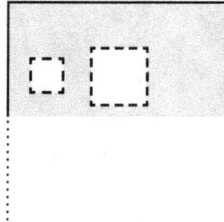

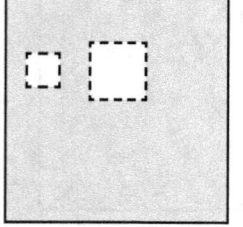 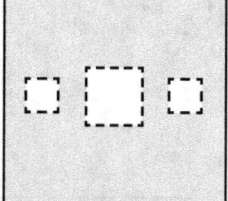 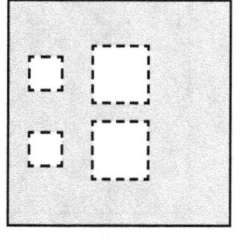 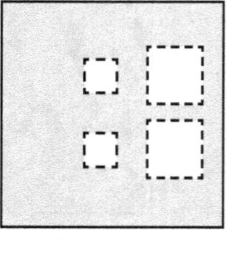

(A)　　　　　　　(B)　　　　　　　(C)　　　　　　　(D)

6.

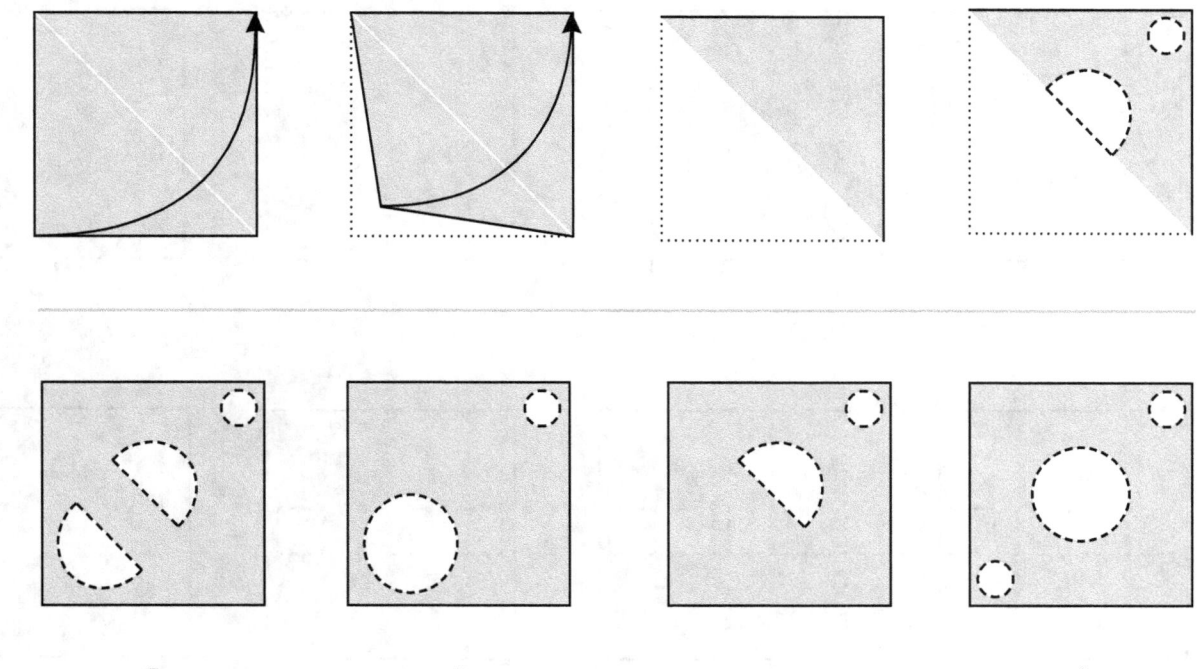

7.

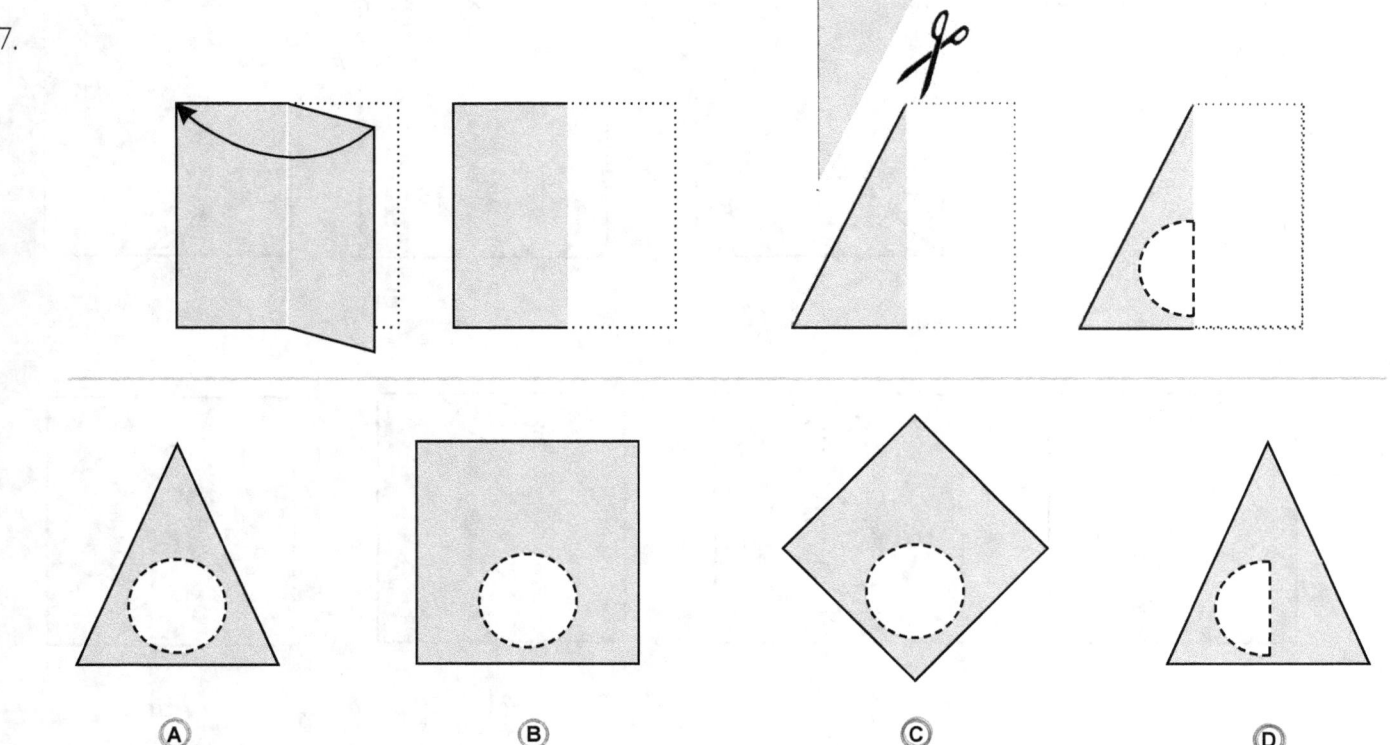

8.

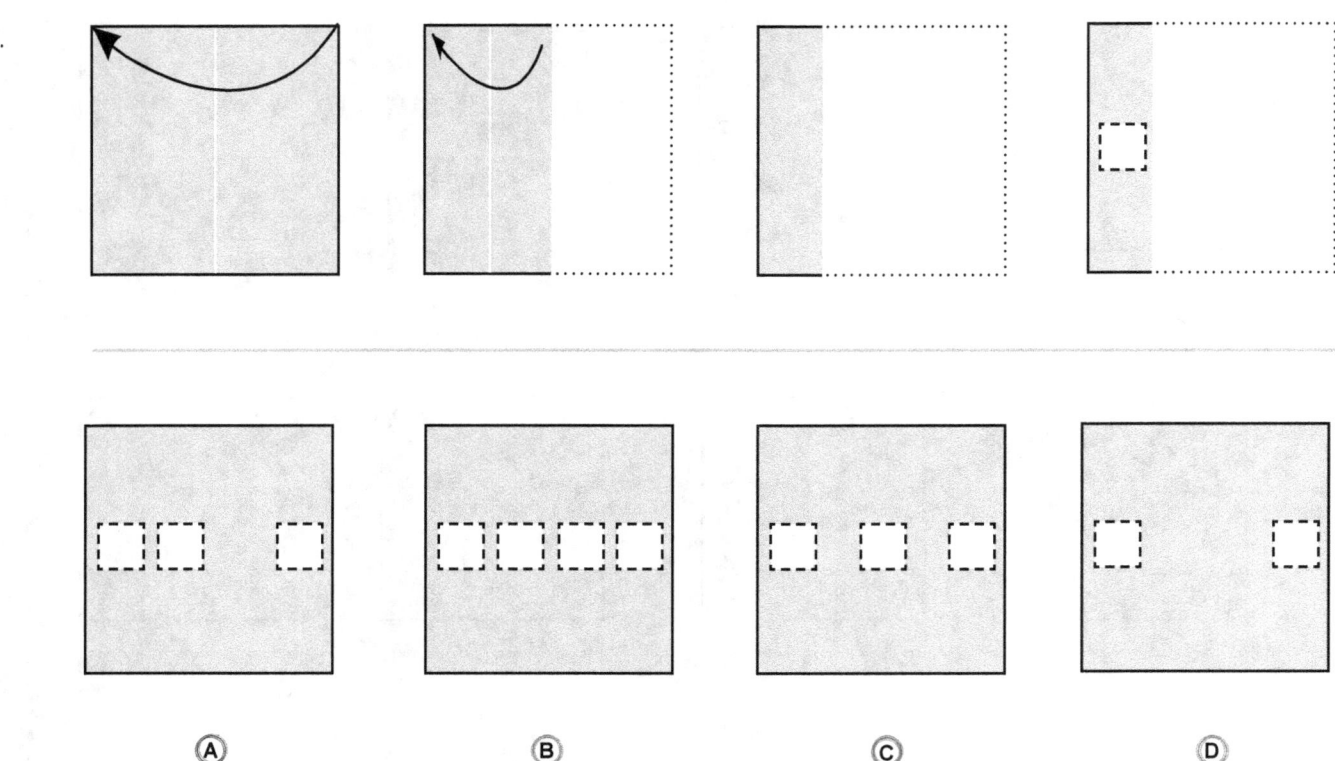

Ⓐ Ⓑ Ⓒ Ⓓ

9.

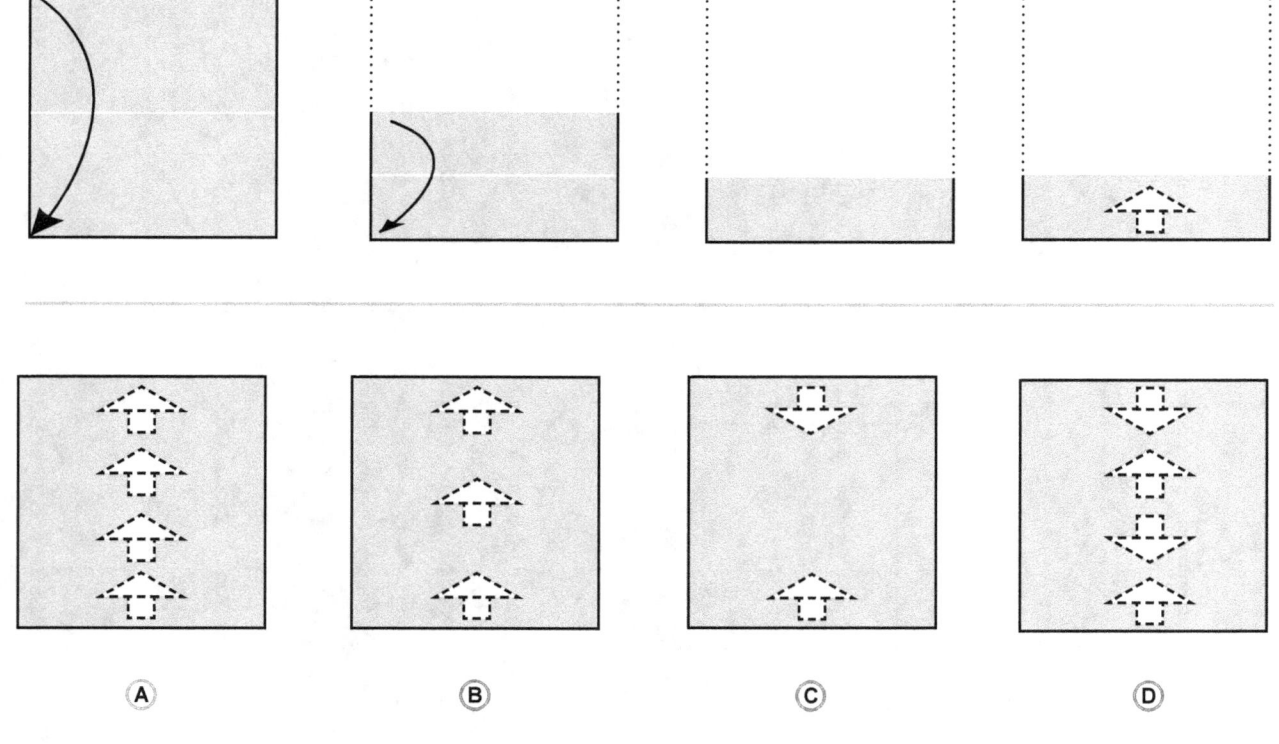

Ⓐ Ⓑ Ⓒ Ⓓ

10.

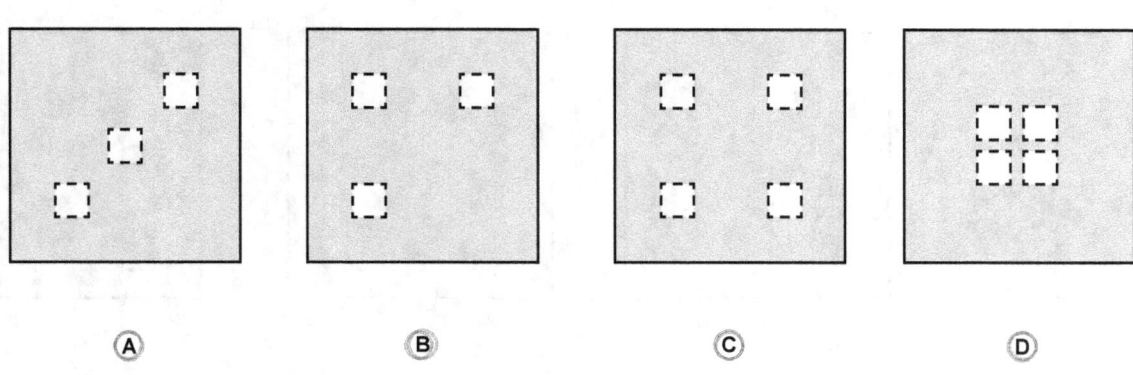

(A) (B) (C) (D)

11.

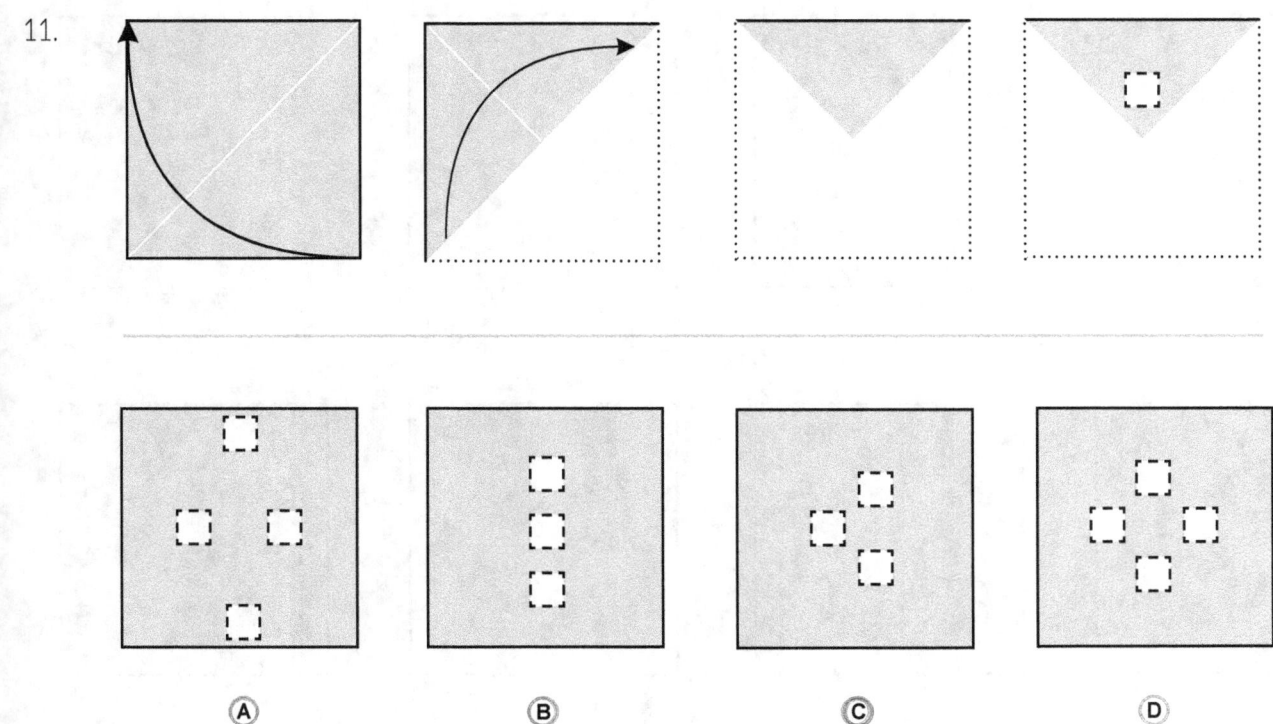

(A) (B) (C) (D)

59

12.

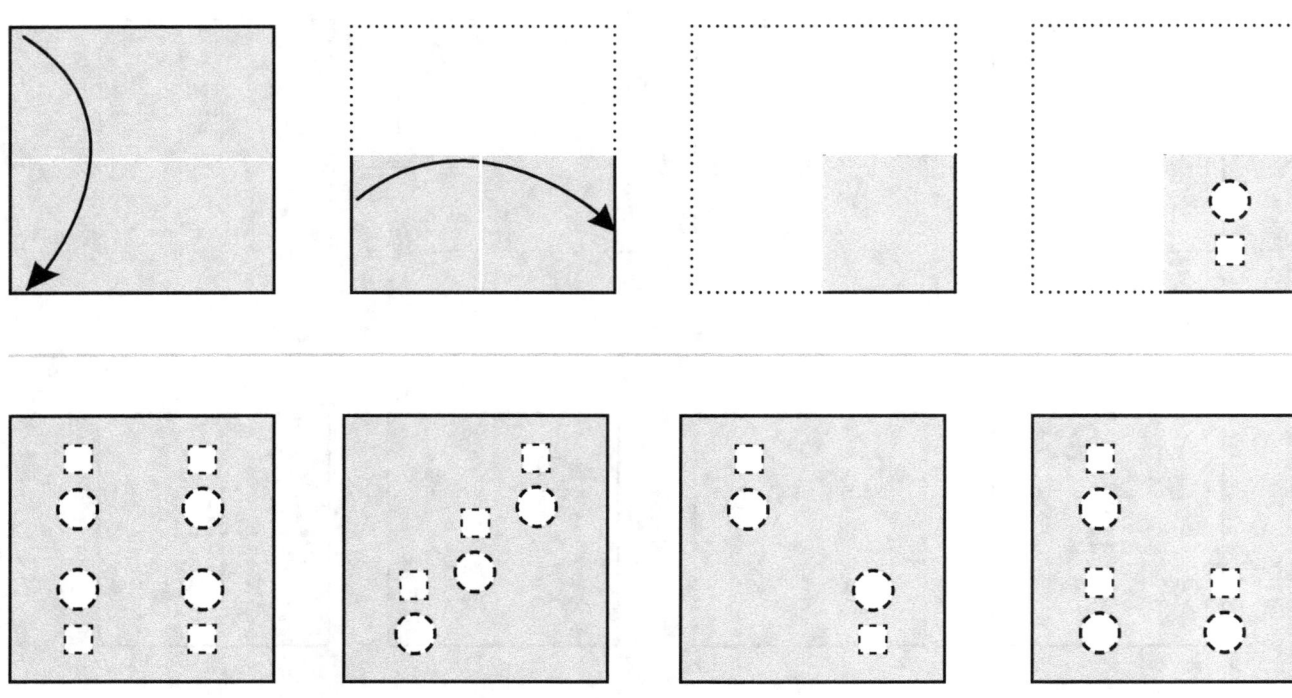

13.

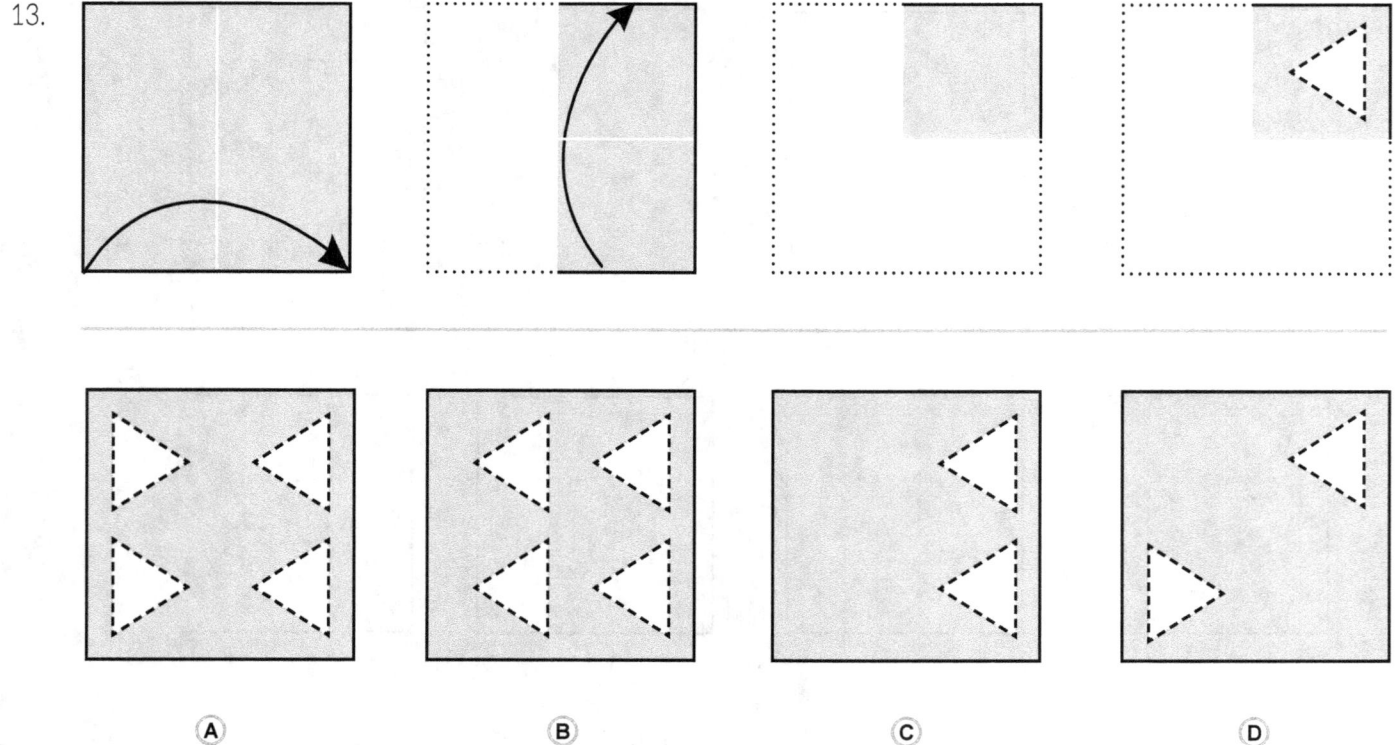

Ⓐ   Ⓑ   Ⓒ   Ⓓ

60

14.

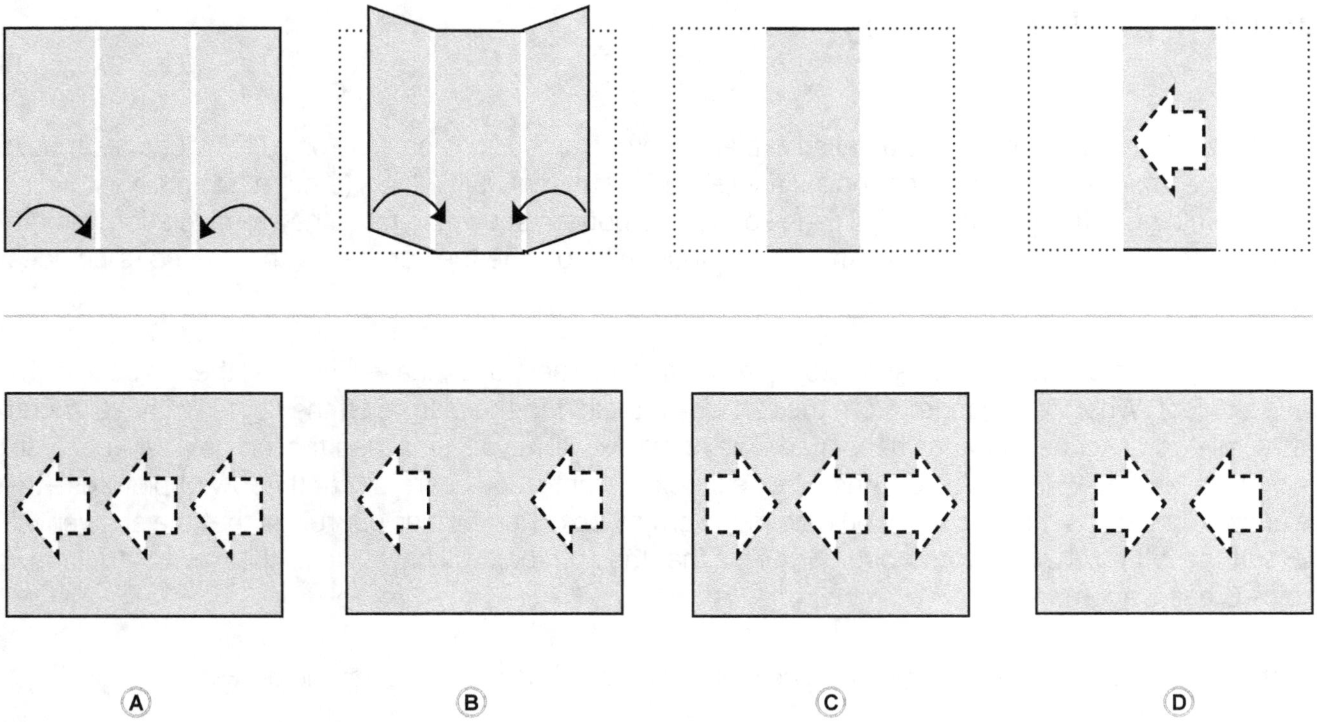

A   B   C   D

15.

A   B   C   D

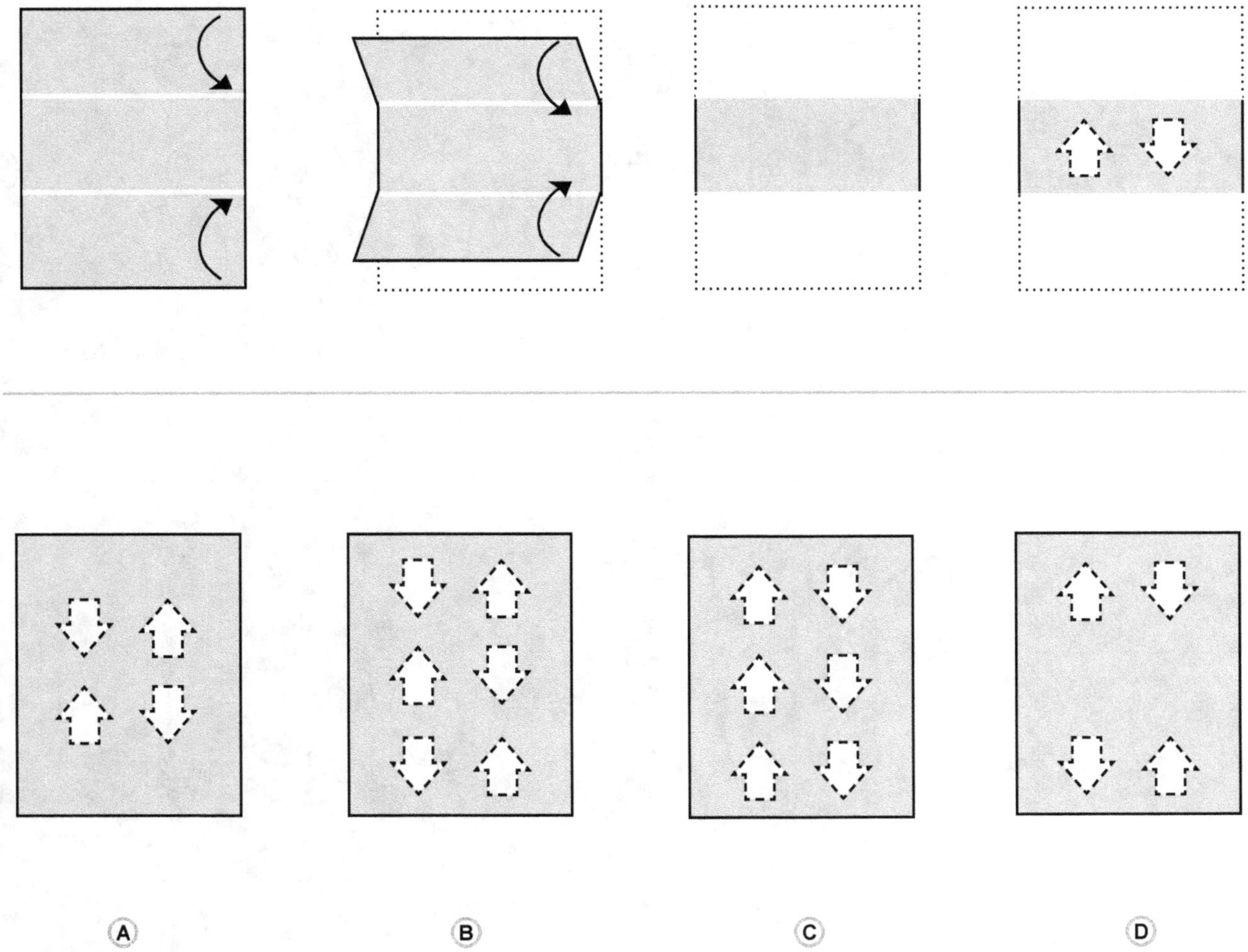

NUMBER ANALOGIES

Explanation (for parents): A more detailed explanation of Number Analogies is on p.17. Your child must figure out how the images in the top set of boxes are related mathematically. Then, (s)he must figure out which answer choice would go with the bottom left image so that the bottom set would have the same relationship. After counting the objects in the boxes, you may want your child to write the number by the box, so (s)he does not forget the quantity.

Directions for the example: Look at the top box on the left. There are 4 leaves. Look at the top box on the right. There is 1 leaf. What has changed from the picture on the left to the picture on the right? We need to come up with a "rule" to describe what has happened. The right box will have 3 less than the left box. What do you see in the bottom left box? There are 5 acorns. The next box is empty. Look carefully at the row of pictures - these are the answer choices. Which choice would go in the empty box? Remember, our rule is that the answer will have 3 less. If the left box has 5 acorns, and our rule is that the right box will have 3 less, that means the answer is 2. Choice C has 2 acorns.

Directions for the rest: Which answer choice would go inside the empty box at the bottom?

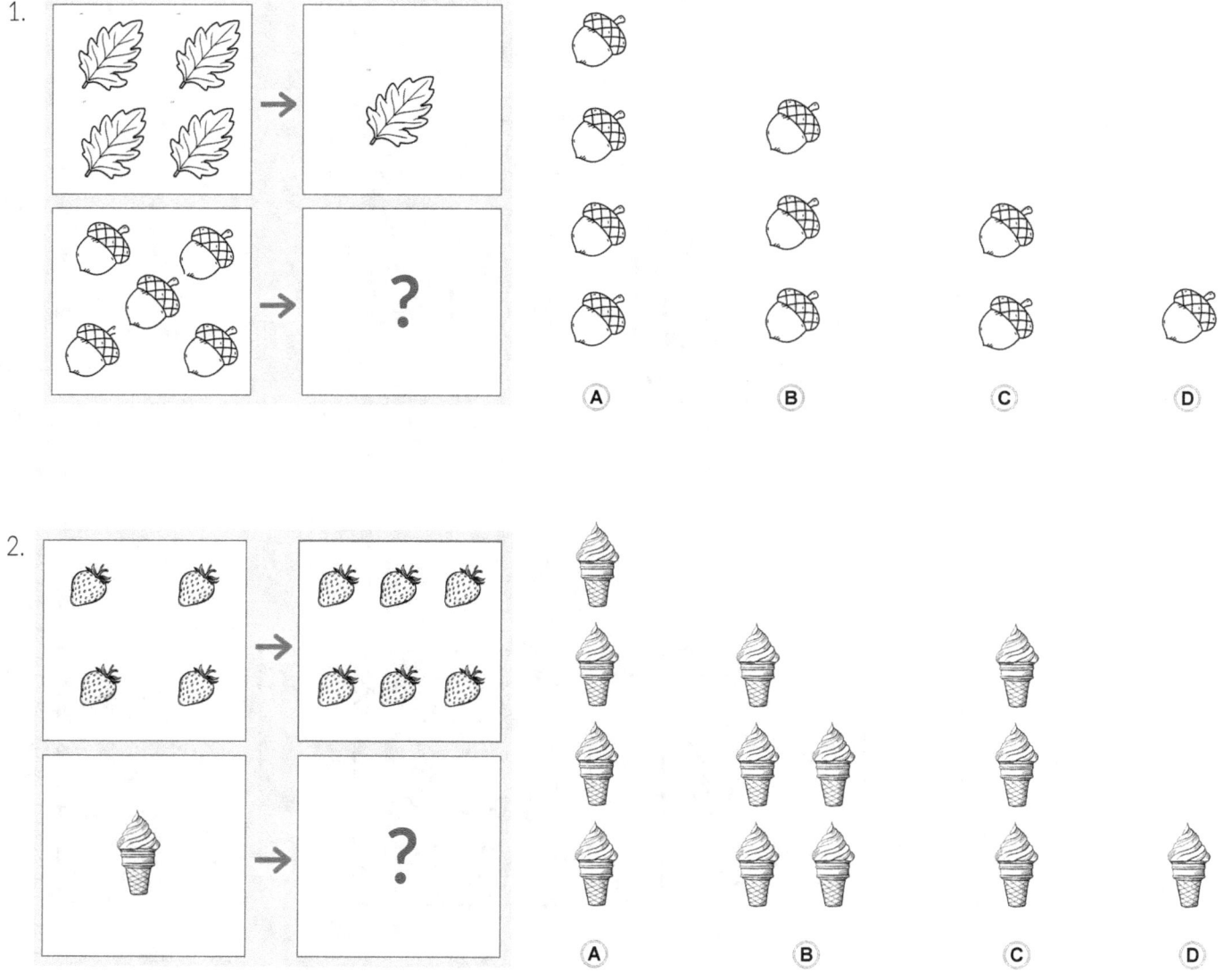

3.

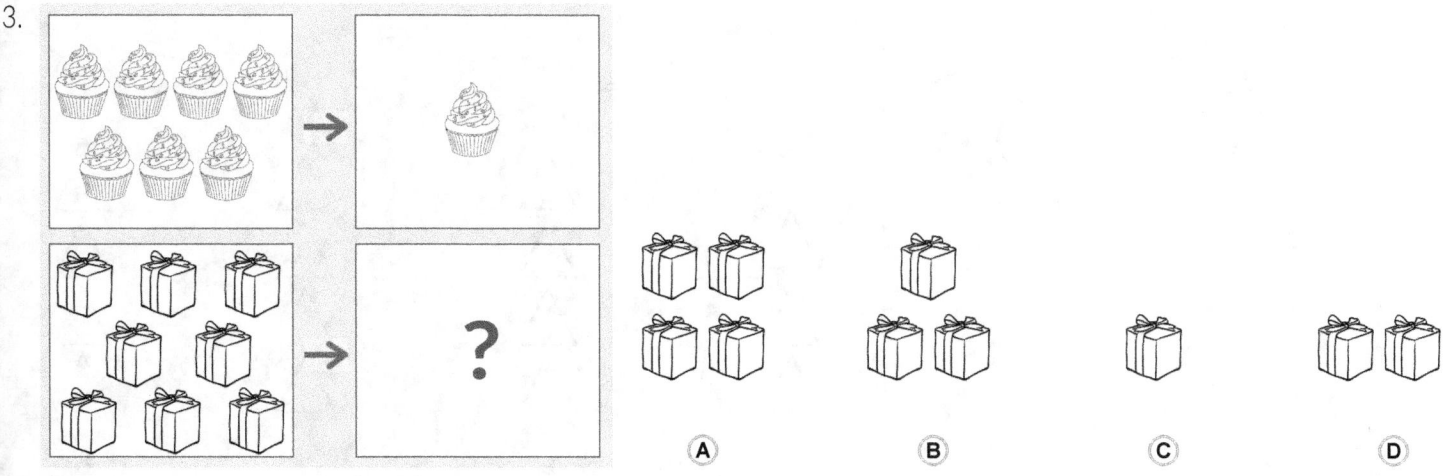

A   B   C   D

4.

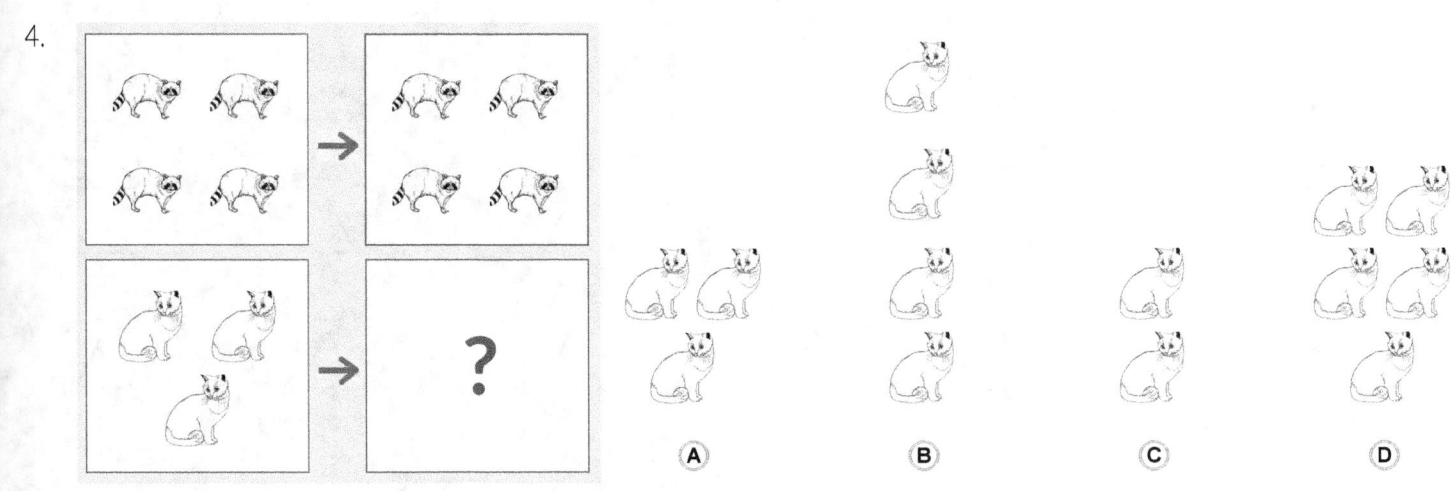

A   B   C   D

5.

A   B   C   D

6.

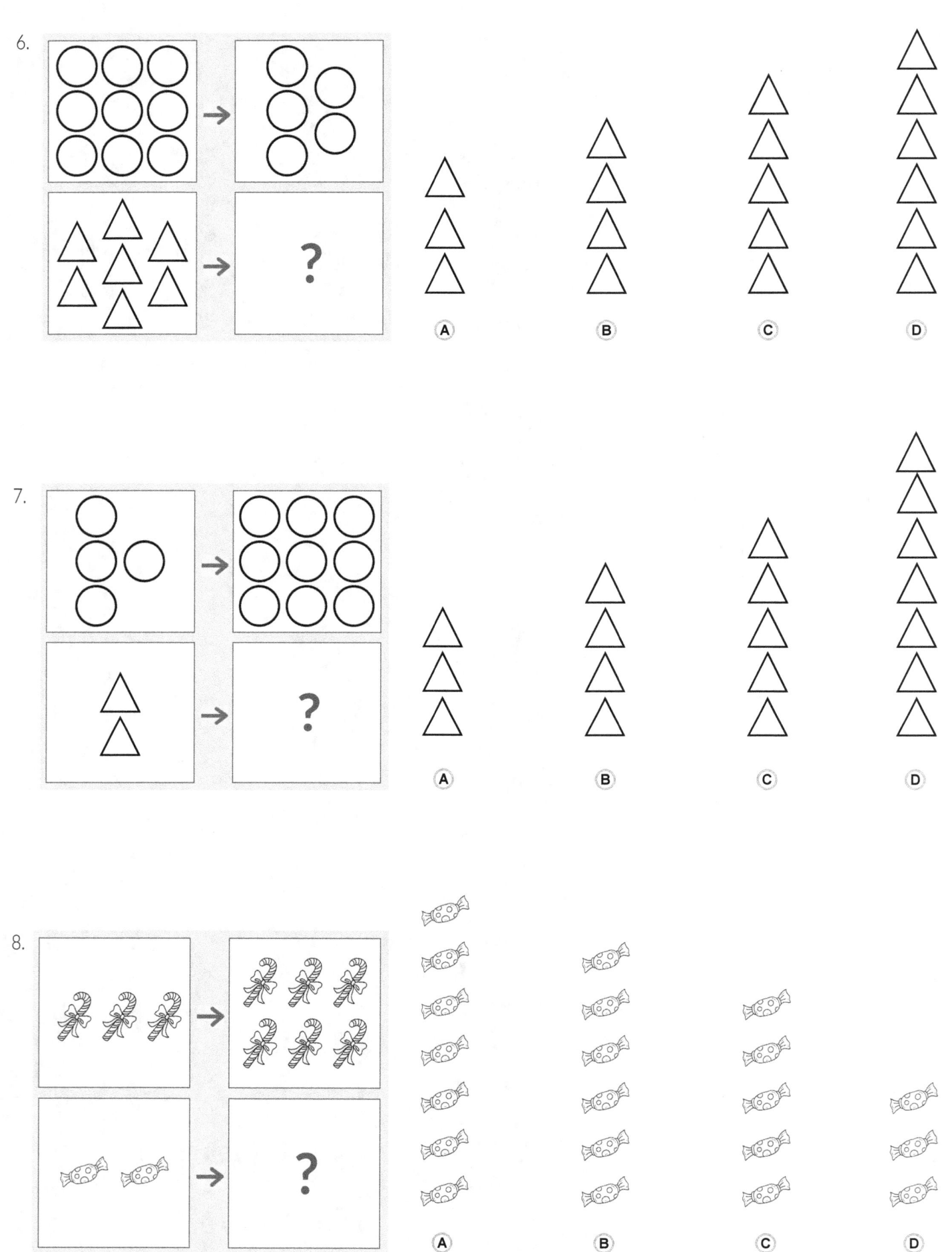

7.

8.

64

9.

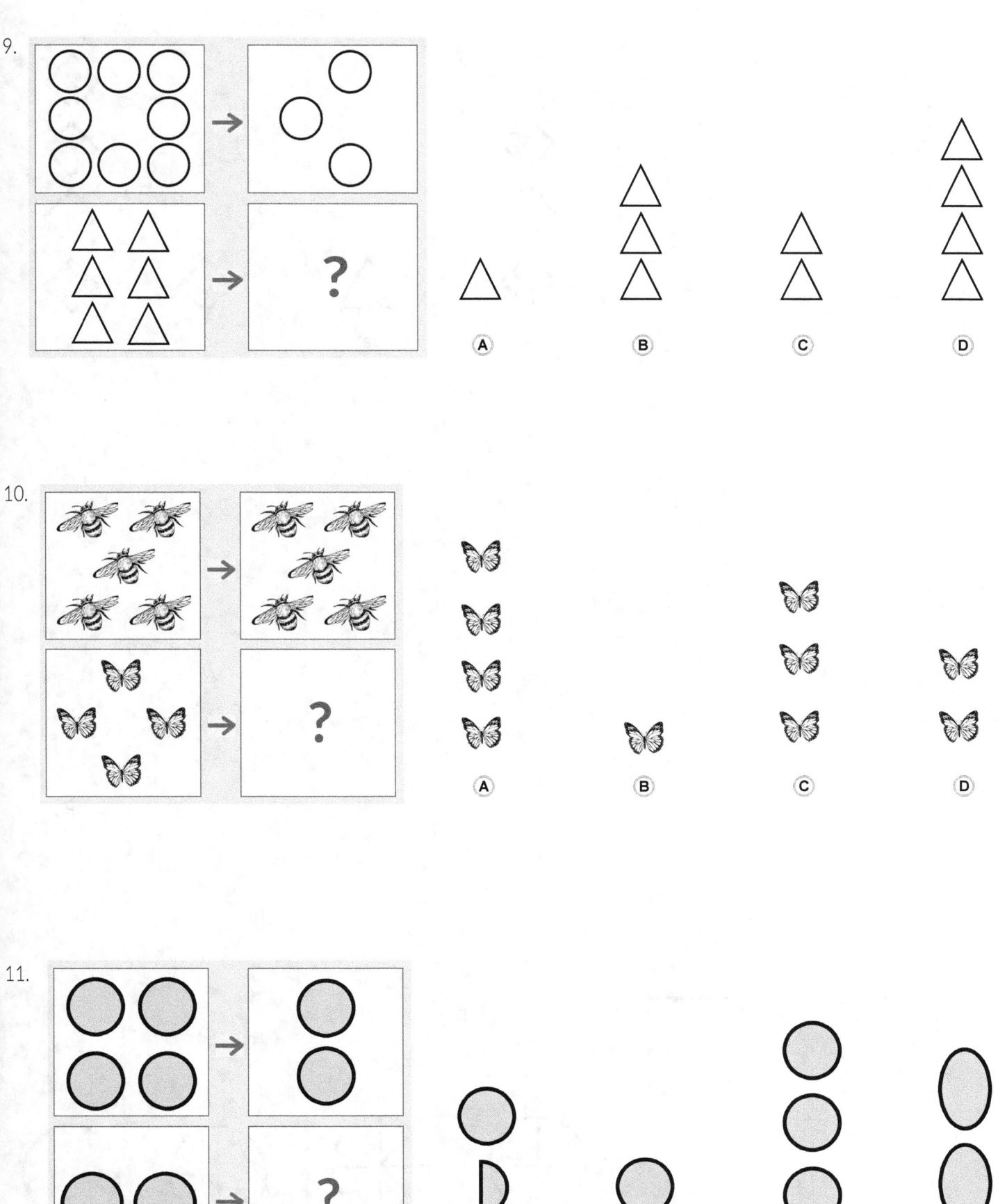

10.

11.

12.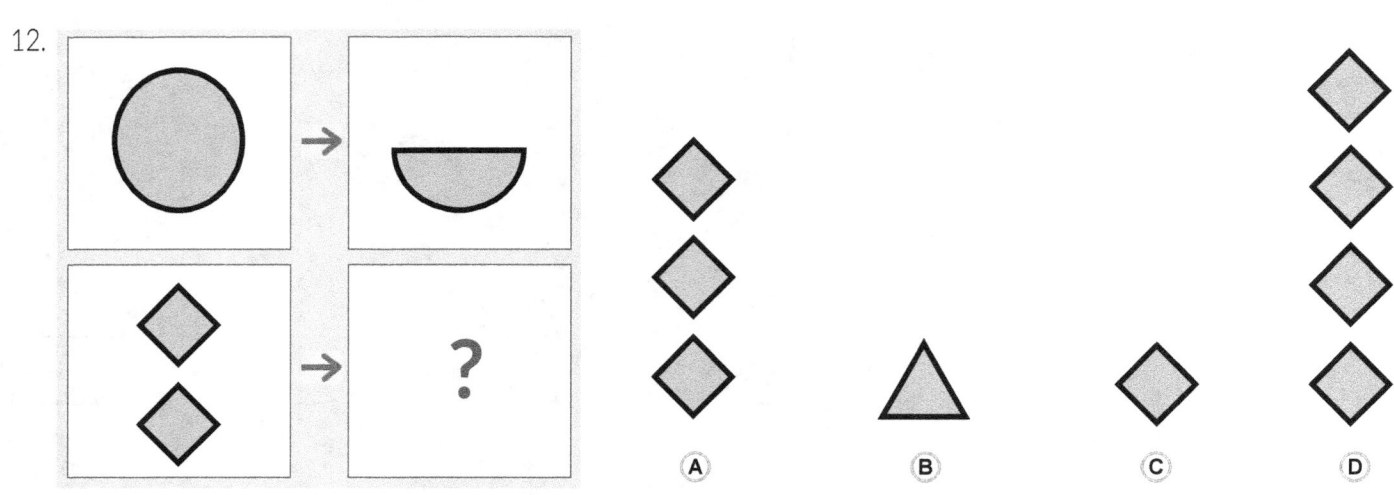

13.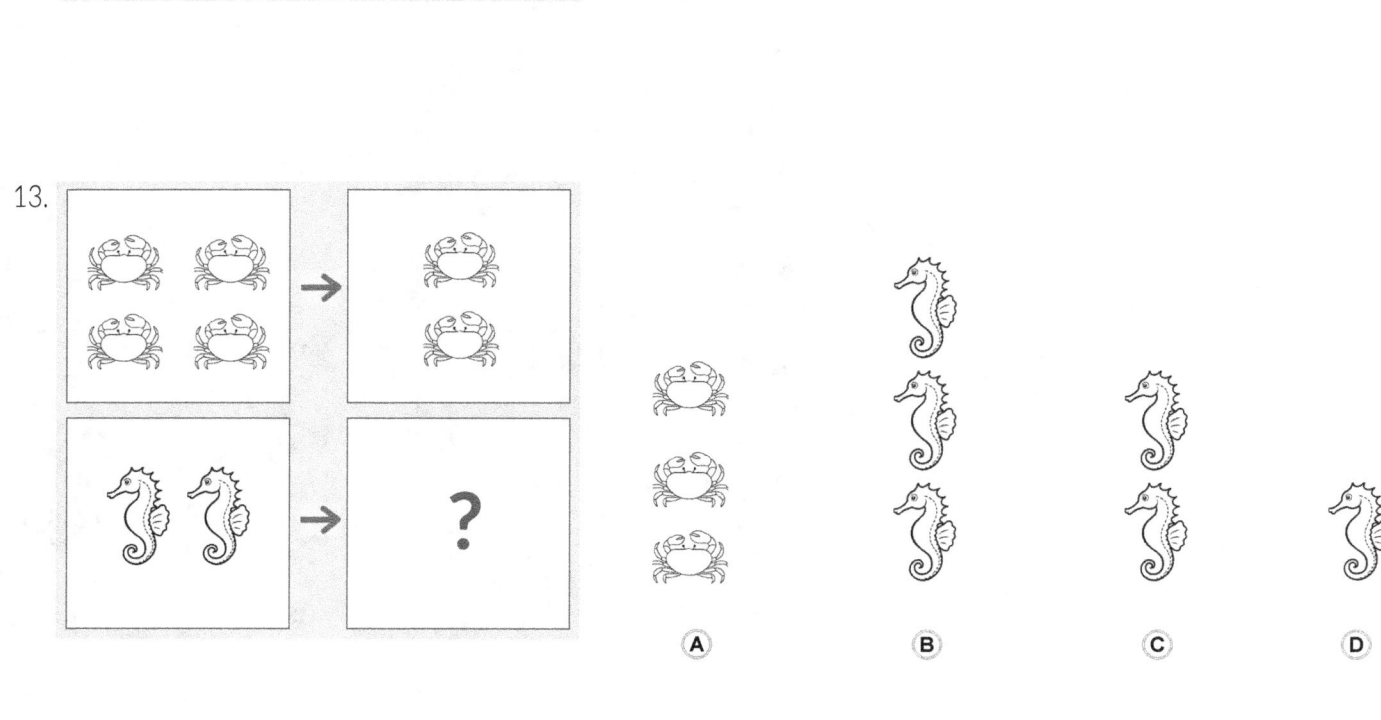

14.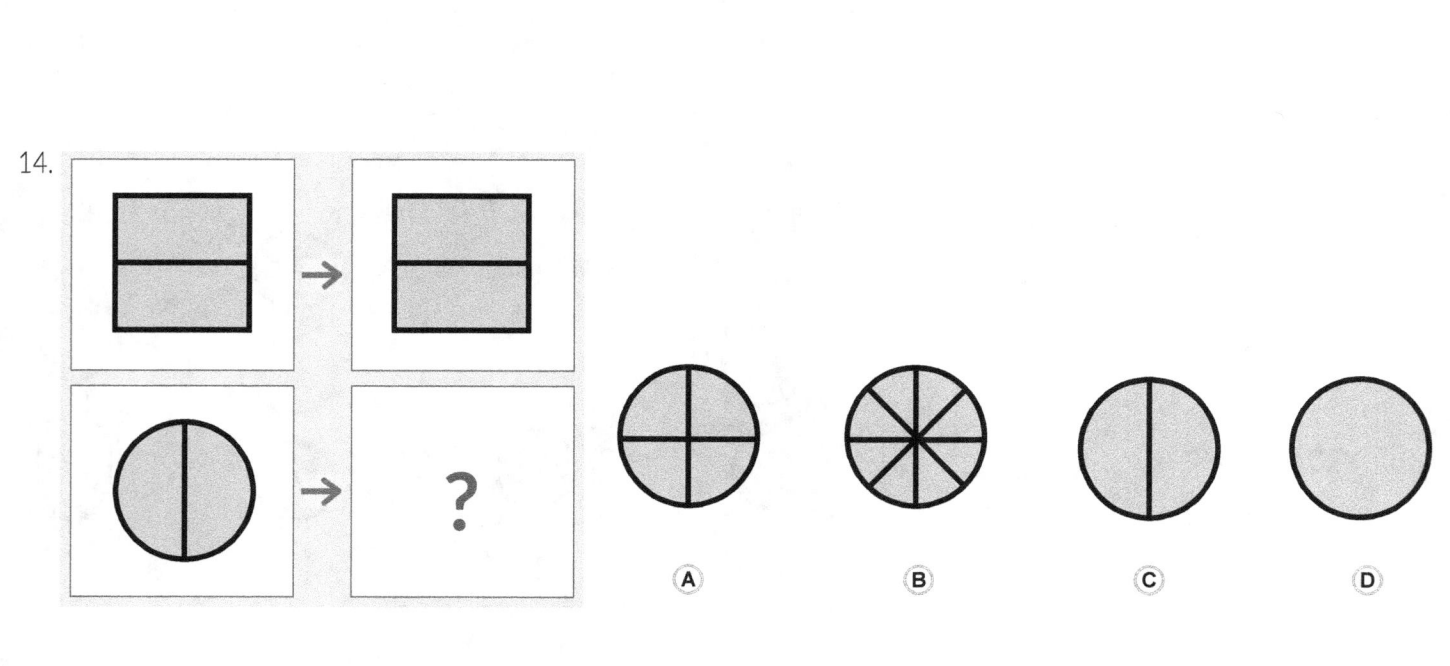

66

15.

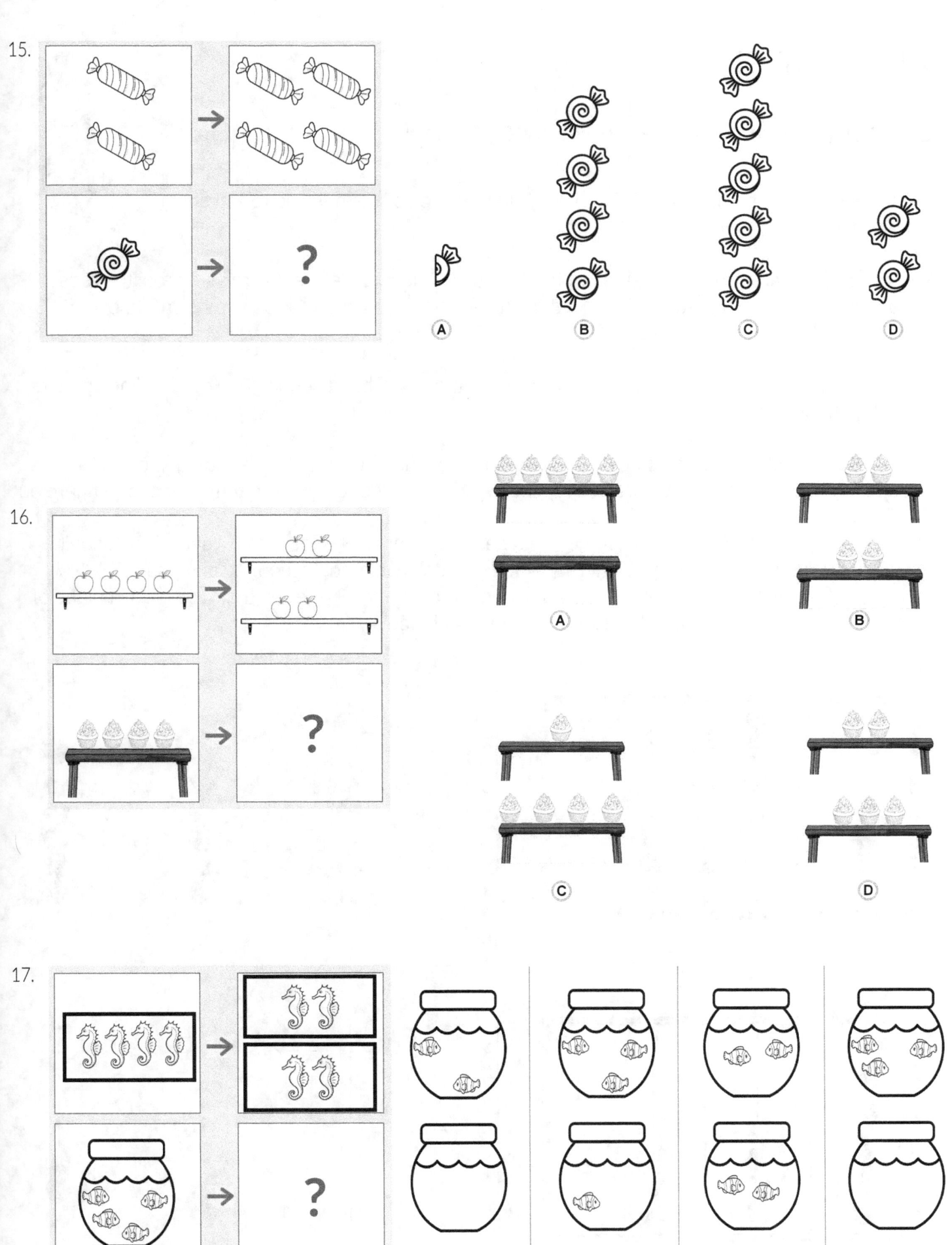

A   B   C   D

16.

17.

NUMBER SERIES

"Let's figure out the pattern!" Maya says.

Maya

Directions (read to child): Which rod should go in the place of the missing rod to finish the pattern?

Explanation (for parents): The final rod of the abacus is missing. Before this missing rod, the rods of the abacus have made a pattern. Your child must look closely to determine the pattern. Go over p.18 with your child, if you haven't already.

Note that some rods do not have any beads. Rods without any beads equal "0." The gray line appears above the 5th bead's place.

Example (read to child): The picture below shows an abacus. The abacus has rods going from the bottom to the top. On these rods are beads. These rods have made a pattern that we need to figure out.

First, we see a rod with 5 beads. Then, we see 5 beads, 7 beads, 7 beads, and 3 beads. Then, finally there is a missing rod. What is the pattern that these rods have made? Each rod is repeated: 5, 5, 7, 7, and then 3. If this is the pattern, what should the next rod be after 3 (the rod that would go in place of the missing rod on the abacus)? The rod with 3 beads, choice A.

1.

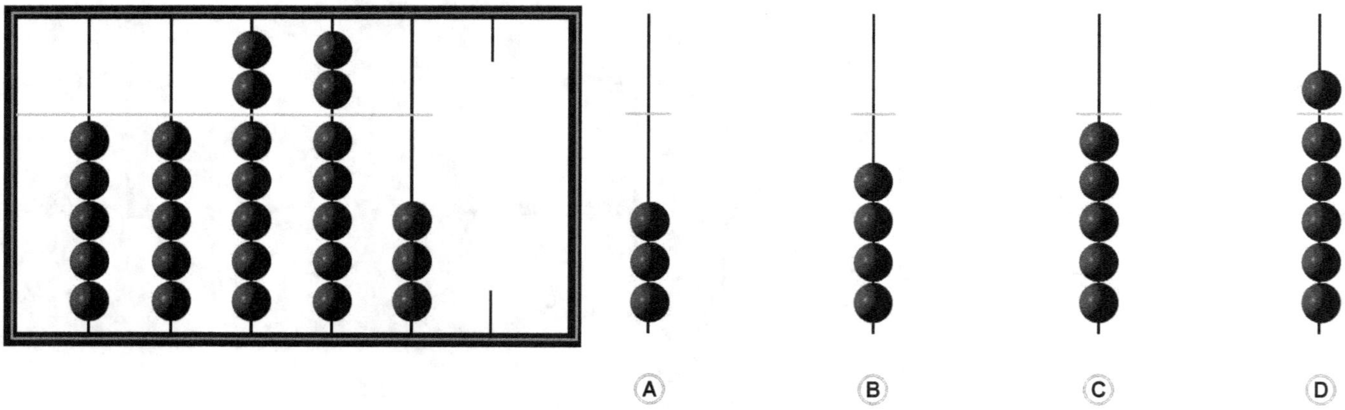

Ⓐ   Ⓑ   Ⓒ   Ⓓ

2.

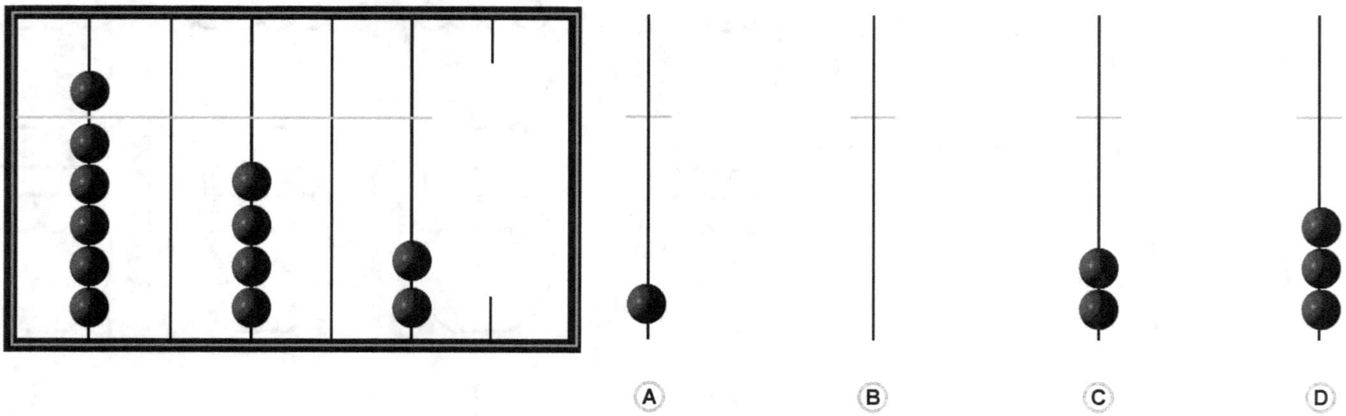

Ⓐ   Ⓑ   Ⓒ   Ⓓ

3.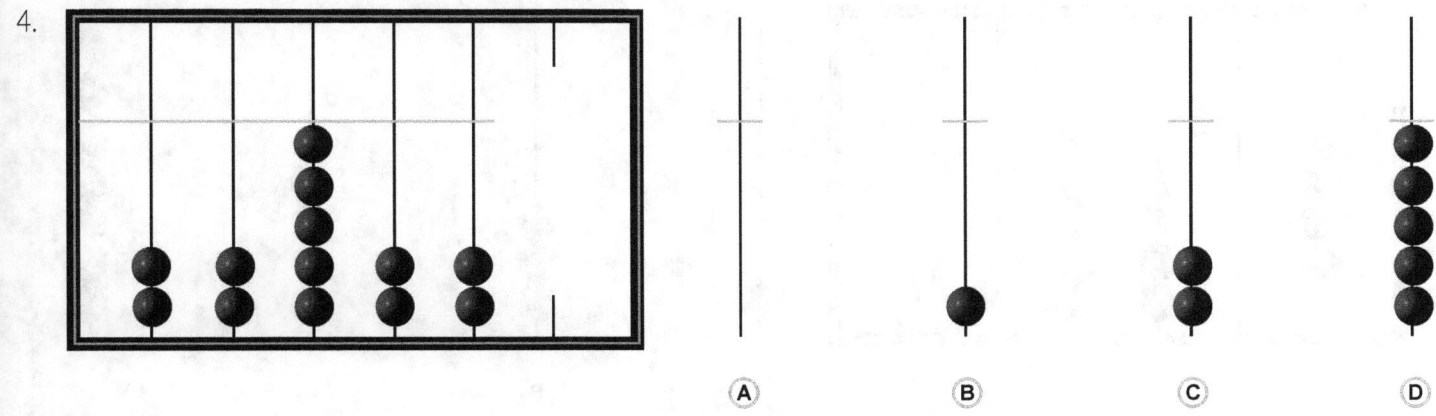

4.

5.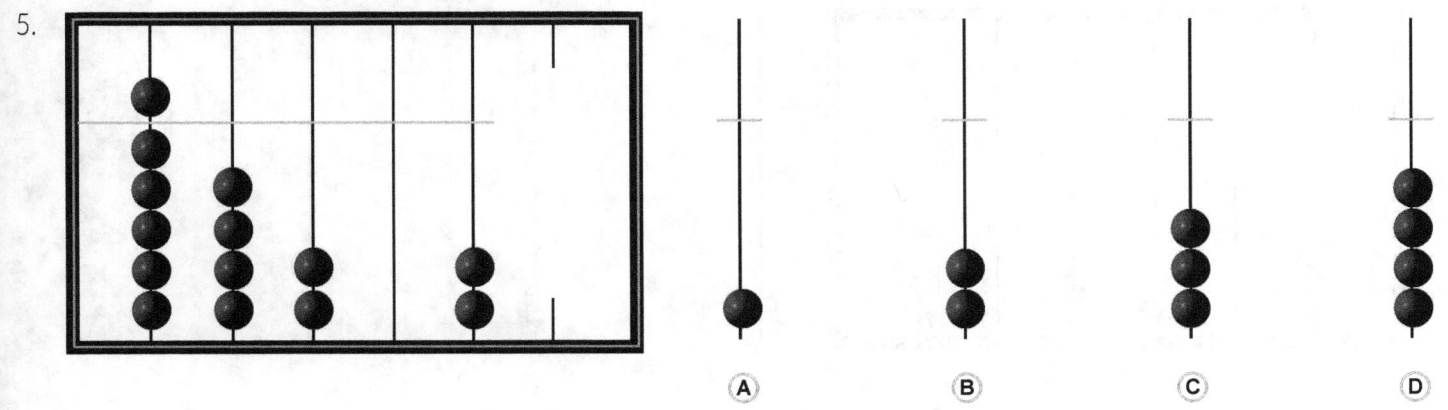

6.

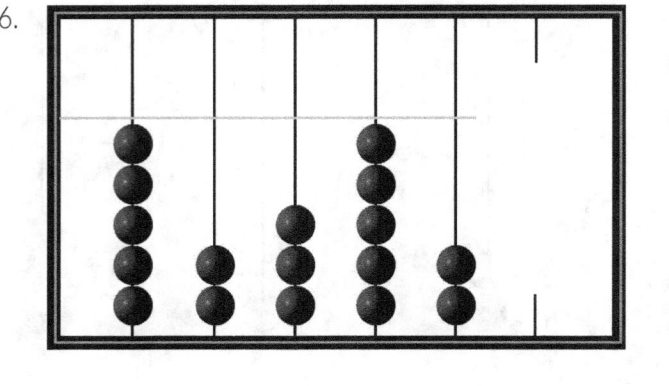

(A)   (B)   (C)   (D)

7.

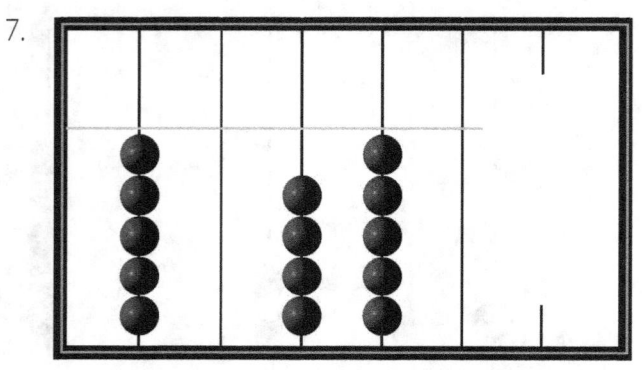

(A)   (B)   (C)   (D)

8.

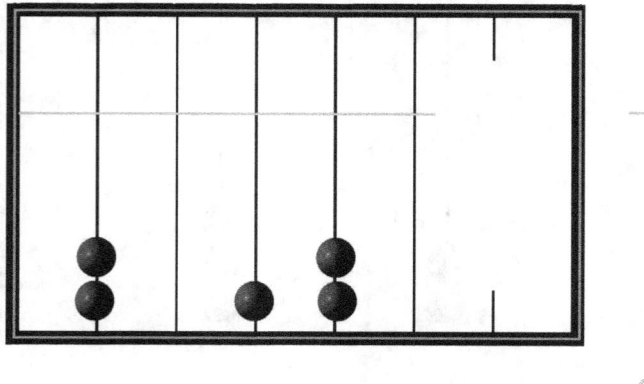
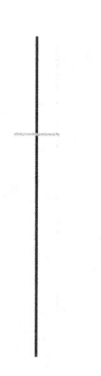

(A)   (B)   (C)   (D)

9.

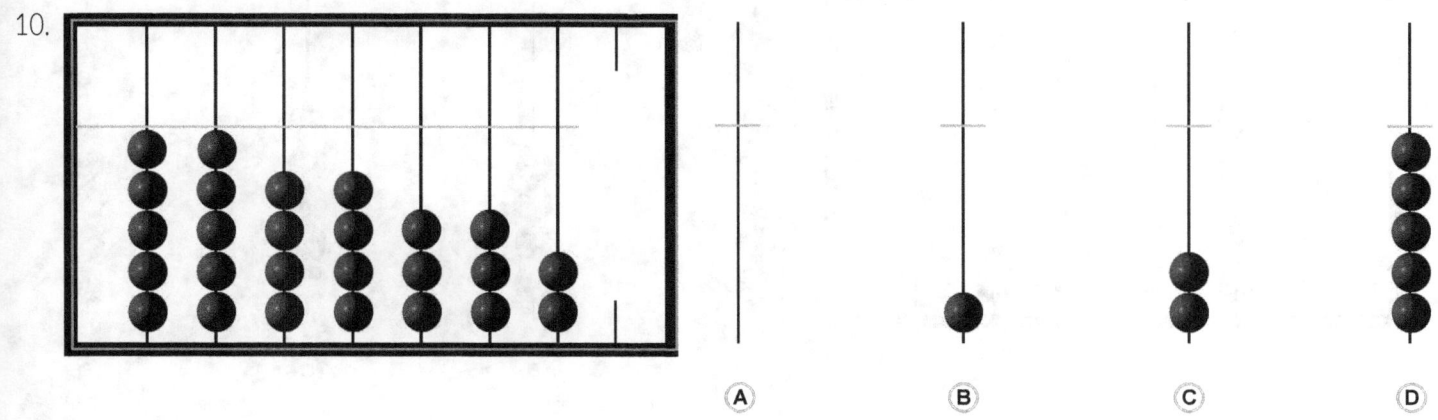

A   B   C   D

10.

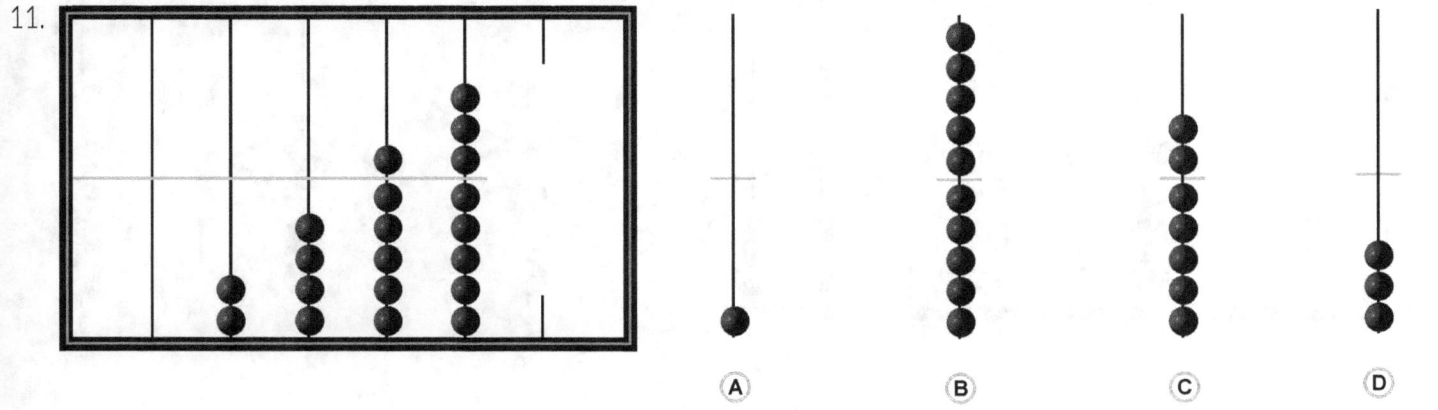

A   B   C   D

11.

A   B   C   D

12.

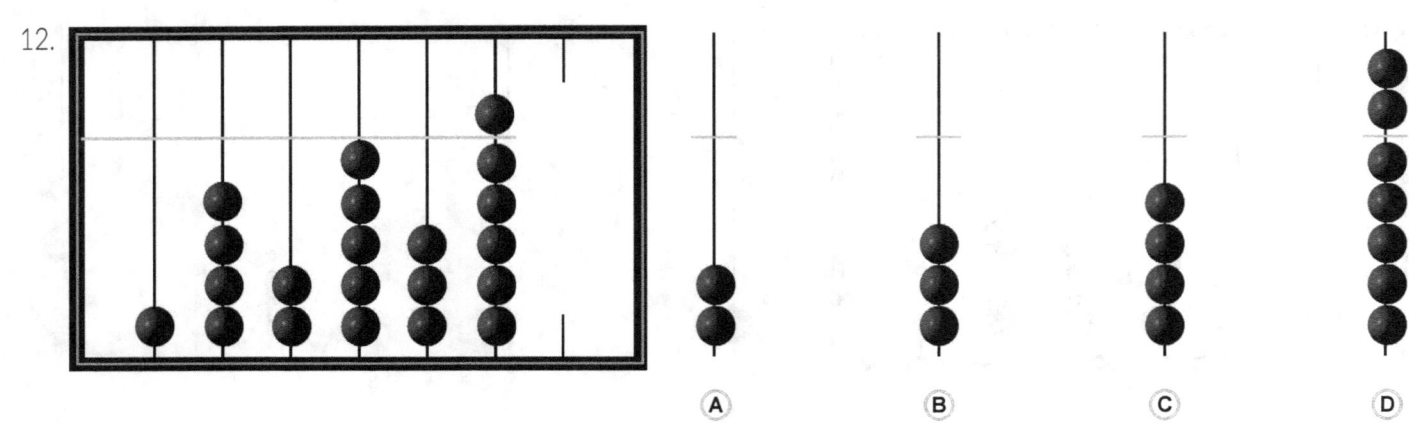

A   B   C   D

13.

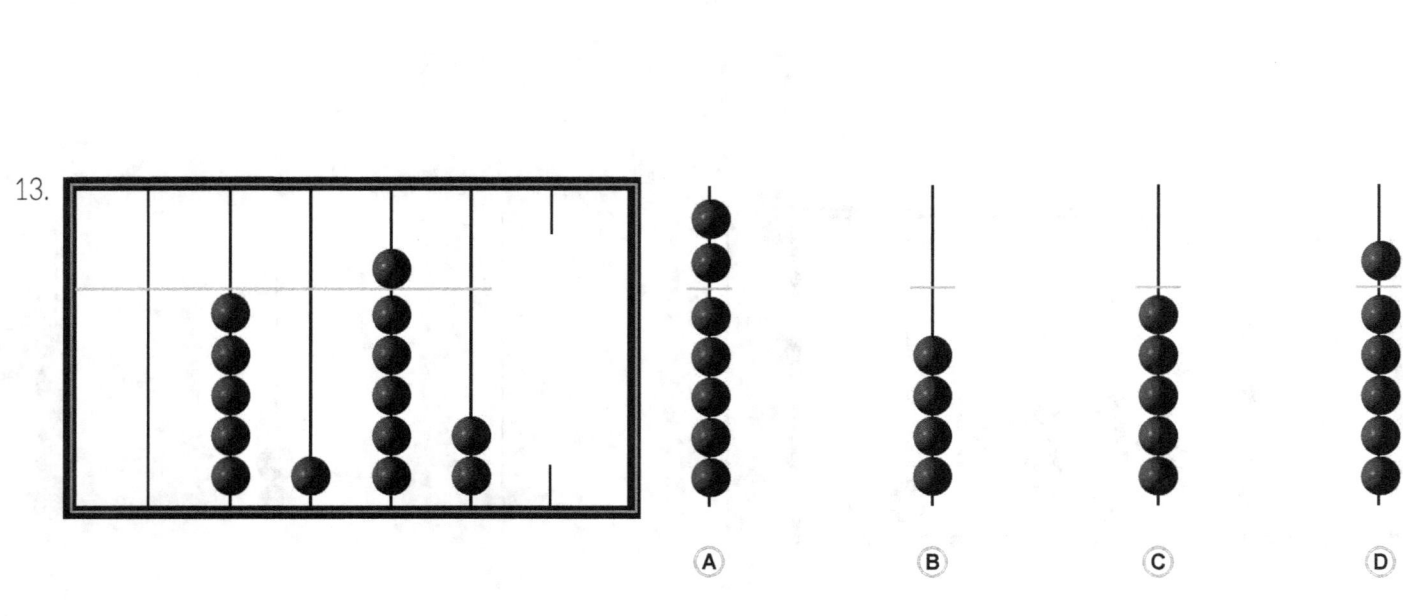

A   B   C   D

14.

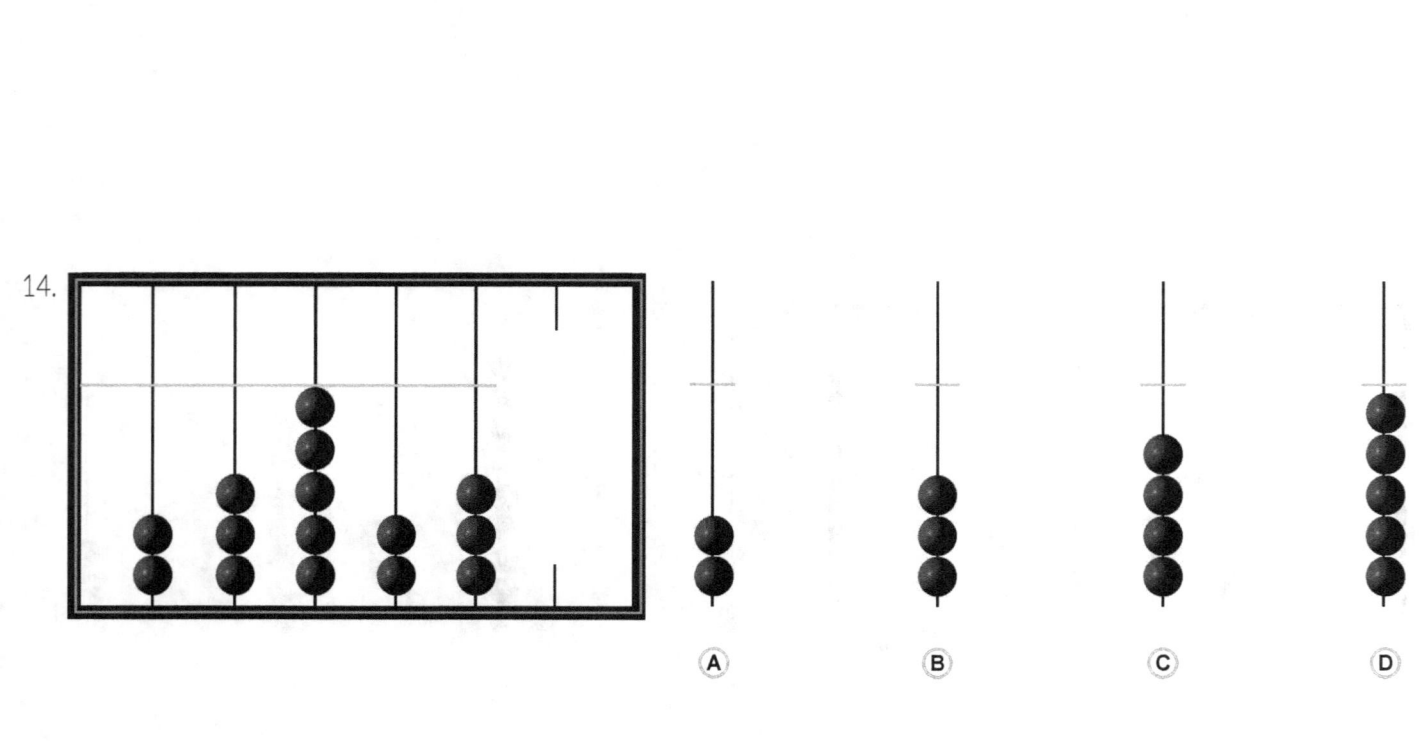

A   B   C   D

15.

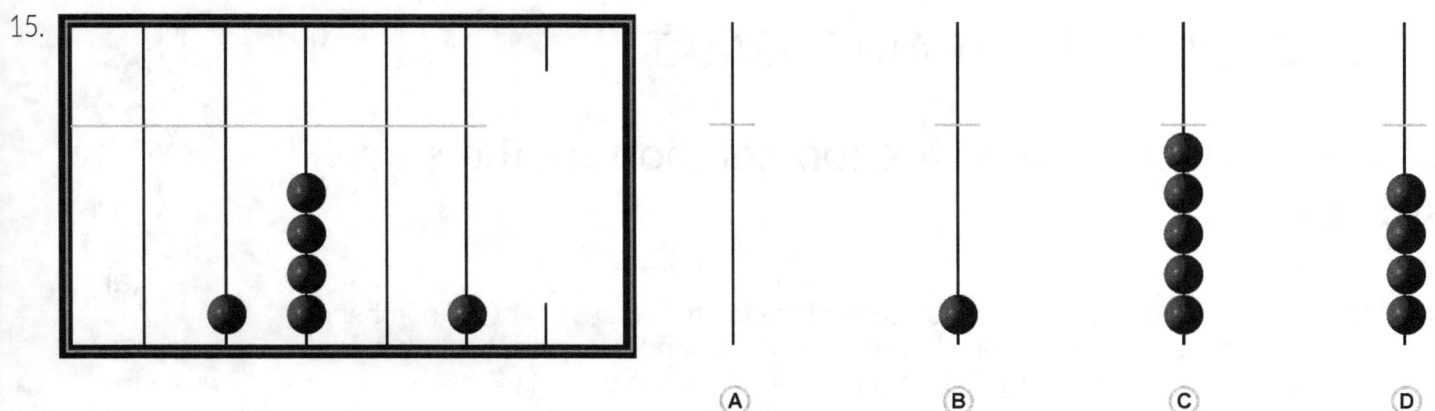

16.

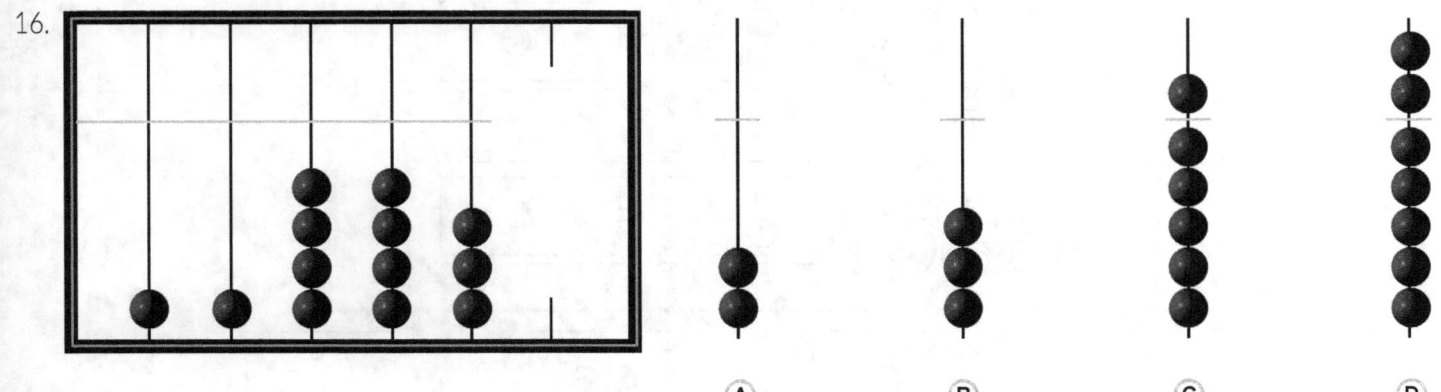

Zoe

NUMBER PUZZLES, TRAIN FORMAT

"Which train car makes the top and bottom the same?" Kai asks.

Kai

Directions for Question #1 (read to child): Look at the top train. Let's count the number of things it's carrying inside the train cars. It is carrying 7 gray circles. Look at the bottom train. The bottom train has 3 circles inside the left train car. The right train car has a question mark. We must figure out which train car in the answer choices would go in place of the train car with the question mark so that the top train and the bottom train carry the same number of gray circles inside. Remember that the top train has 7 gray circles. So, the bottom train car on the right must have 4 gray circles. Three plus 4 equals 7. Which answer choice has 4 gray circles? Choice C is the answer. (**Note:** If you haven't gone over p.20 with your child, do so now.)

Directions for the rest (read to child): Which train car should you choose so that the top train carries the same number of items as the bottom train?

1.

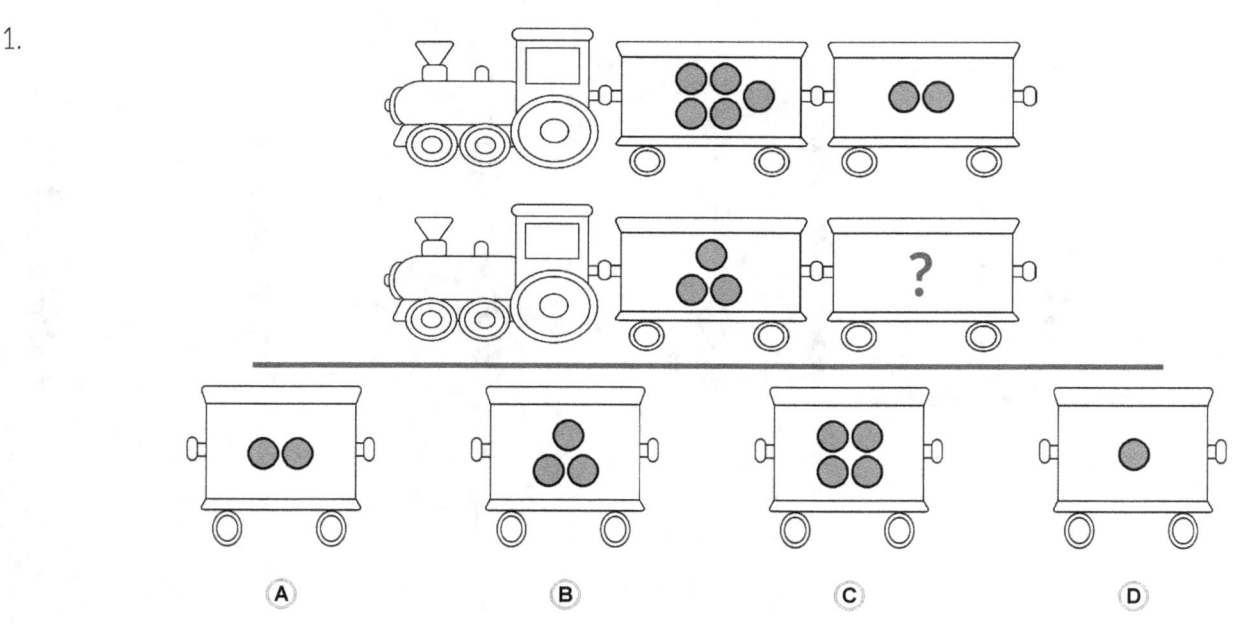

2.

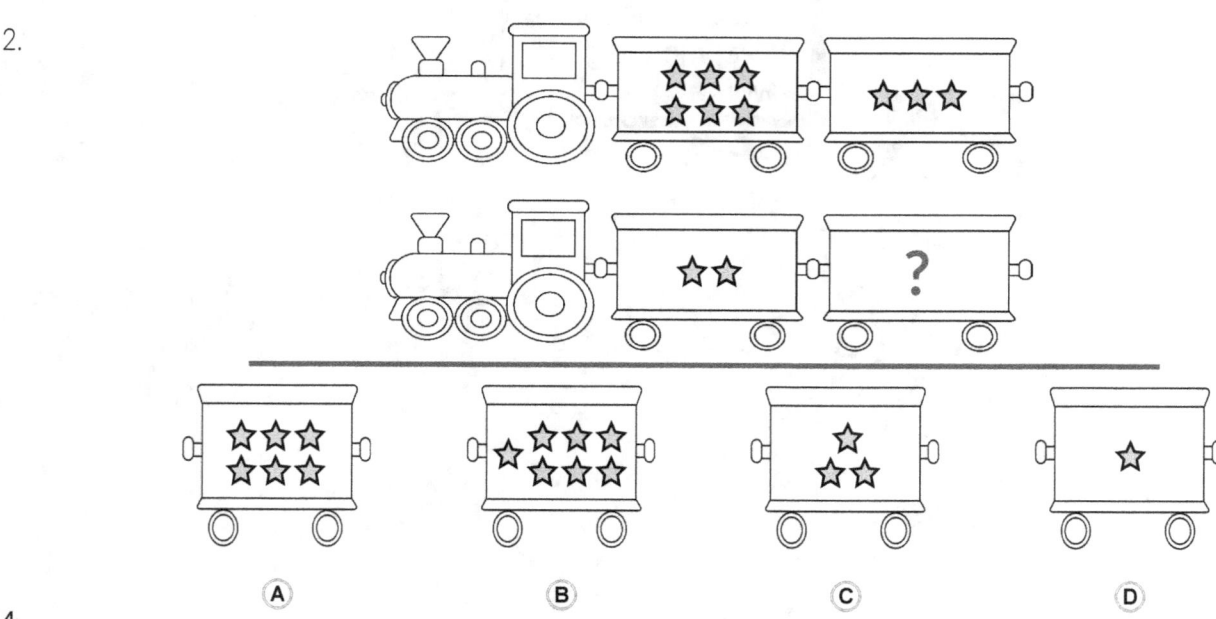

74

3.

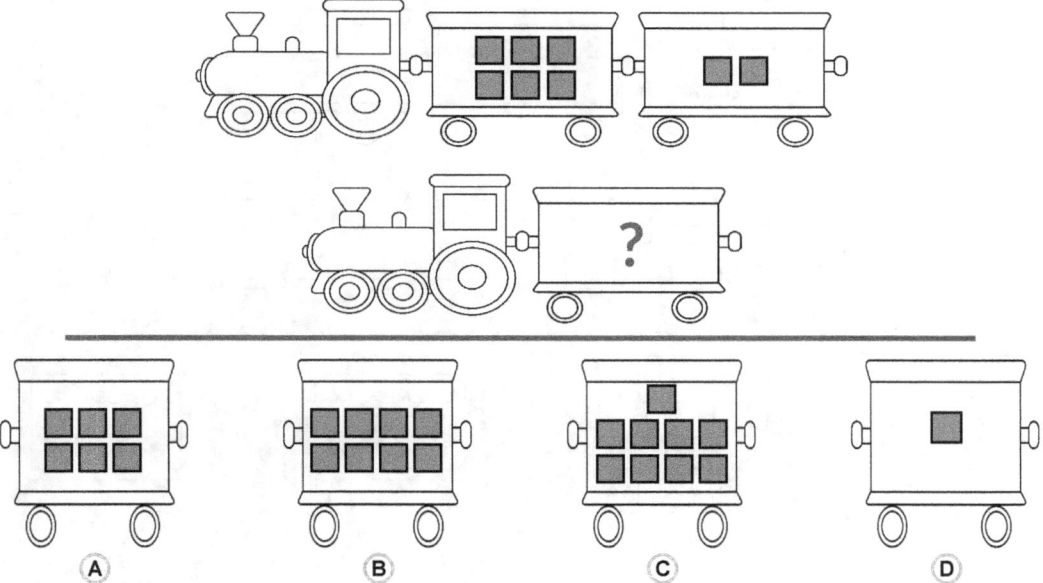

A	B	C	D

4.

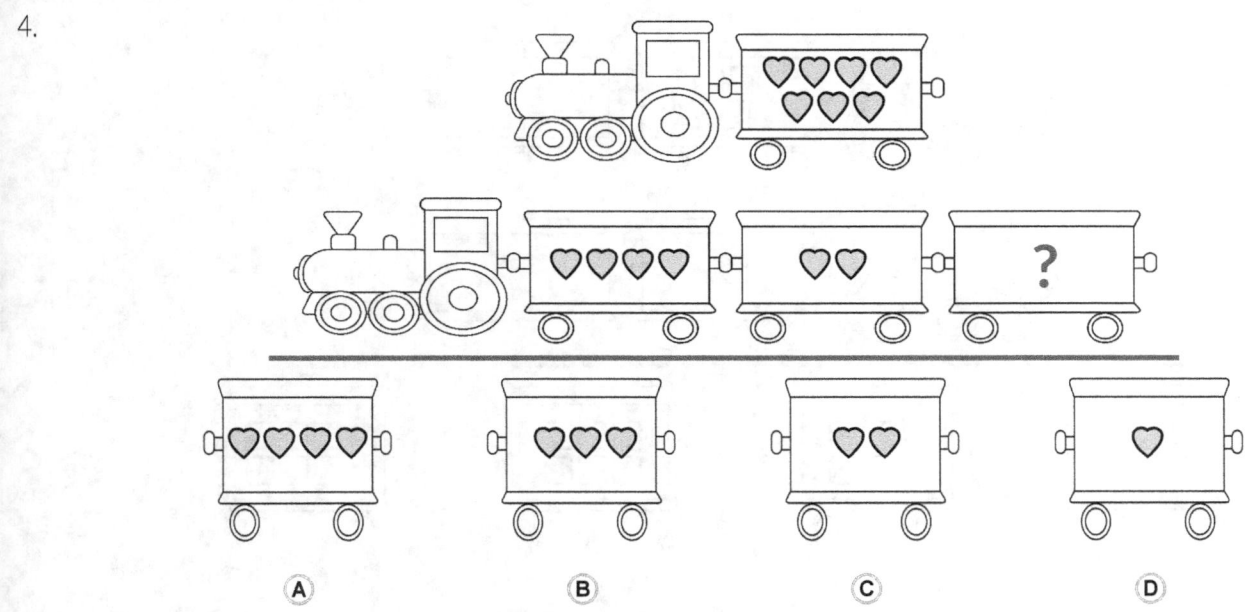

A	B	C	D

5.

6.

A   B   C   D

7.

A   B   C   D

8.

A   B   C   D

NUMBER PUZZLES (subtraction)

• **Explanation for the next questions (read to child):** In the next group of questions, remember that if something has an "X" on it, this means that it would be taken away from the train.

Which train car should you choose so that the top train carries the same number of items as the bottom train?

9.

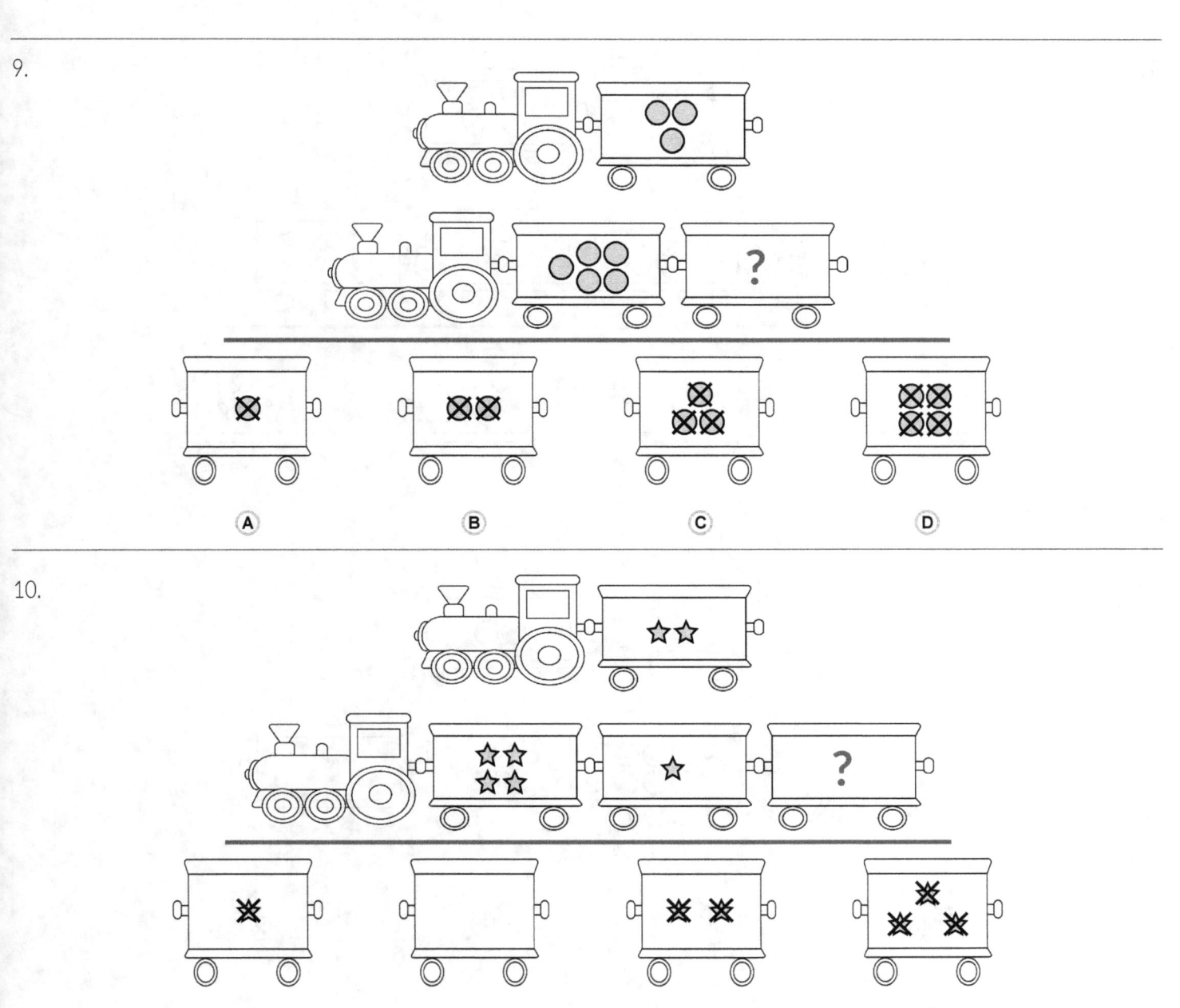

10.

11.

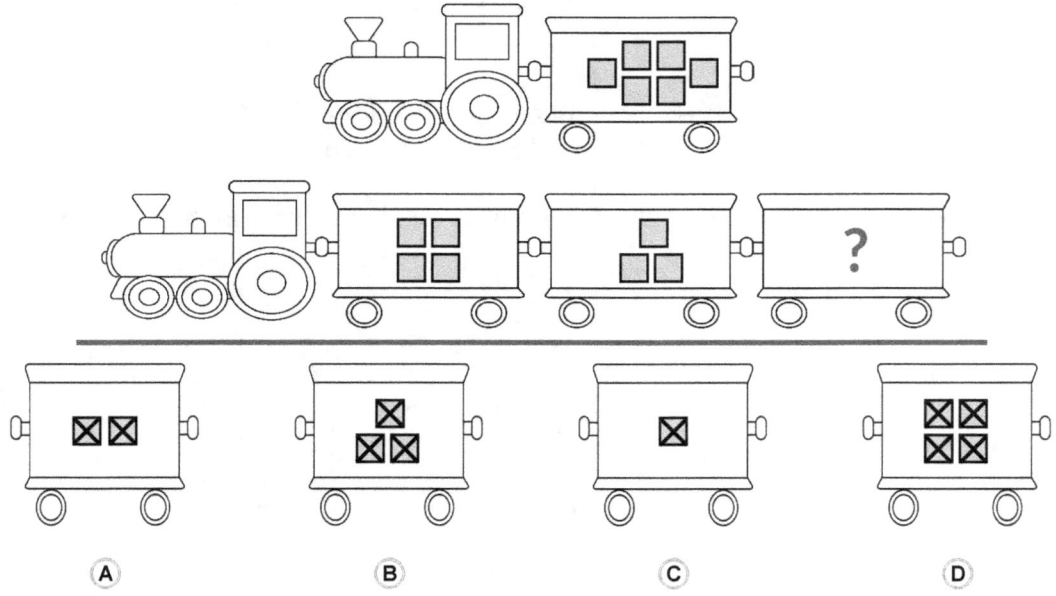

A	B	C	D

12.

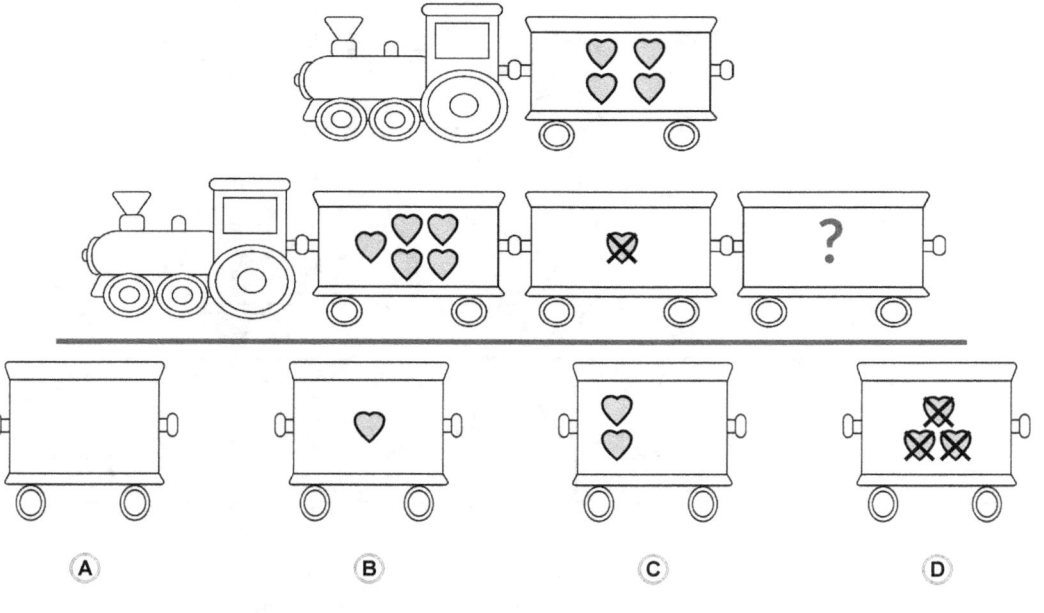

A	B	C	D

13.

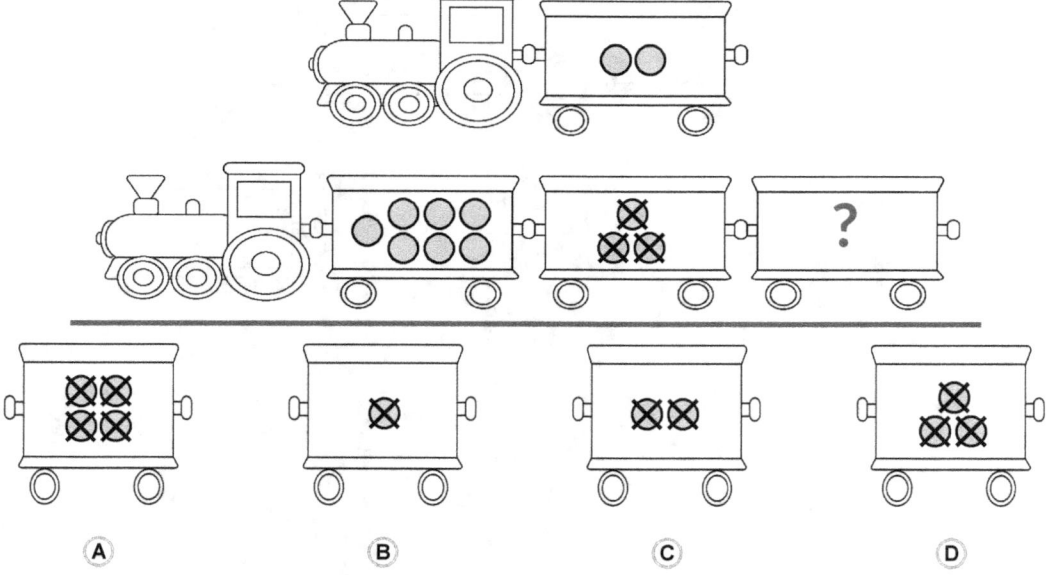

A	B	C	D

NUMBER PUZZLES, EQUATION FORMAT

Directions: Look at the box that has the question mark. Which number would go here so that both of the sides of this equal sign (point to the equal sign) would have the same amount?

Parent Note: Some exercises require three numbers to be added/subtracted. In these, be sure your child correctly distinguishes between the addition and subtraction signs and completes the entire exercise before selecting an answer.

1.

$$9 = 3 + \boxed{?}$$

4	5	6	7
(A)	(B)	(C)	(D)

2.

$$9 = 10 - \boxed{?}$$

7	5	3	1
(A)	(B)	(C)	(D)

3.

$$2 = 10 - 5 - \boxed{?}$$

1	2	3	4
(A)	(B)	(C)	(D)

4.

$$11 = 6 + 5 + \boxed{?}$$

0	1	2	3
Ⓐ	Ⓑ	Ⓒ	Ⓓ

5.

$$12 = 9 + 5 - \boxed{?}$$

4	3	2	1
Ⓐ	Ⓑ	Ⓒ	Ⓓ

6.

$$2 = 12 + 1 - \boxed{?}$$

8	9	10	11
Ⓐ	Ⓑ	Ⓒ	Ⓓ

7.

$$5 = 3 + 13 - \boxed{?}$$

11	9	8	7
Ⓐ	Ⓑ	Ⓒ	Ⓓ

8.

$$10 = 1 + 12 - \boxed{?}$$

5	4	3	2
Ⓐ	Ⓑ	Ⓒ	Ⓓ

9.

$$6 = 12 - 5 - \boxed{?}$$

2	1	0	3
Ⓐ	Ⓑ	Ⓒ	Ⓓ

10.

$$12 = 10 - 9 + \boxed{?}$$

   9   12   11   10
   Ⓐ   Ⓑ   Ⓒ   Ⓓ

11.

$$13 = 15 - 8 + \boxed{?}$$

   0   4   5   6
   Ⓐ   Ⓑ   Ⓒ   Ⓓ

12.

$$3 = 15 - 9 - \boxed{?}$$

   6   5   4   3
   Ⓐ   Ⓑ   Ⓒ   Ⓓ

13.

$$3 = 14 - 7 - \boxed{?}$$

   7   6   5   4
   Ⓐ   Ⓑ   Ⓒ   Ⓓ

14.

$$15 = 8 + 3 + \boxed{?}$$

   10   4   5   6
   Ⓐ   Ⓑ   Ⓒ   Ⓓ

15.

$$13 = 2 + 4 + \boxed{?}$$

   11   12   7   10
   Ⓐ   Ⓑ   Ⓒ   Ⓓ

COGAT® PRACTICE TEST 2

PICTURE ANALOGIES

Directions: The pictures in the top boxes go together in some way. One of the bottom boxes is empty. Which answer choice goes with the picture in the bottom box in the same way the top pictures do?

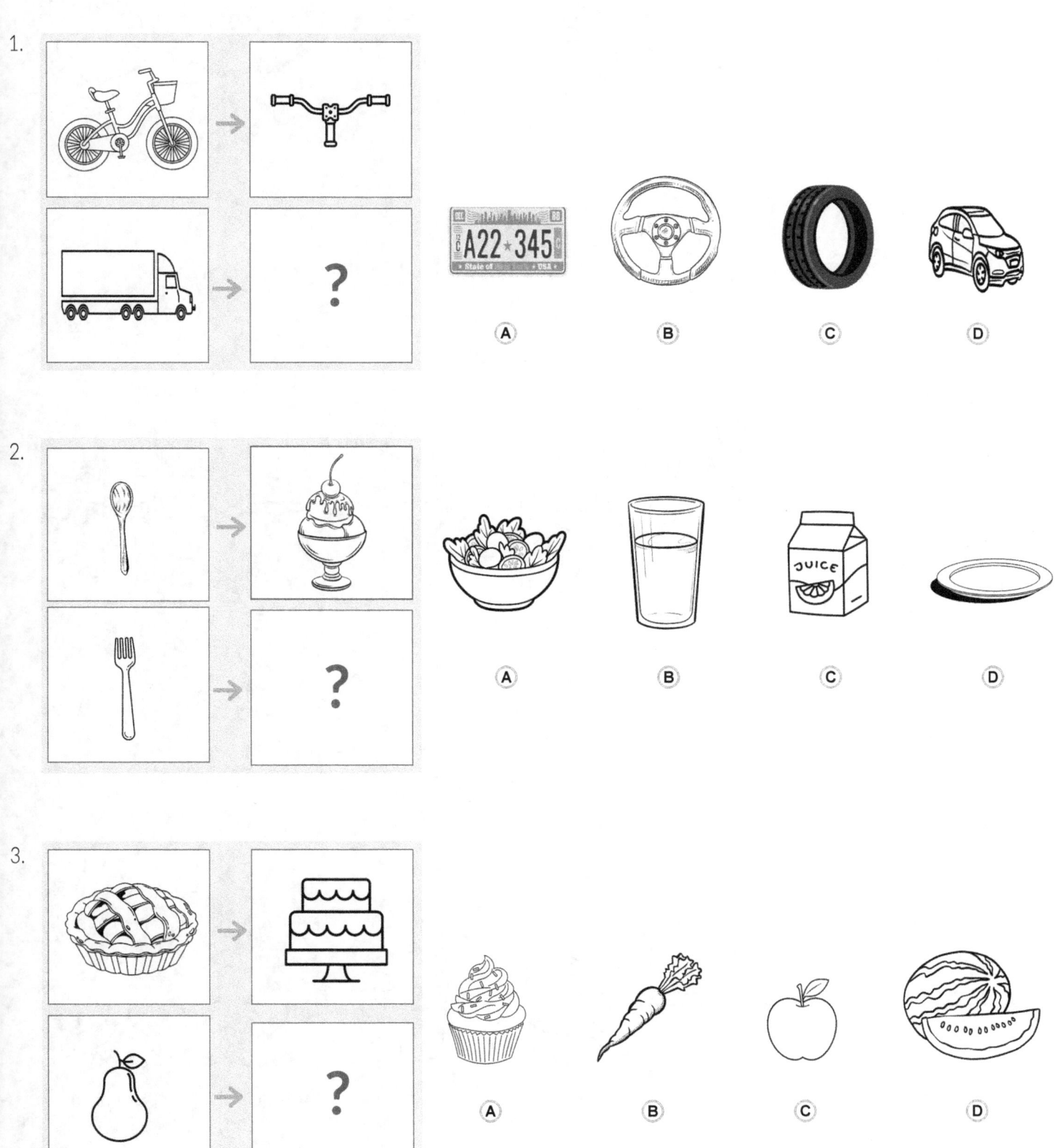

4.

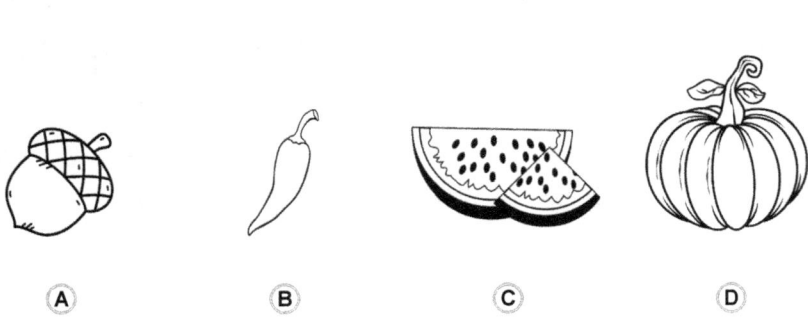

5.

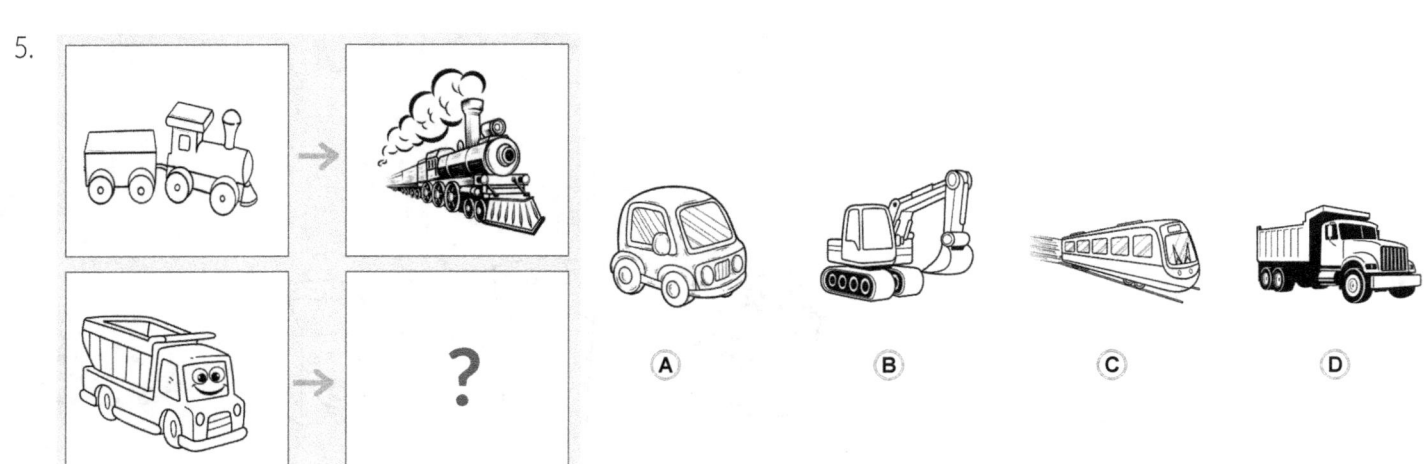

6.

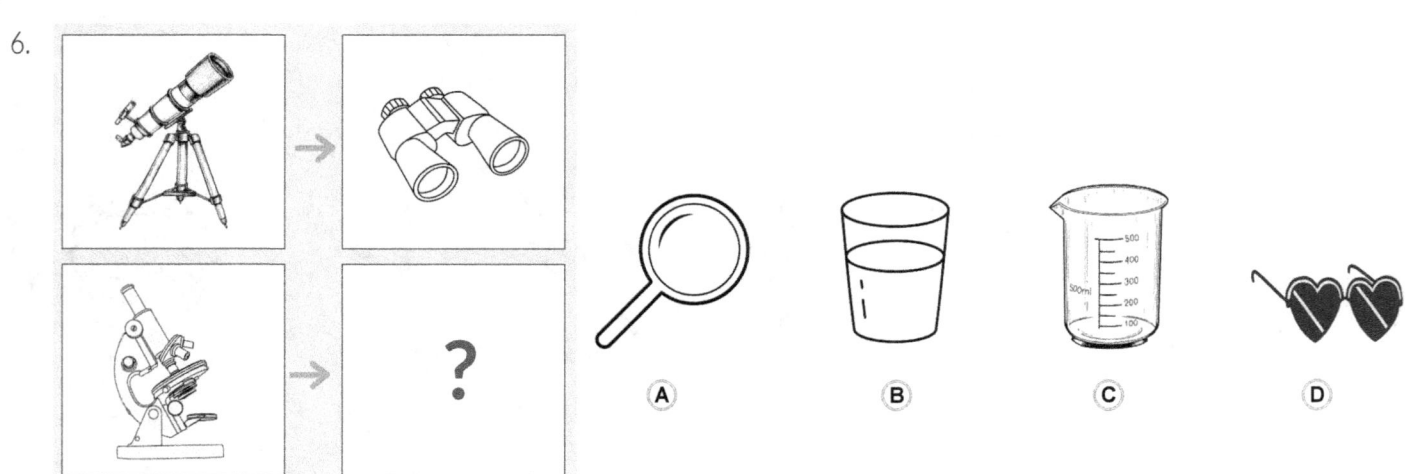

84

7.

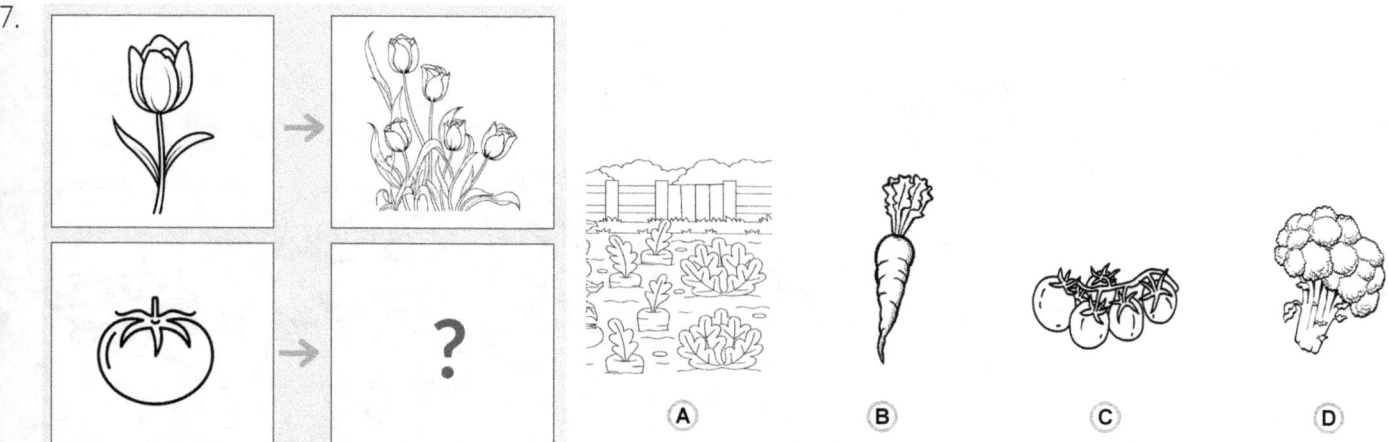

8.

9.

10.

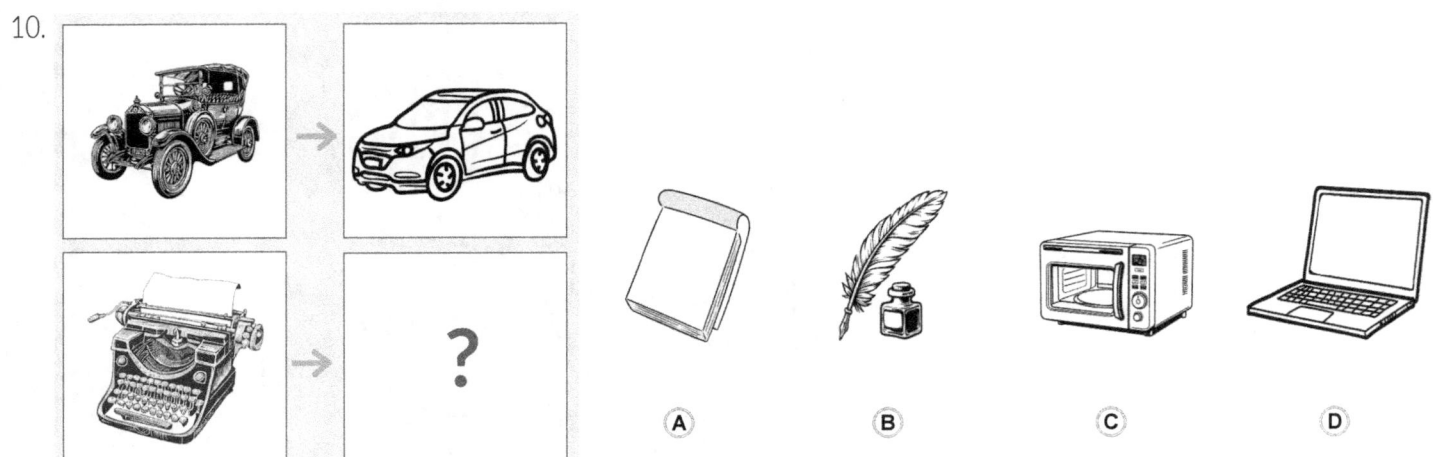

11.

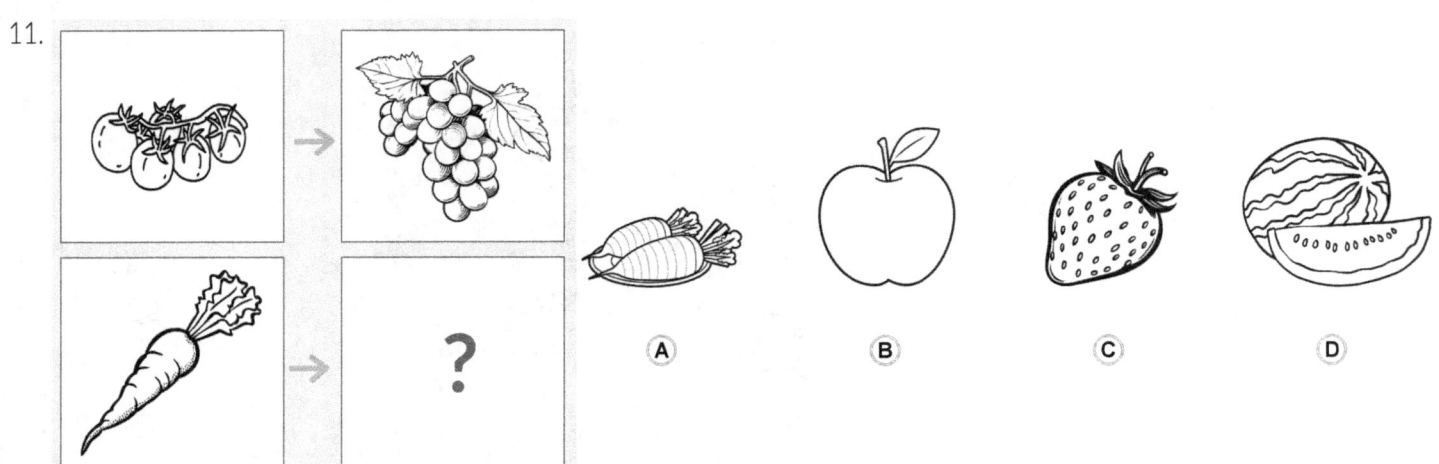

12.

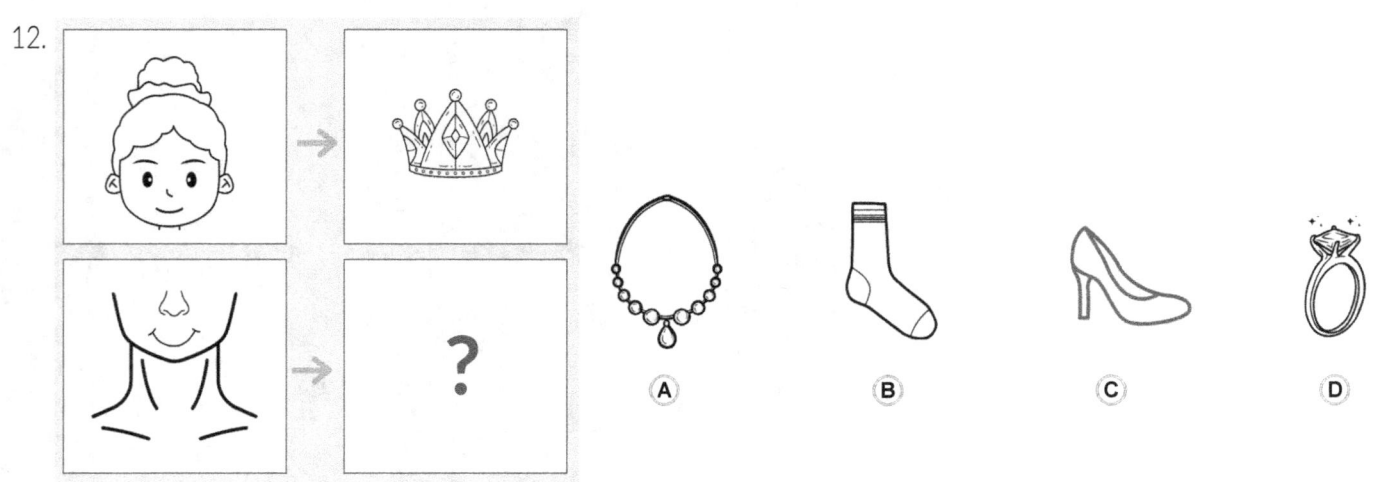

86

13.

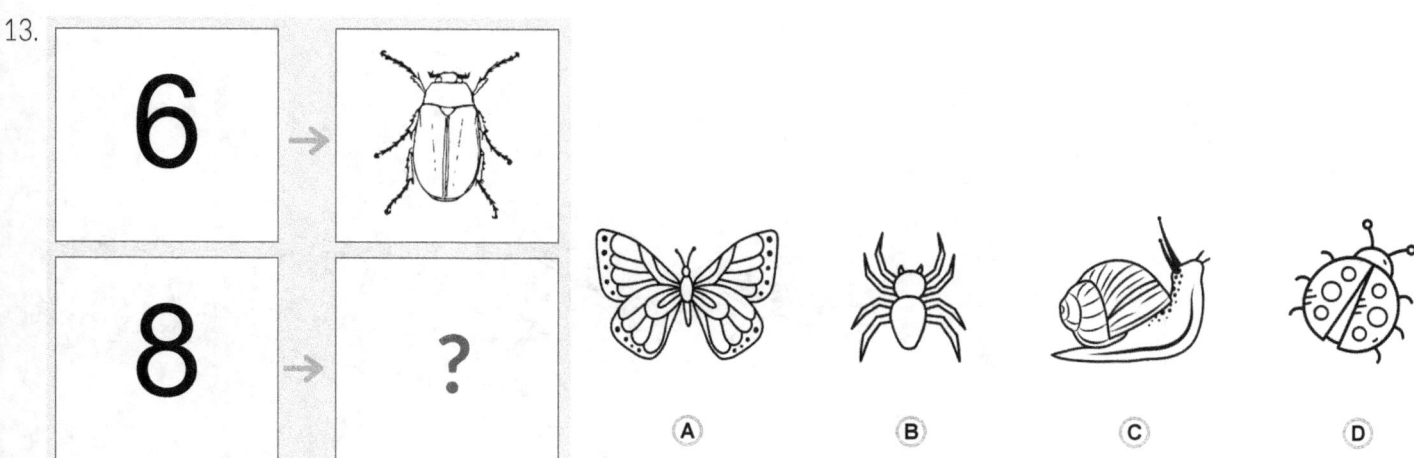

14.

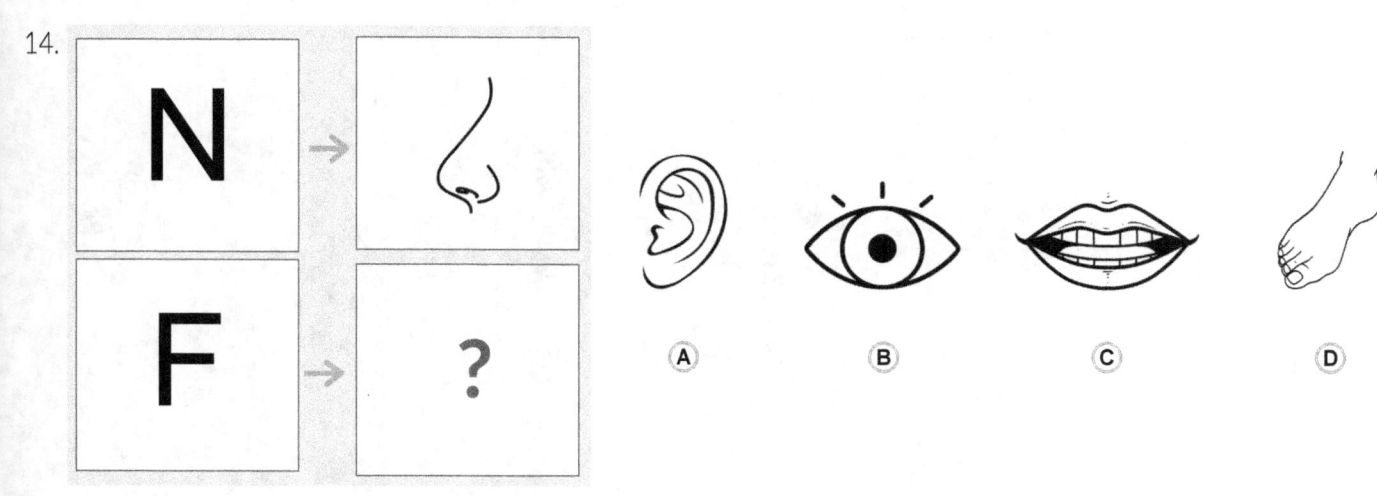

15.

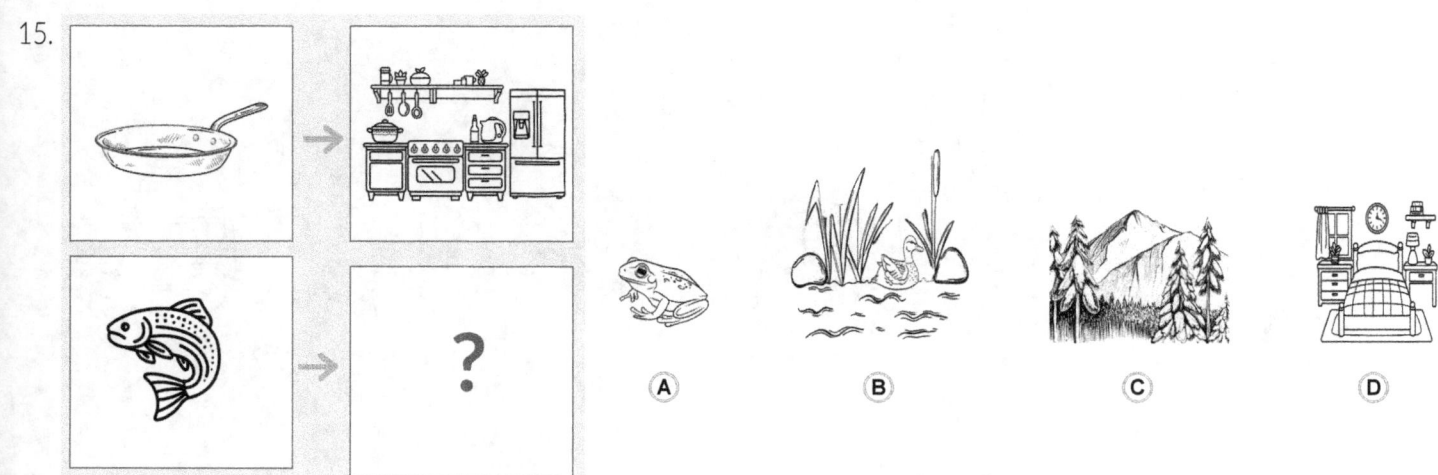

16.

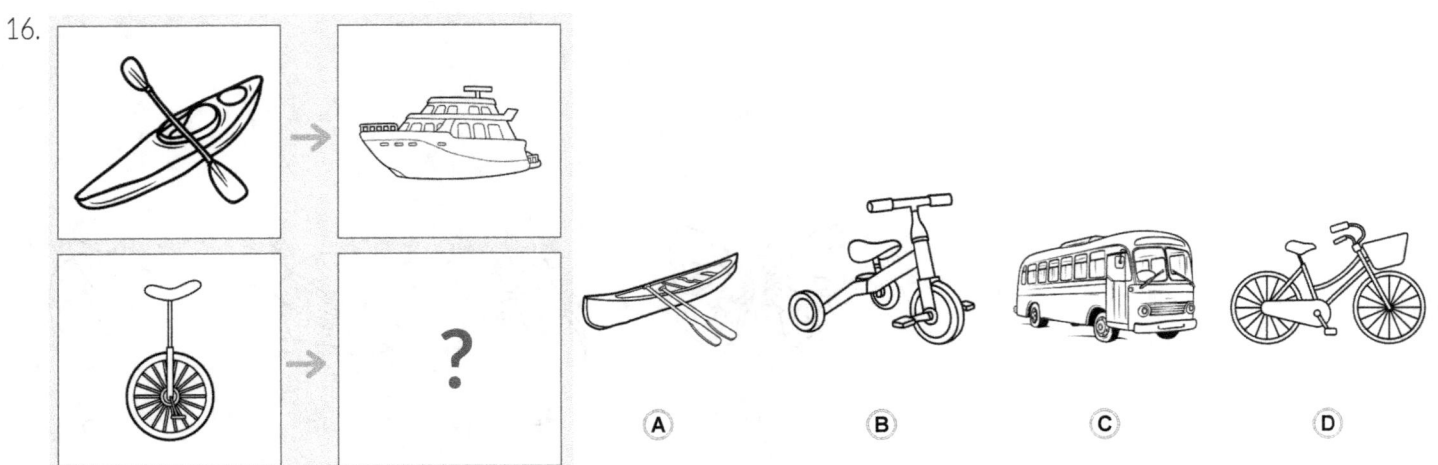

17.

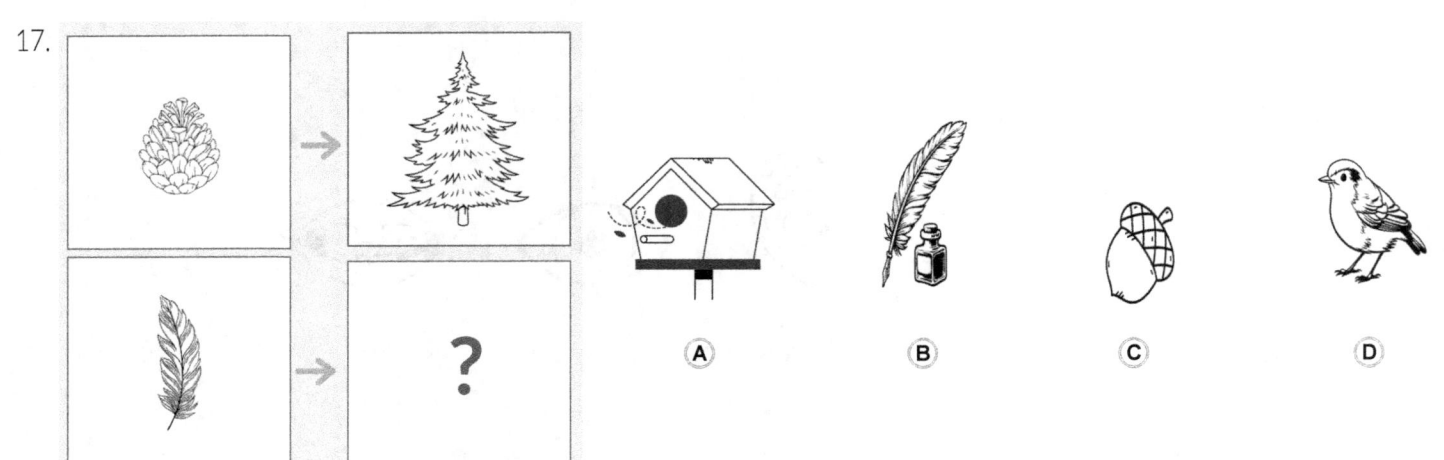

18.

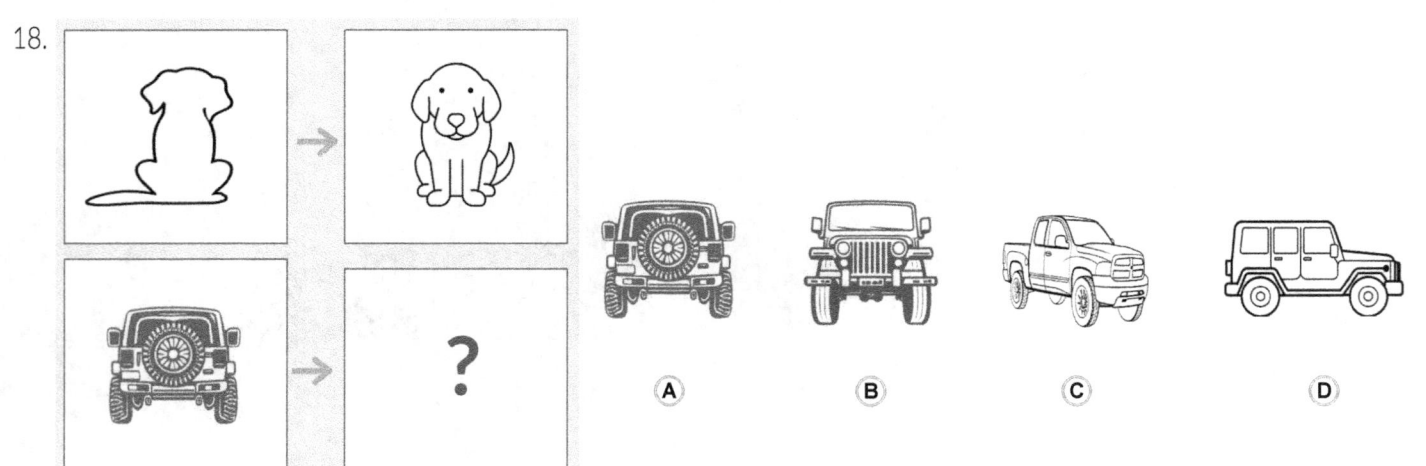

PICTURE CLASSIFICATION
Directions: The top row shows three pictures that are alike in some way. Look at the bottom row. Which bottom picture goes best with the top pictures?

1.

A   B   C   D

2.

A   B   C   D

3.

A   B   C   D

4.

  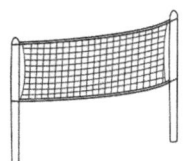

Ⓐ Ⓑ Ⓒ Ⓓ

5.

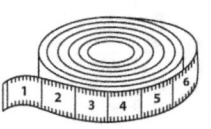 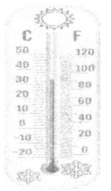 

Ⓐ Ⓑ Ⓒ Ⓓ

6.

 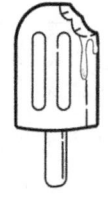  

Ⓐ Ⓑ Ⓒ Ⓓ

7.

(A) (B) (C) (D)

8.

   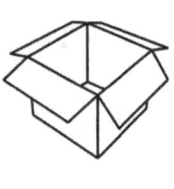

(A) (B) (C) (D)

9.

(A) (B) (C) (D)

10.

(A)   (B)   (C)   (D)

11.

(A)   (B)   (C)   (D)

12.

 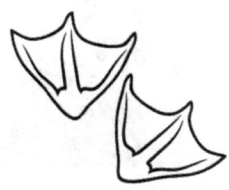 

  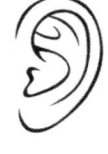 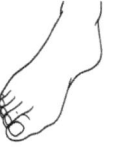

(A)   (B)   (C)   (D)

13.

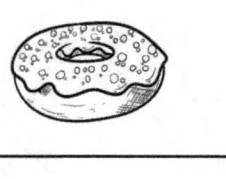  

(A)   (B)   (C)   (D)

14.

  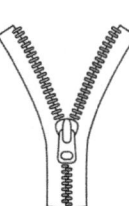

   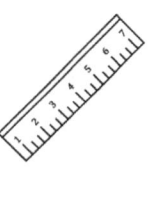

(A)   (B)   (C)   (D)

15.

  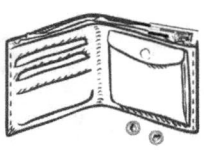

 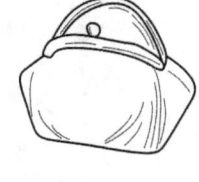 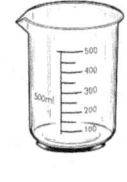 

(A)   (B)   (C)   (D)

16.

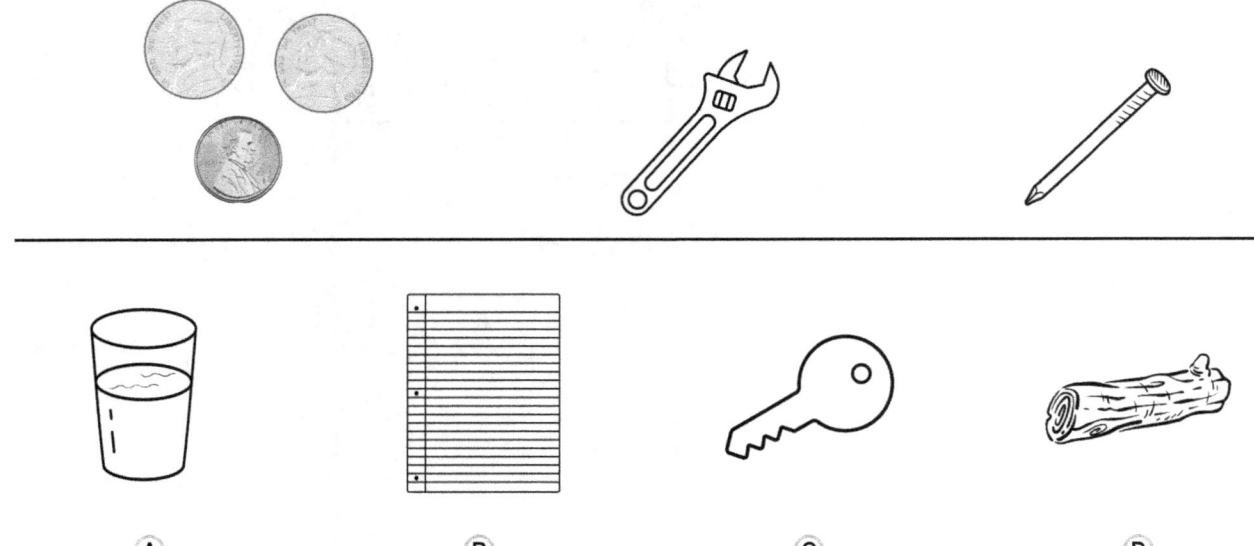

(A)   (B)   (C)   (D)

SENTENCE COMPLETION

Directions: Listen to the question, then choose the best answer.

1. If you were in a science lab, which one of these would you see?

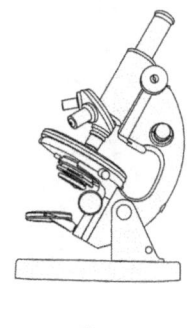

(A)   (B)   (C)   (D)

2. Which one of these would you <u>not</u> see at a doctor's office?

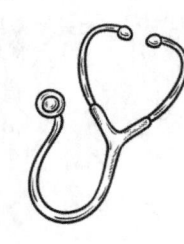

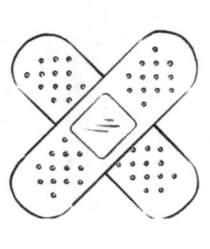

(A)   (B)   (C)   (D)

3. Which of these would you see in the Arctic?

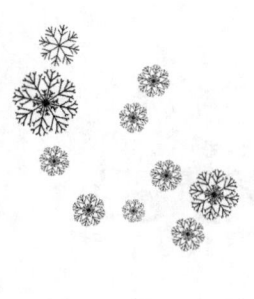

(A)   (B)   (C)   (D)

4. The weather report says that there will be a lot of precipitation tomorrow. Which one of these should you make sure that you have?

A   B   C   D

5. Ana's favorite animal has 8 legs. Which picture shows Ana's favorite animal?

A   B   C   D

6. The book you're reading is about an extinct animal. Which picture shows the animal that your book is about?

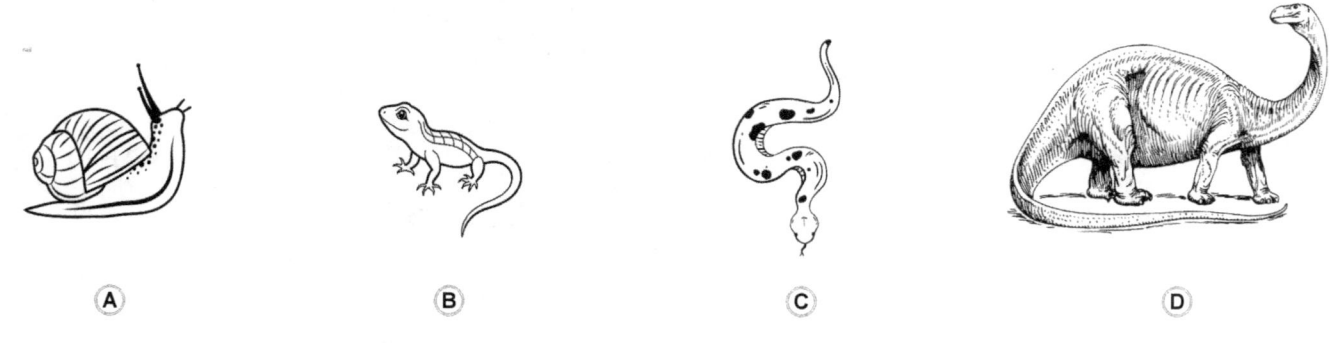

A   B   C   D

7. Your friend is reading a book about an animal that hibernates. Which picture shows the animal that your friend's book is about?

(A)   (B)   (C)   (D)

8. Which one of these is <u>not</u> used to tell time?

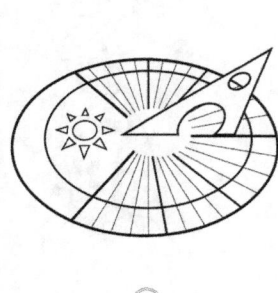

(A)   (B)   (C)   (D)

9. Your grandad is a carpenter. Which one of these would he use while working?

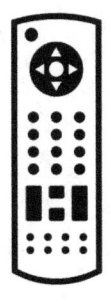

(A)   (B)   (C)   (D)

10. Your friend lives on a farm. Which of these would your friend probably <u>not</u> use there?

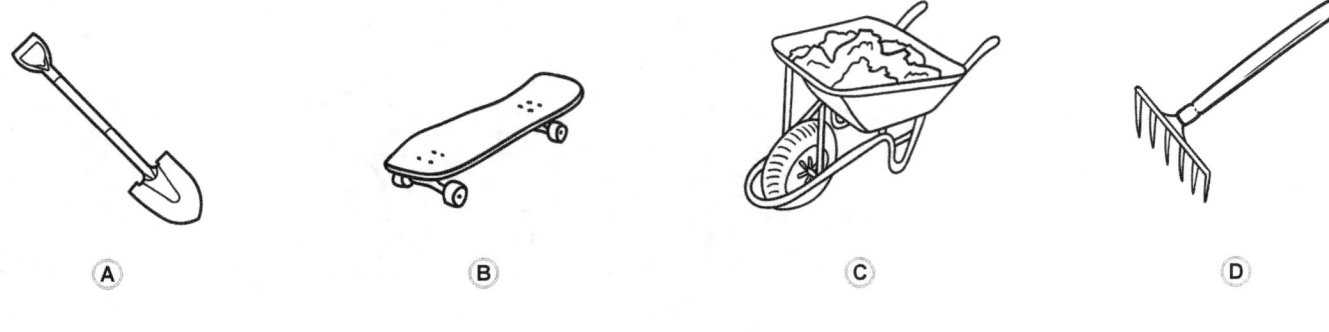

A   B   C   D

11. Which picture shows animals that go through metamorphosis?

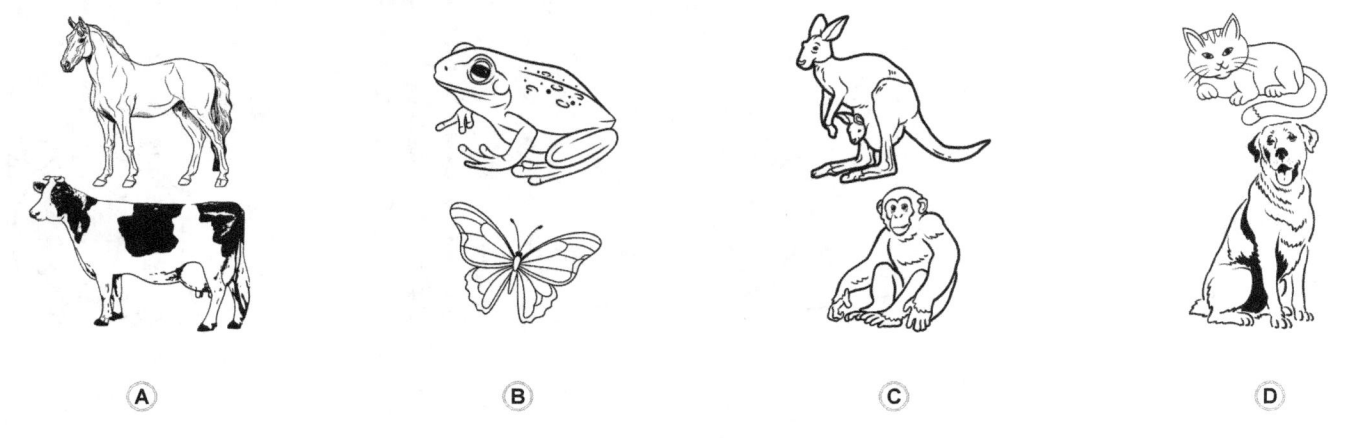

A   B   C   D

12. Which picture shows 1 food that must be peeled before eating and one that does not need to be peeled before eating?

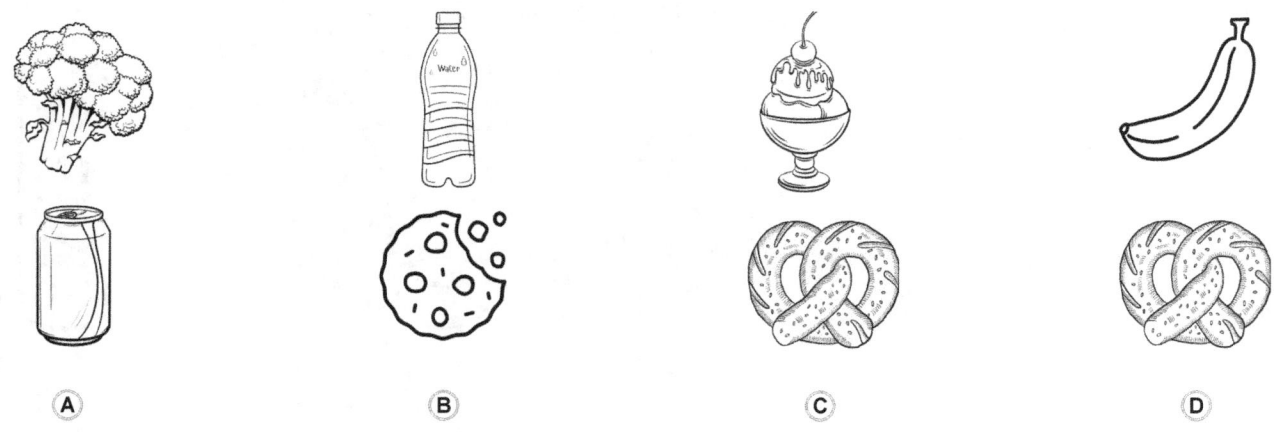

A   B   C   D

98

13. While visiting a farm, you saw 2 mammals and 1 reptile. Which picture shows the animals that you saw?

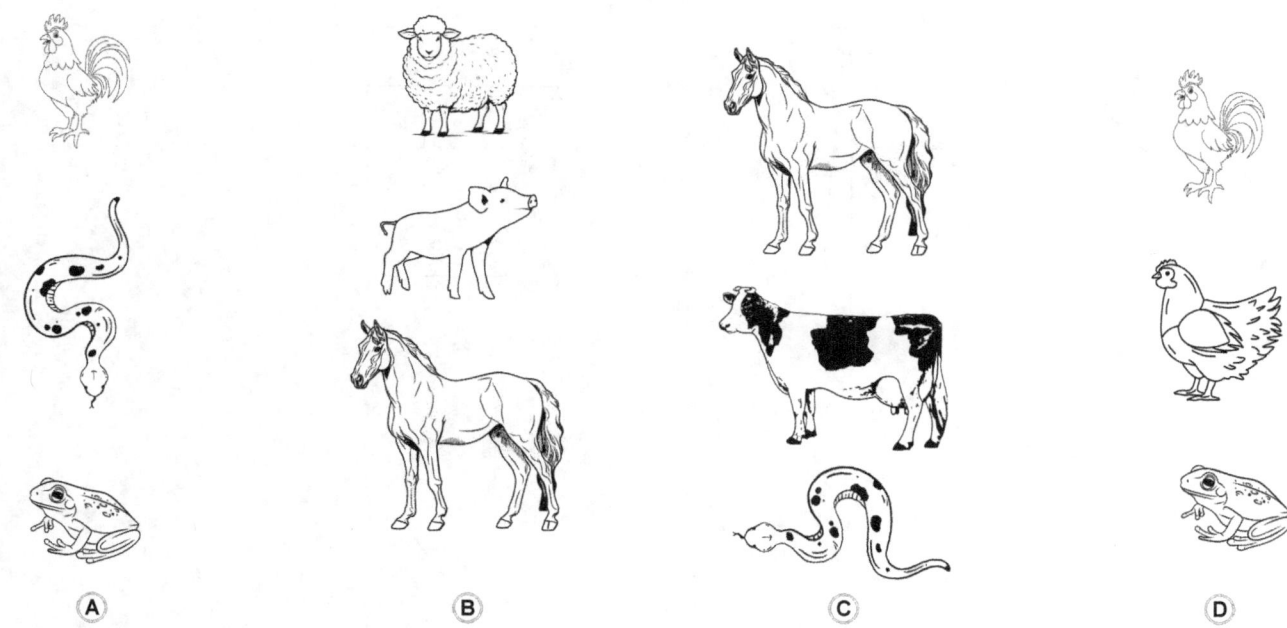

14. If your home lost electricity, which one of these would still work?

15. If you needed to travel quickly between two cities that were far apart, which vehicle would you choose?

16. Which one of these is not used for measuring?

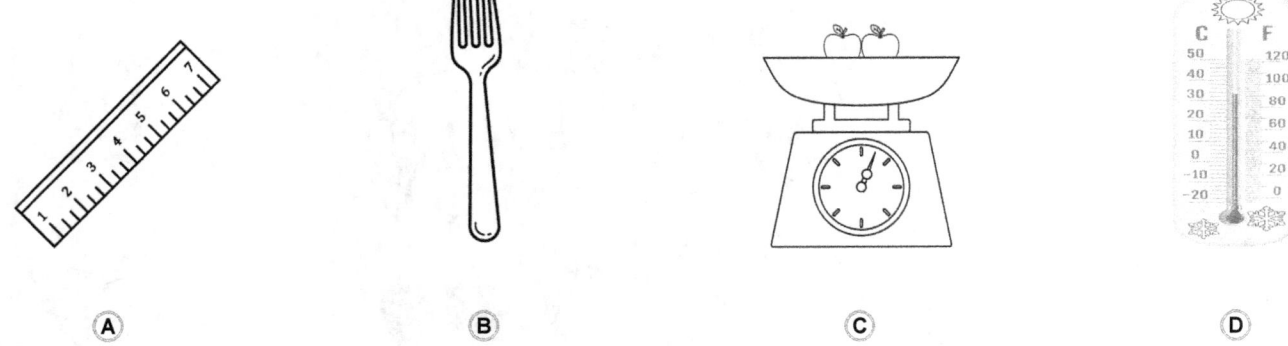

A   B   C   D

FIGURE ANALOGIES

Directions: The pictures in the top boxes go together in some way. One of the bottom boxes is empty. Which answer choice goes with the picture in the bottom box in the same way the top pictures do?

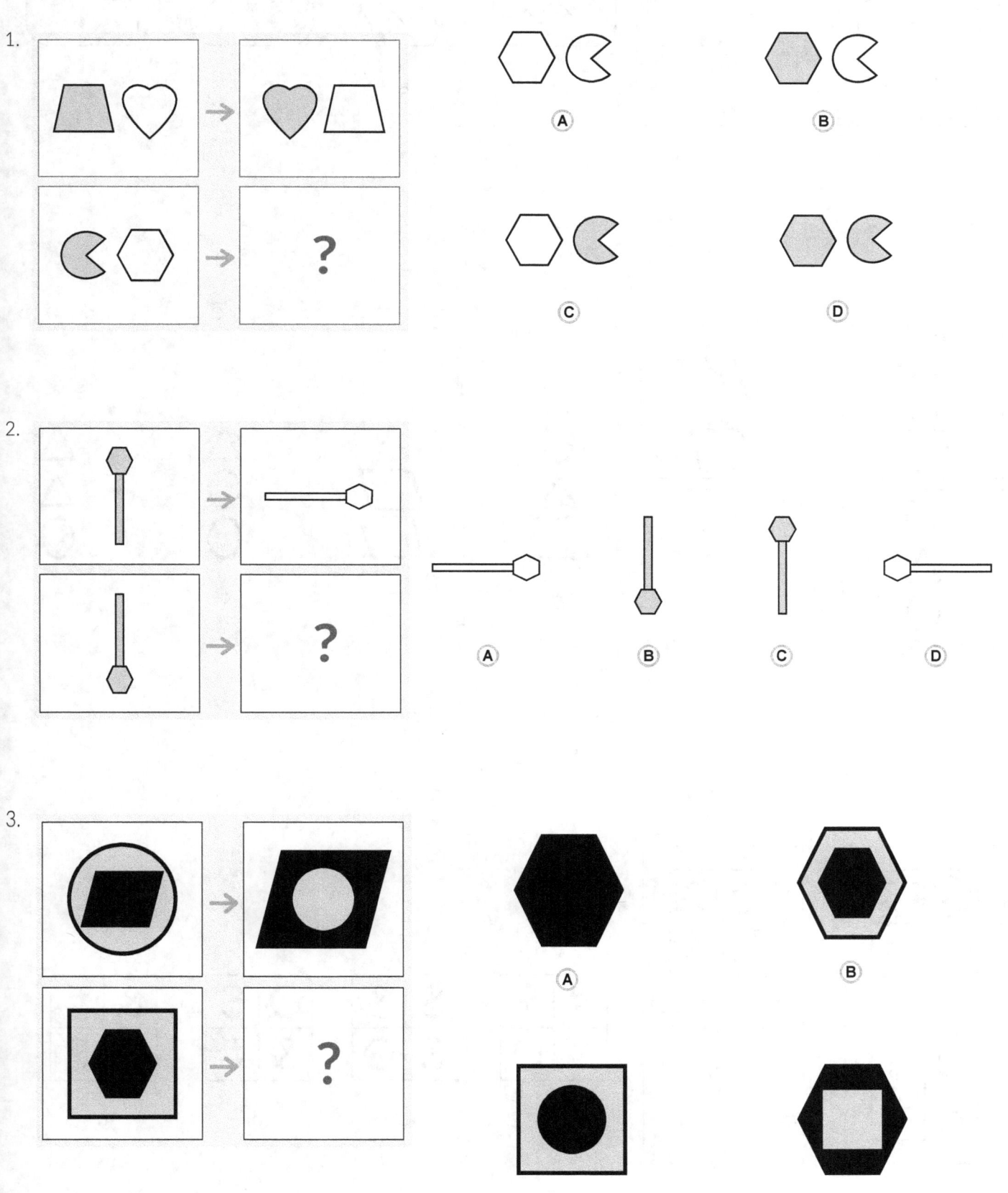

4.

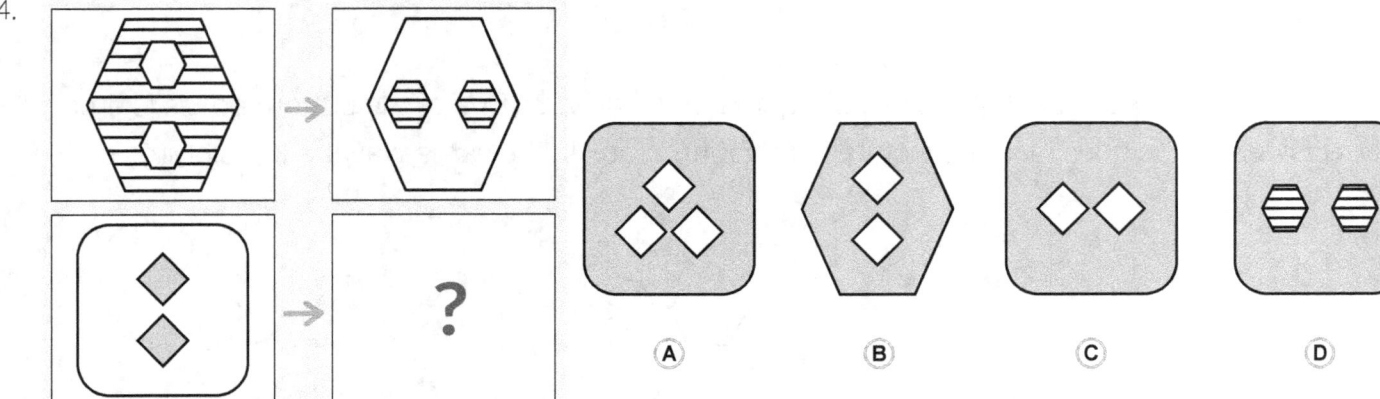

5.

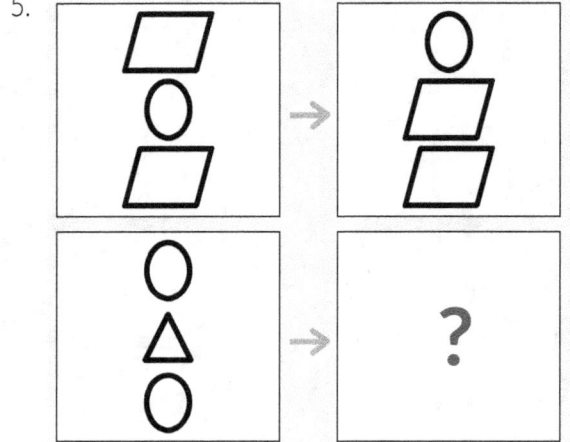

6.

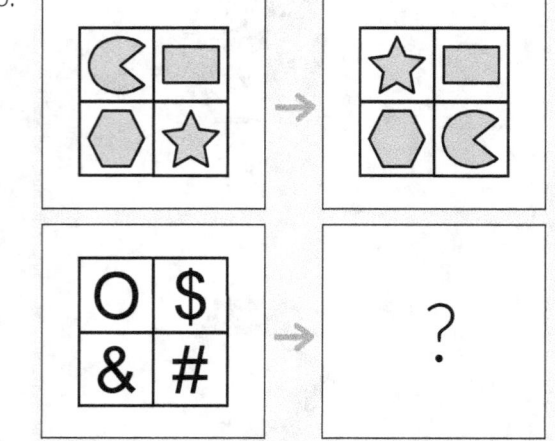

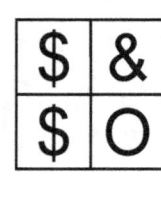 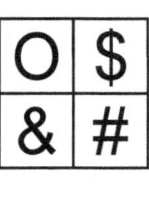 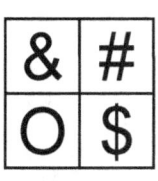

7.

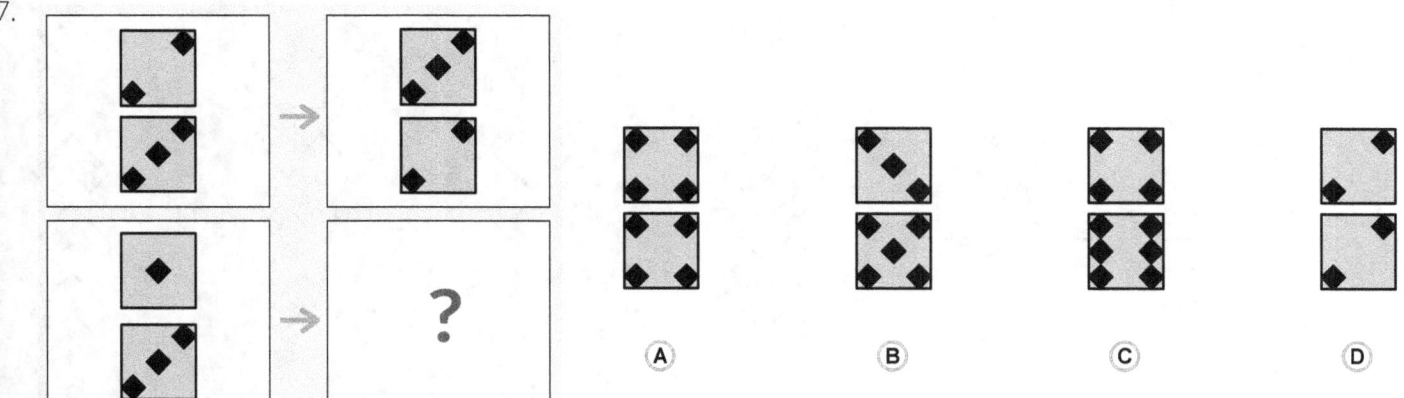

8.

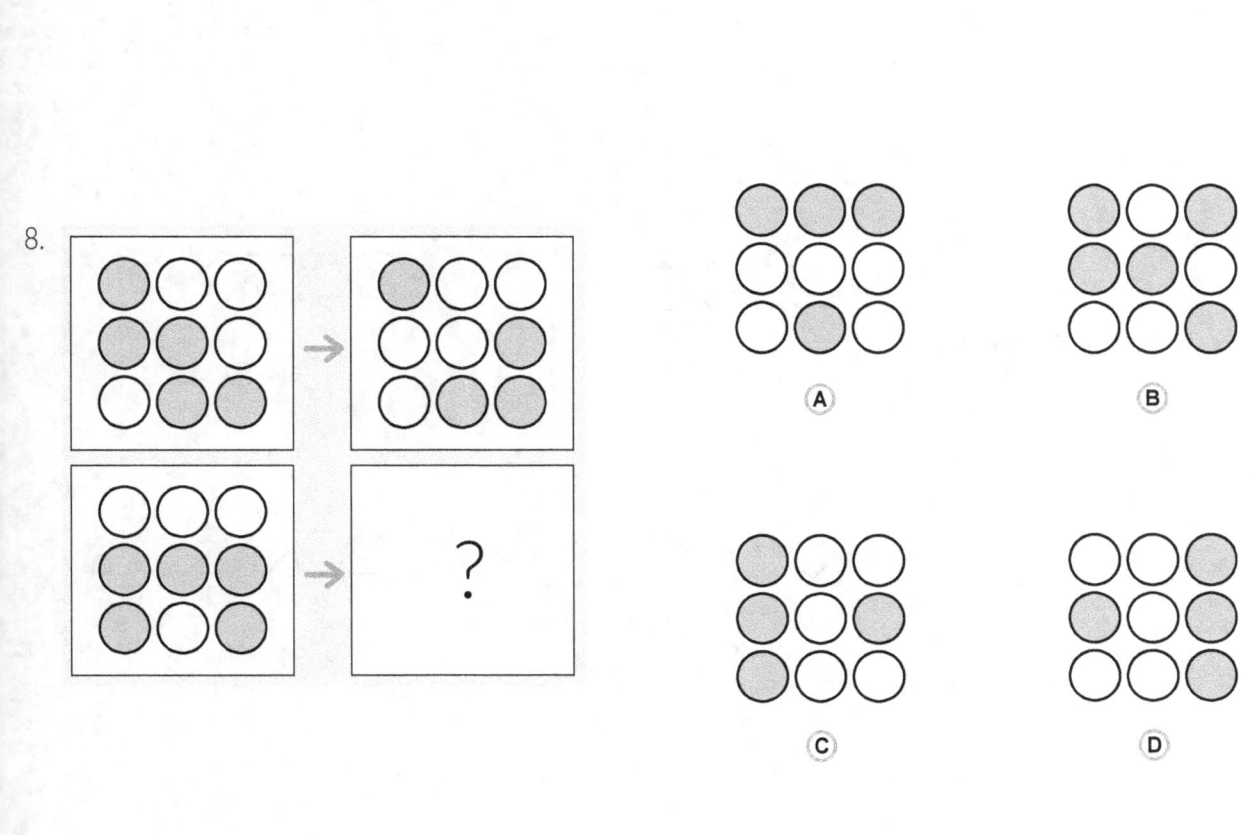

9.

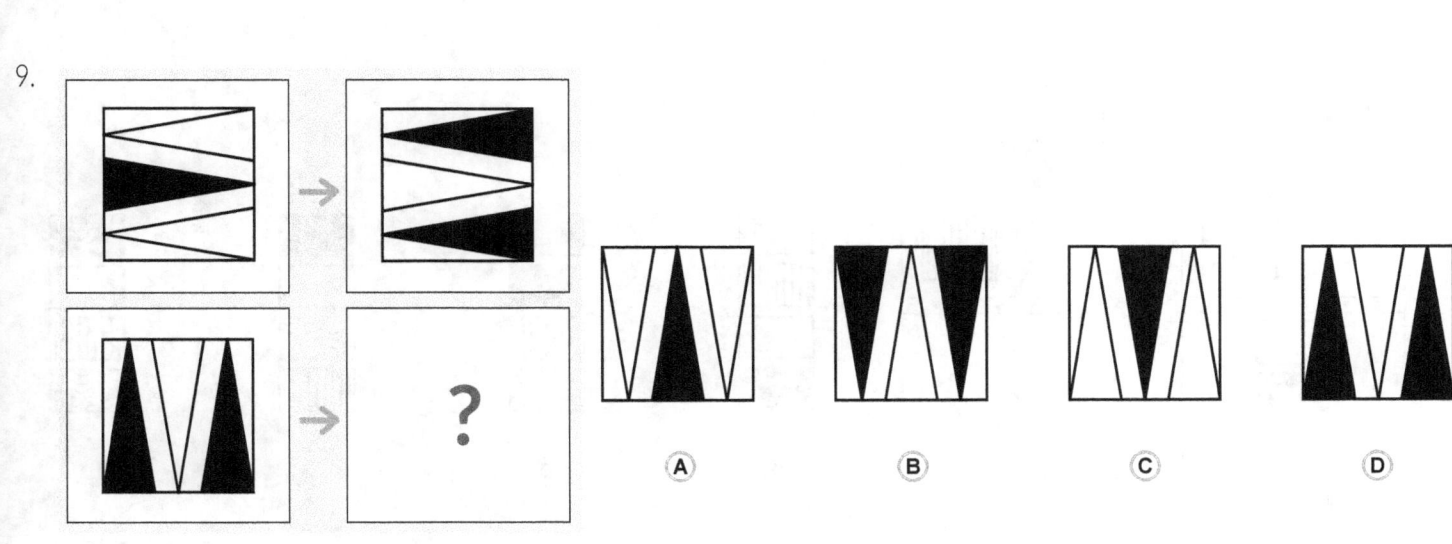

10.

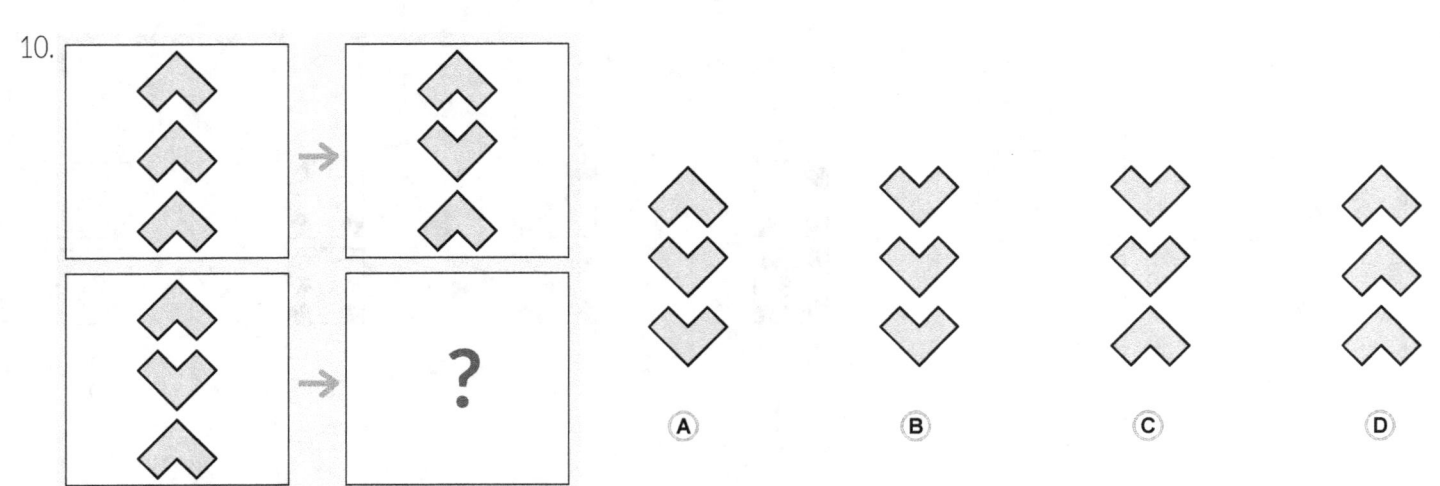

11.

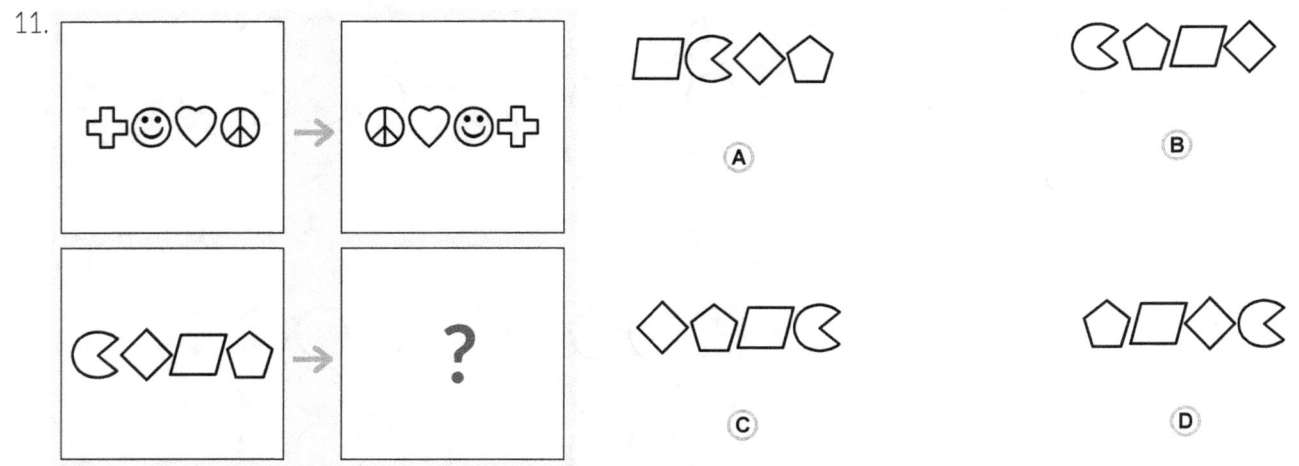

12.

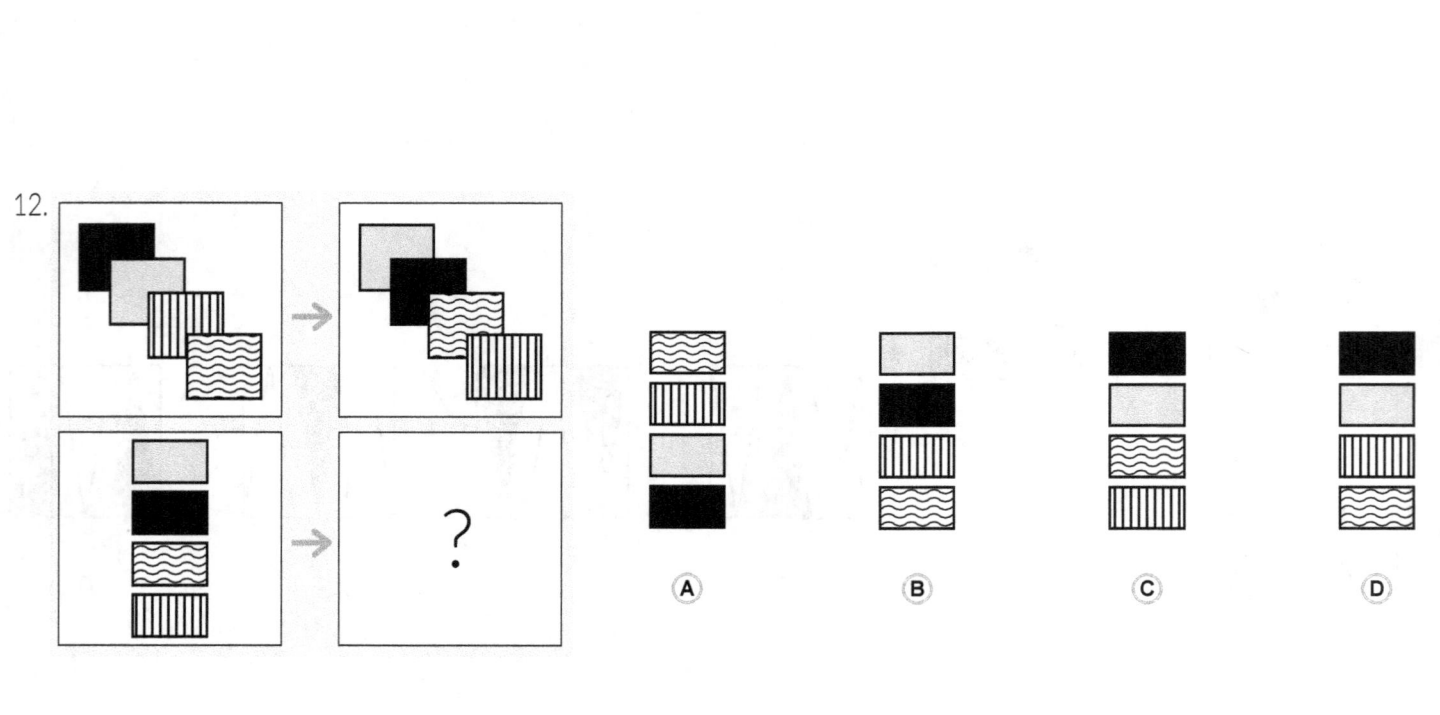

13.

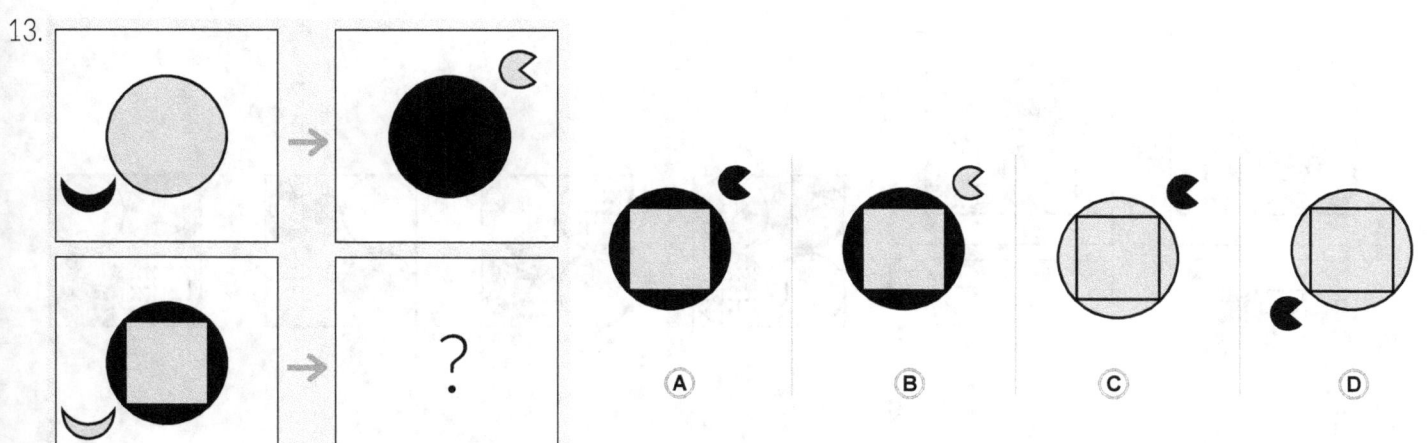

14.

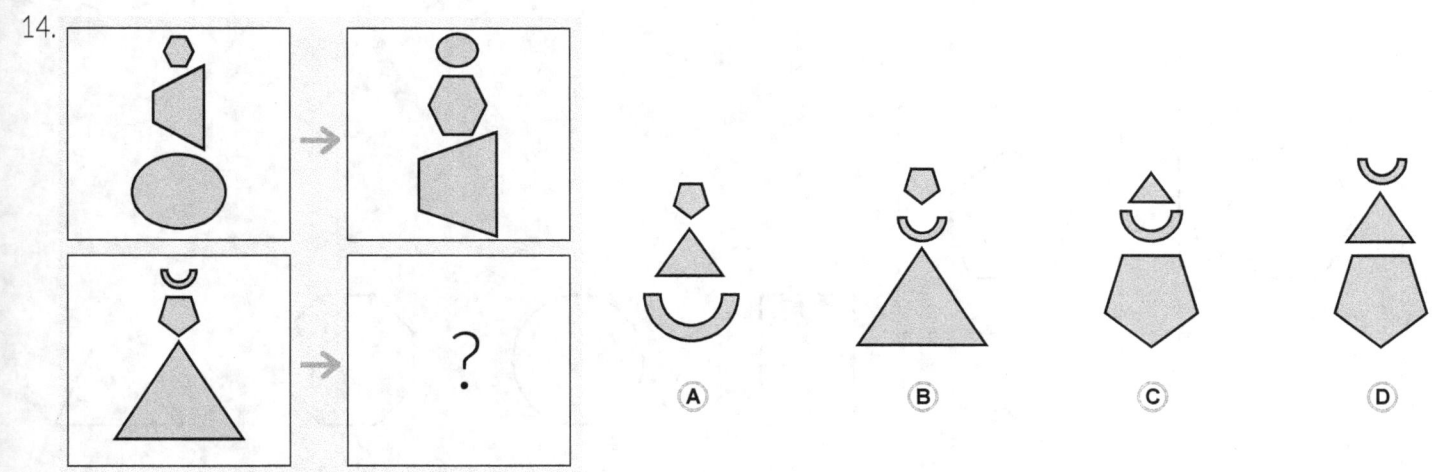

15.

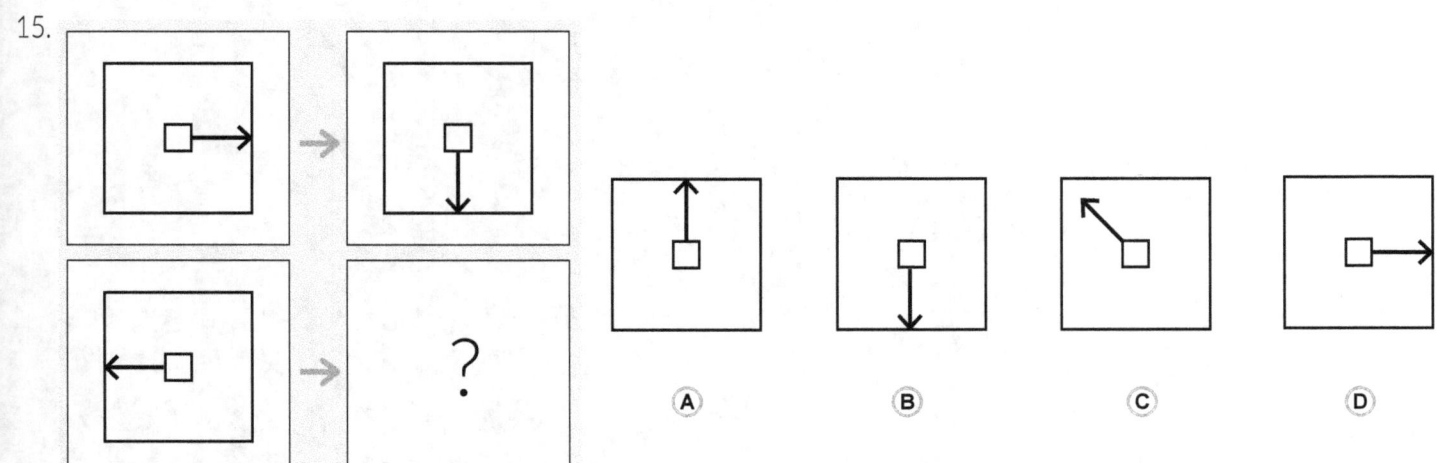

105

16.

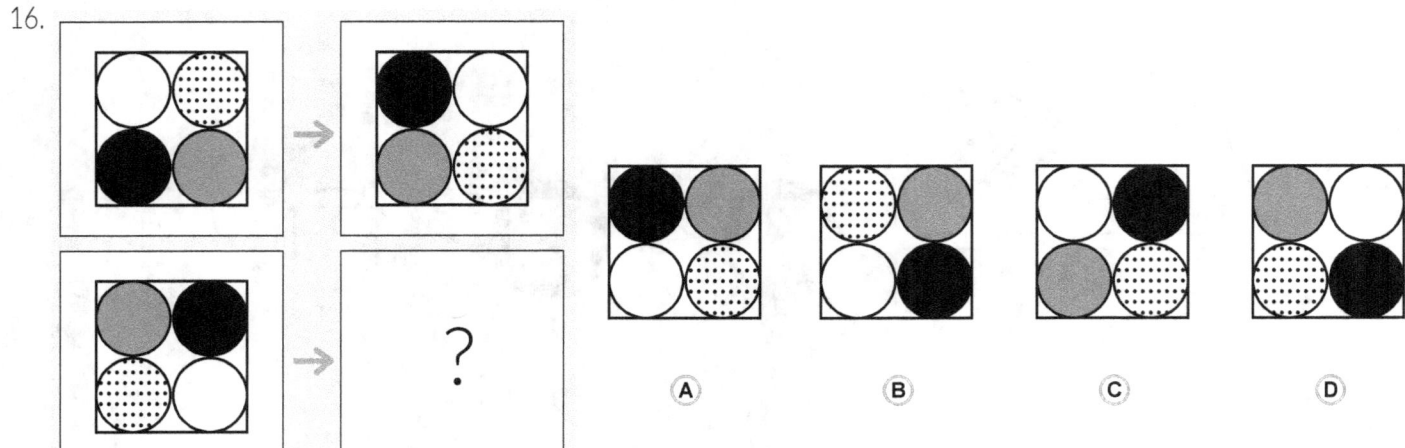

17.

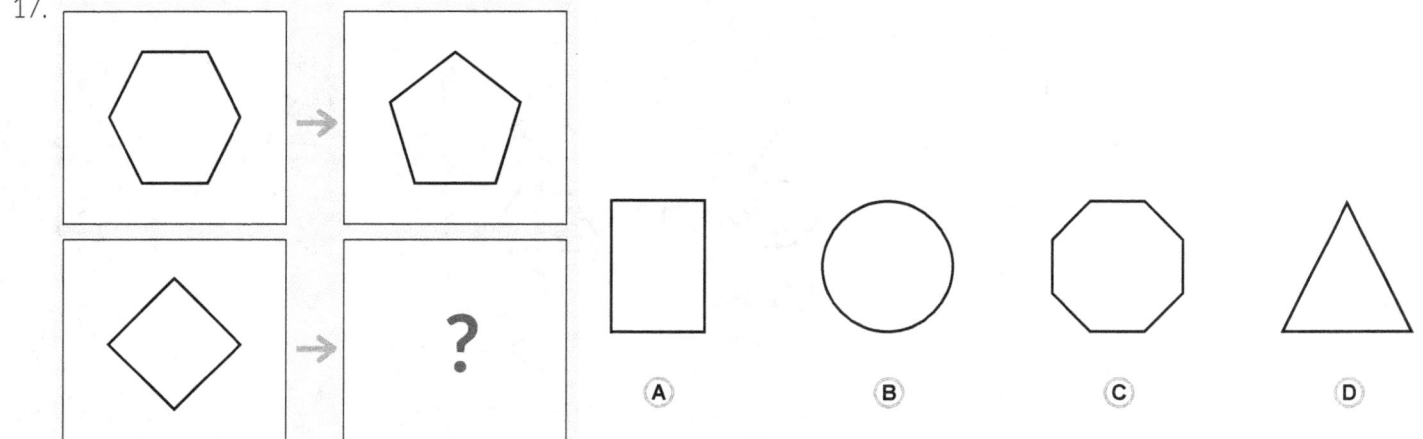

106

FIGURE CLASSIFICATION
Directions: The top row shows three pictures that are alike in some way. Look at the bottom row. Which bottom picture goes best with the top pictures?

1.

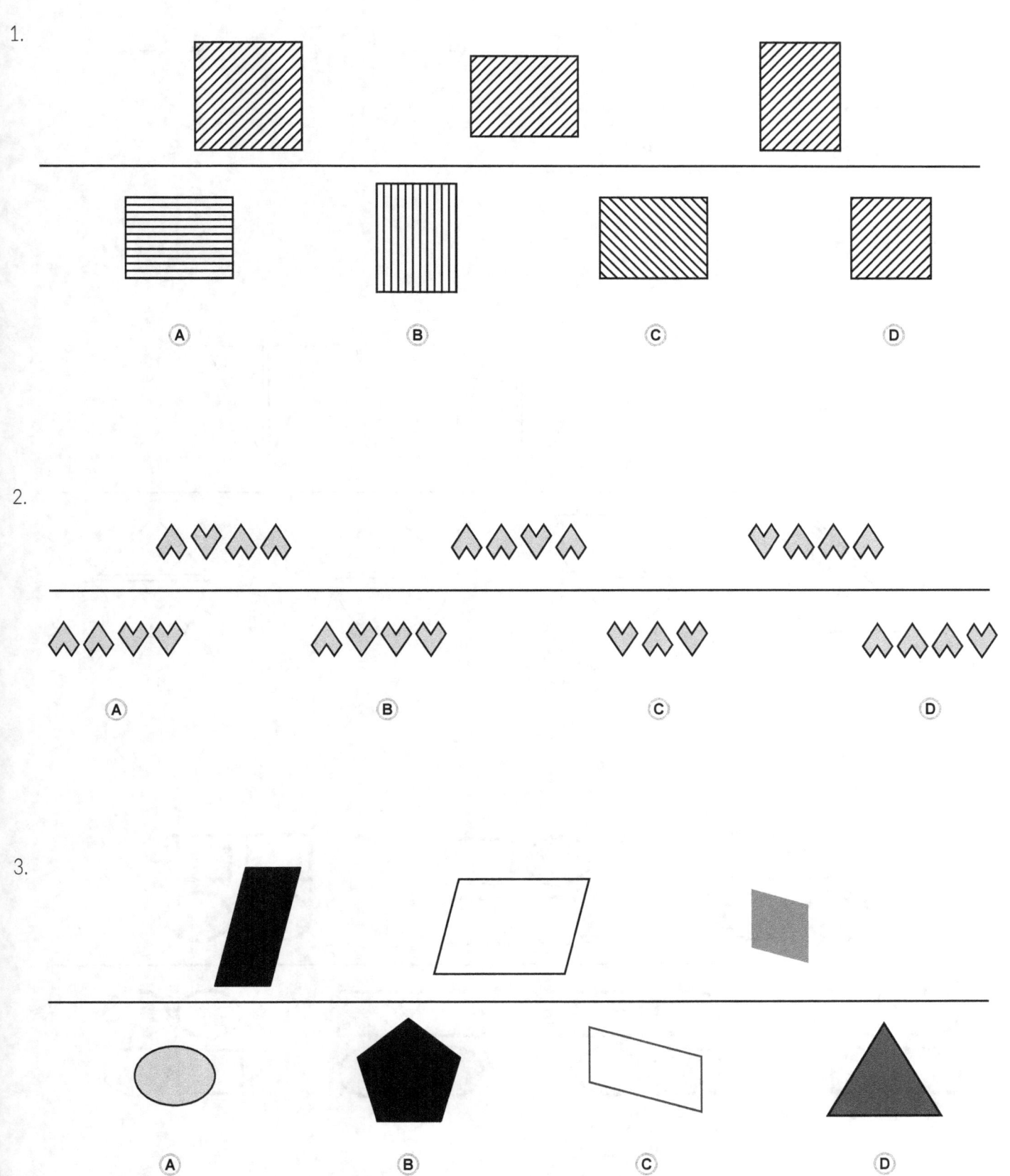

2.

3.

4.

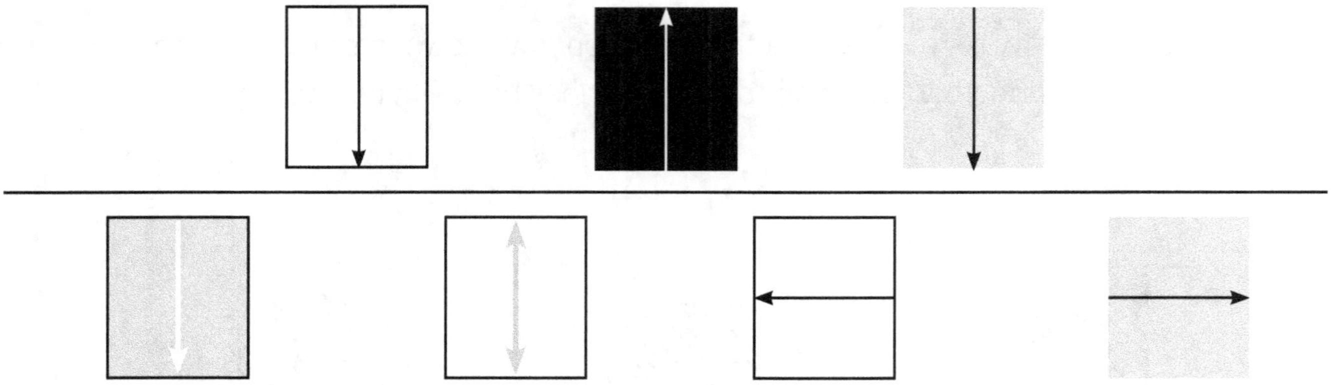

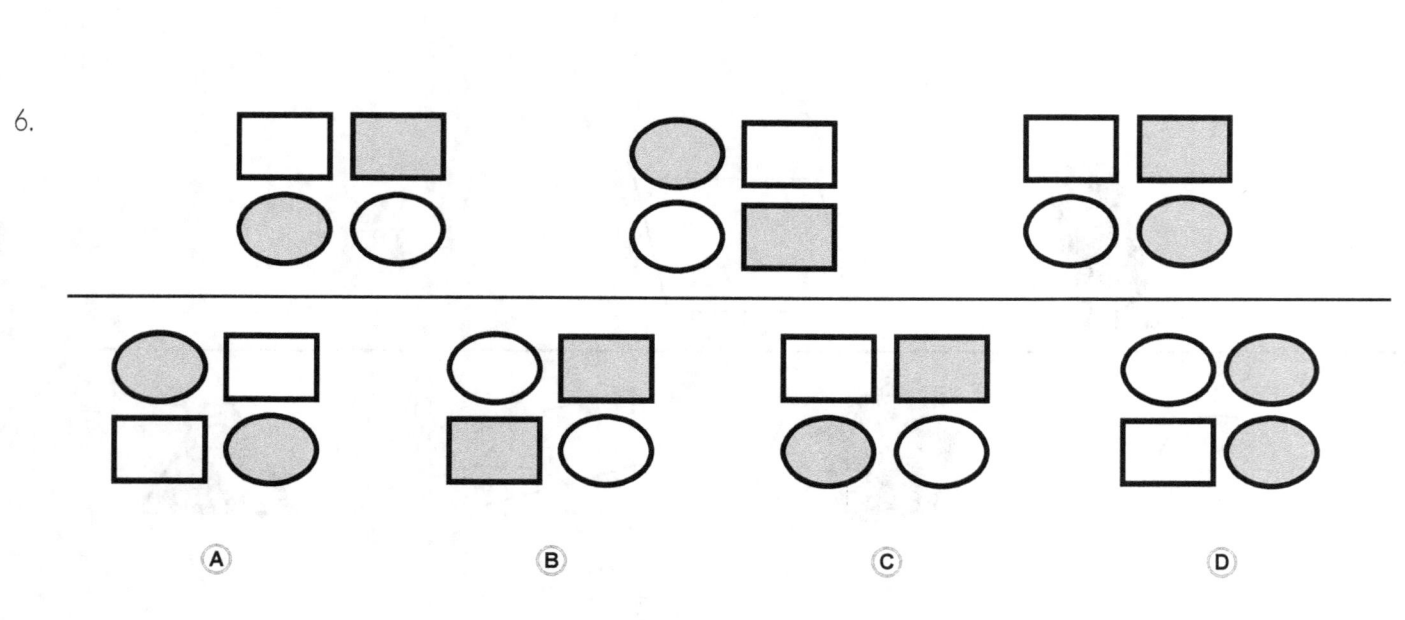

5.

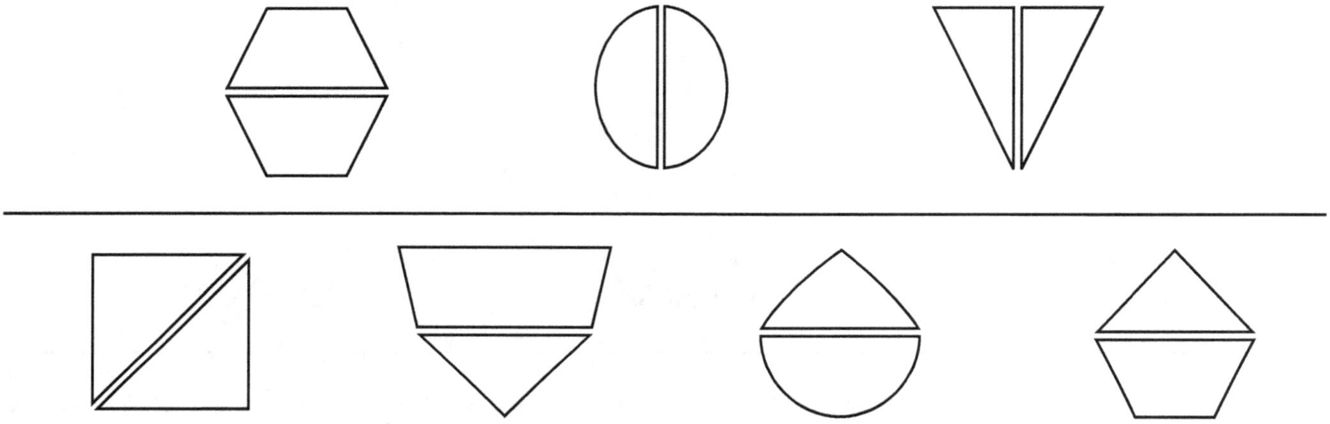

6.

7.

   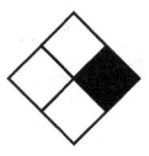

Ⓐ Ⓑ Ⓒ Ⓓ

8.

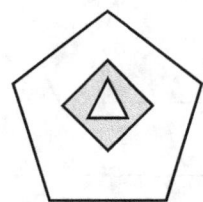 

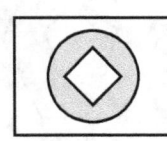 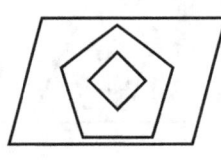 

Ⓐ Ⓑ Ⓒ Ⓓ

9.

Ⓐ Ⓑ Ⓒ Ⓓ

10.

 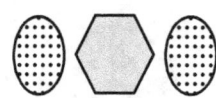 

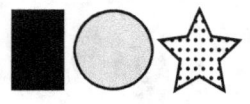  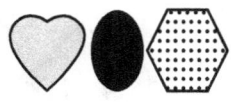 

Ⓐ Ⓑ Ⓒ Ⓓ

11.

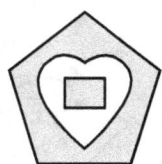  

 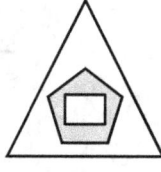 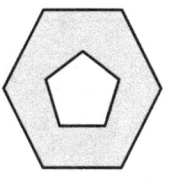 

Ⓐ Ⓑ Ⓒ Ⓓ

12.

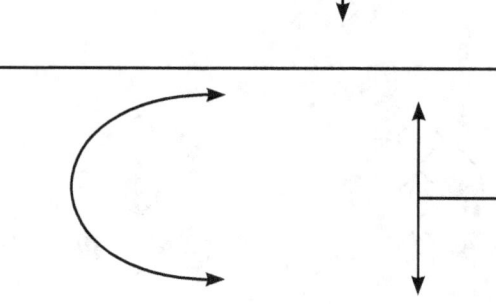 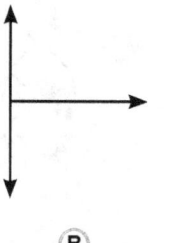  

Ⓐ Ⓑ Ⓒ Ⓓ

13.

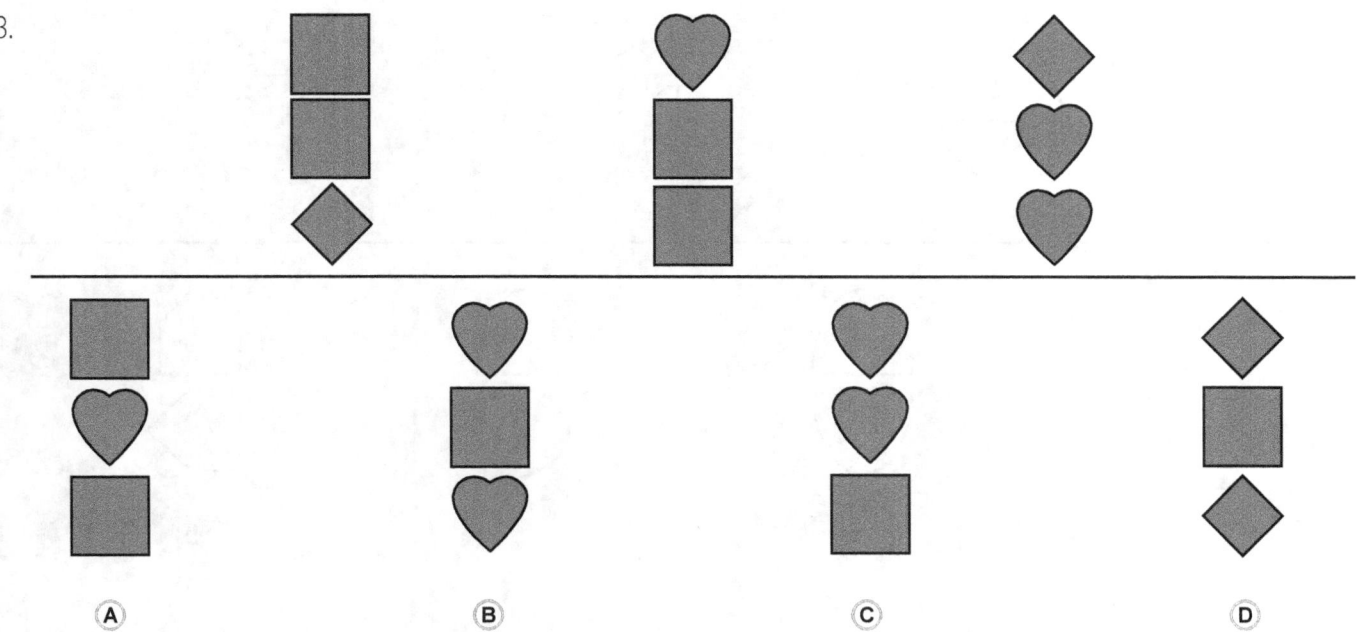

| A | B | C | D |

14.

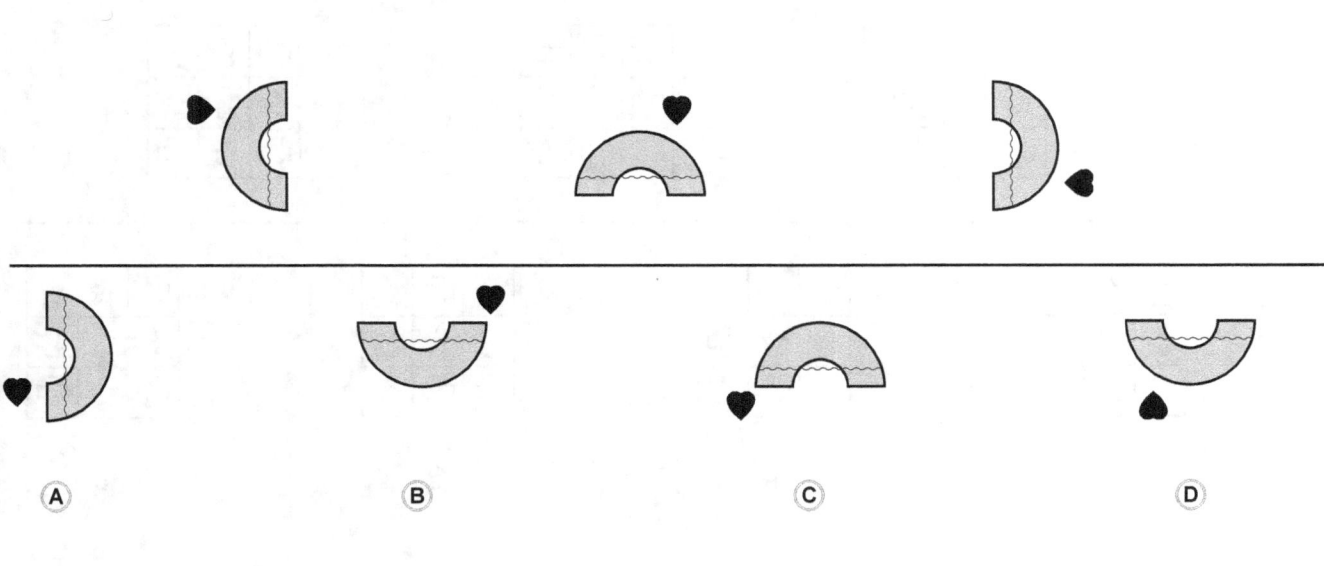

| A | B | C | D |

15.

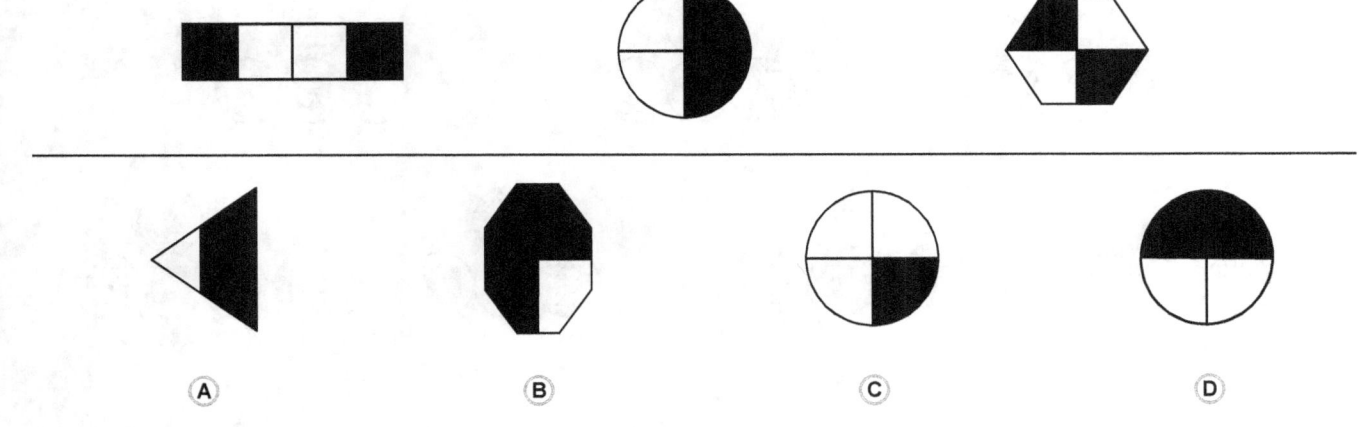

| A | B | C | D |

16.

17.

18.

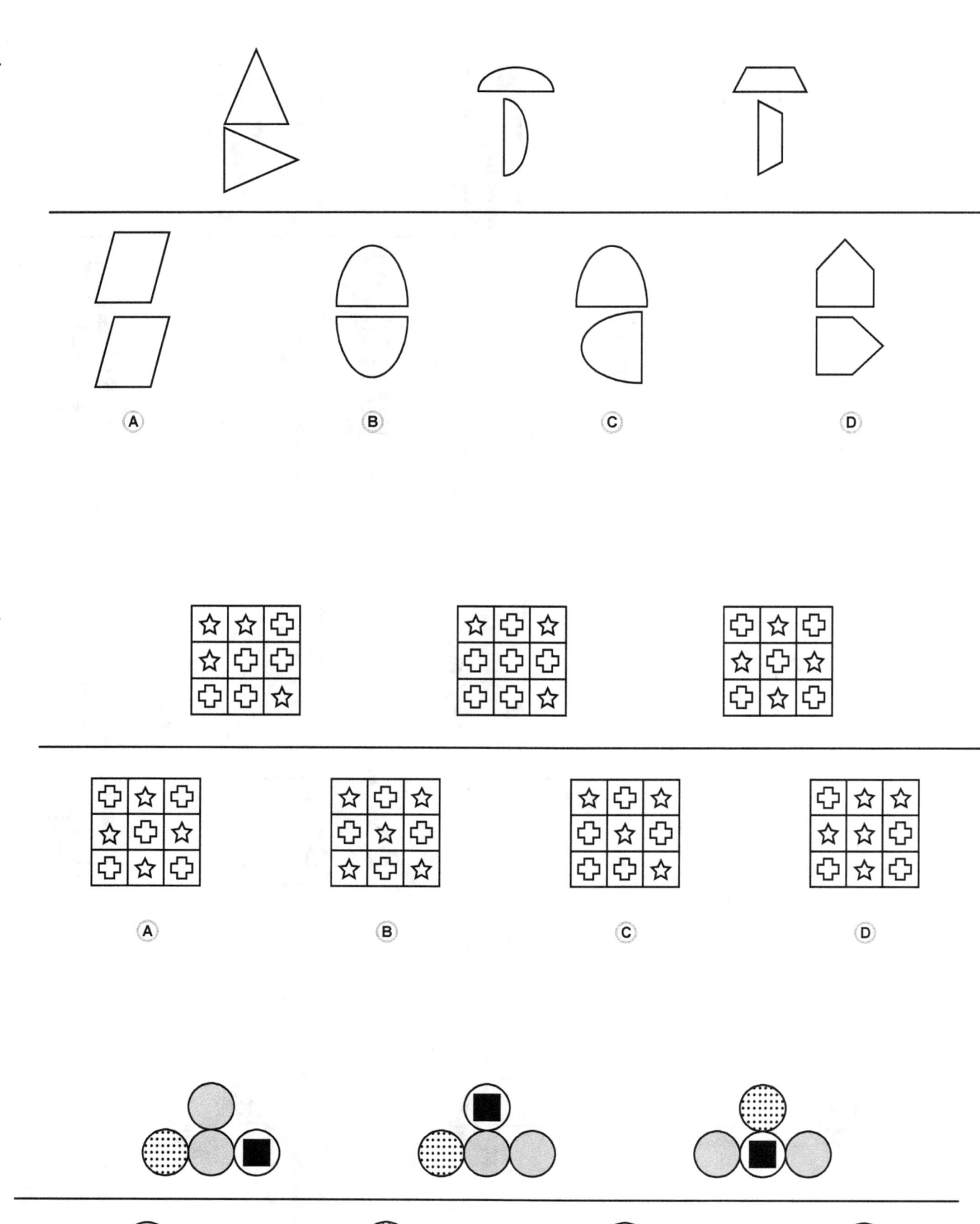

PAPER FOLDING

The top row of pictures shows a sheet of paper. The paper was folded, then something was cut out. Which picture in the bottom row shows how the paper would look after it's unfolded?

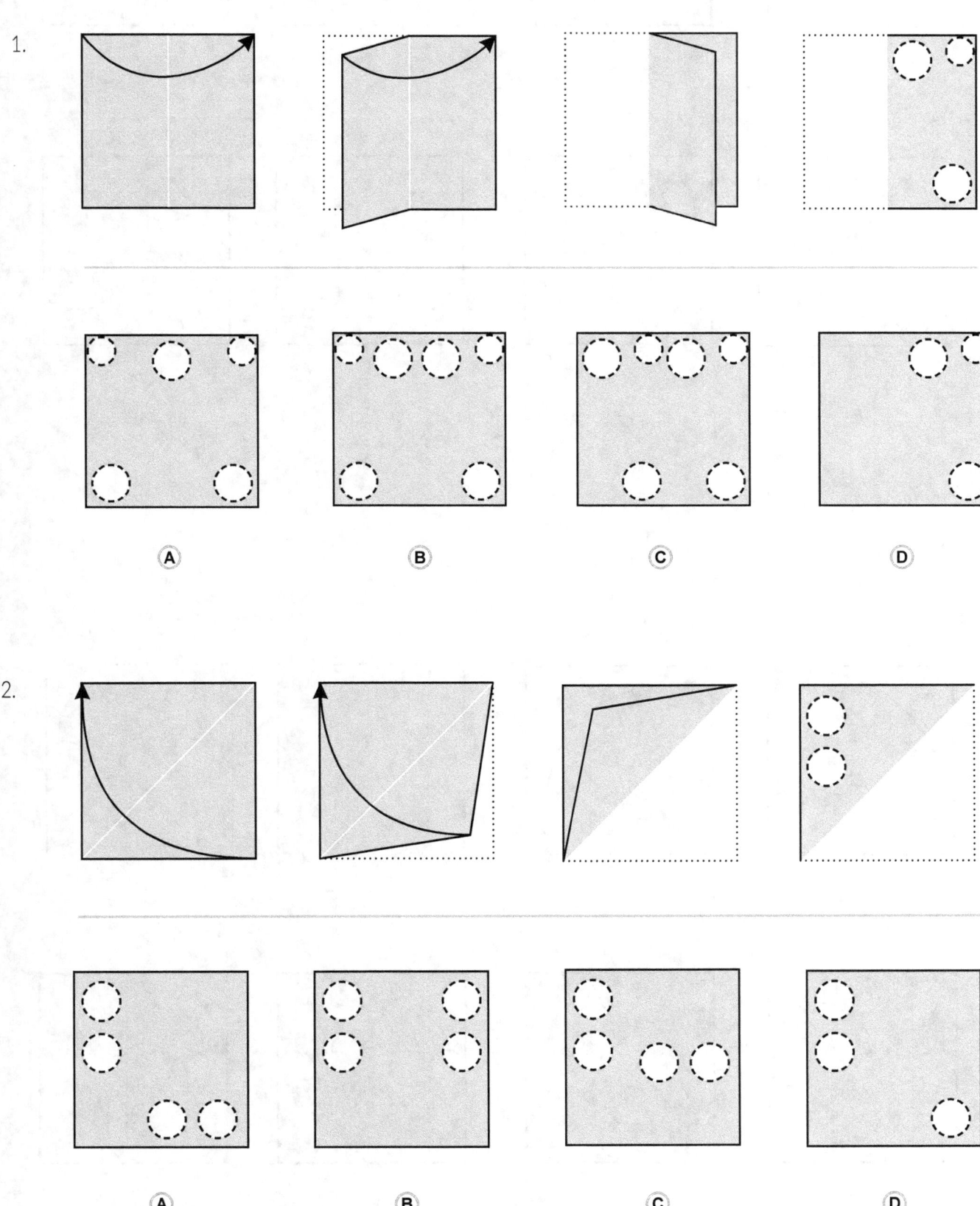

1.

A   B   C   D

2.

A   B   C   D

3.

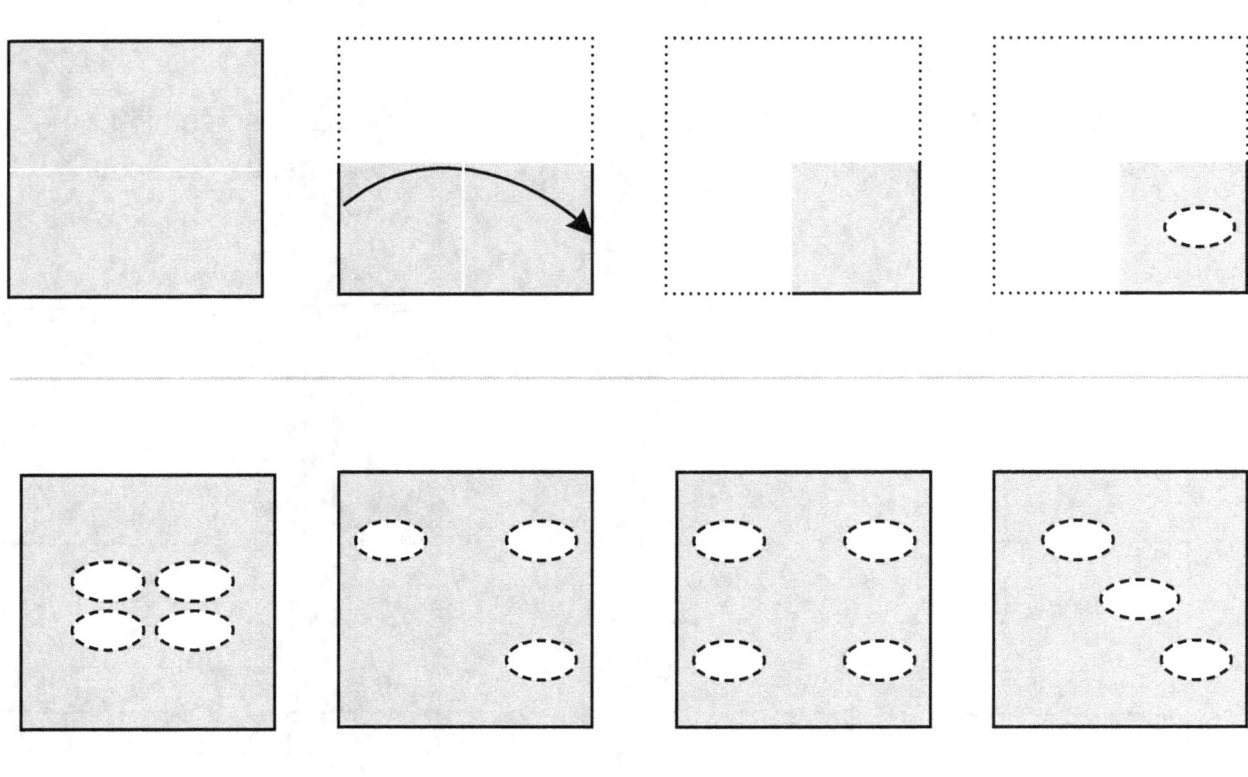

A   B   C   D

4.

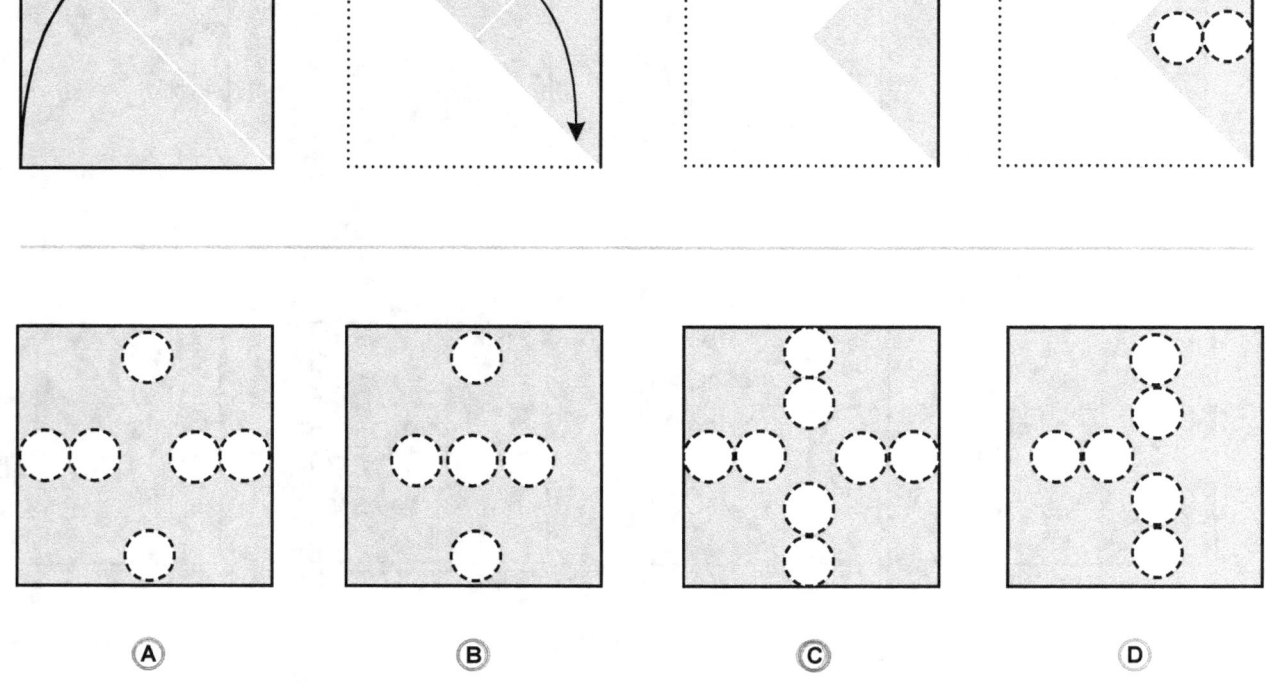

A   B   C   D

114

5.

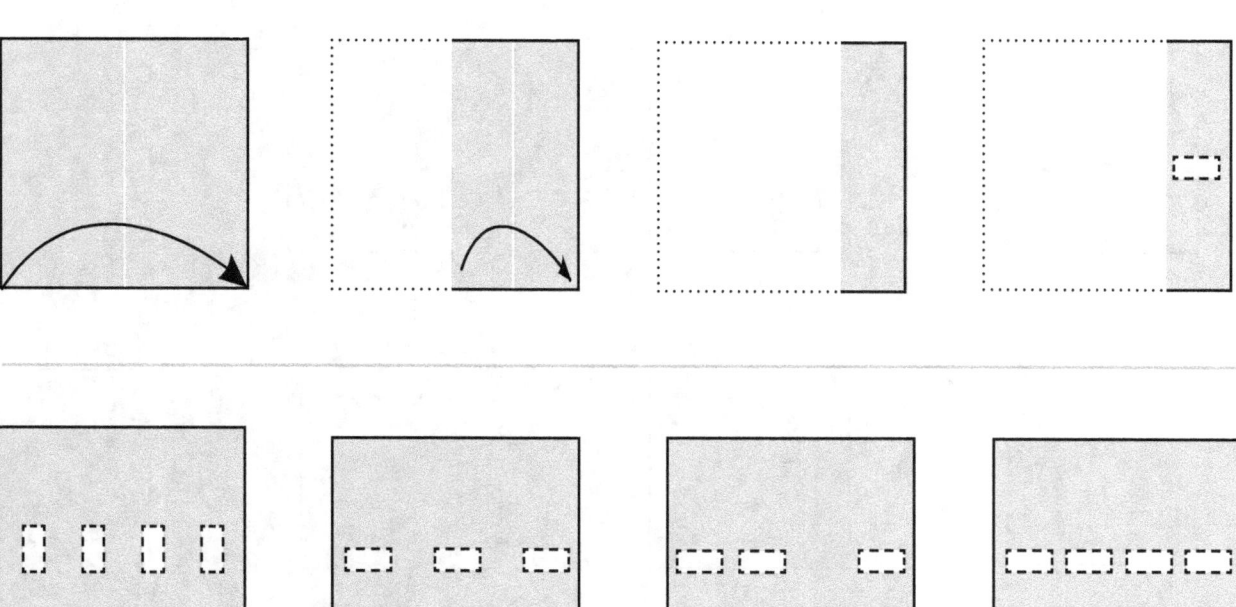

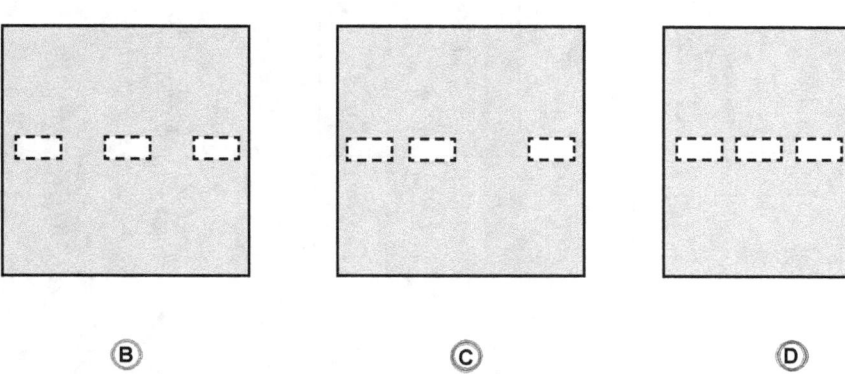

<table>
<tr><td>Ⓐ</td><td>Ⓑ</td><td>Ⓒ</td><td>Ⓓ</td></tr>
</table>

6.

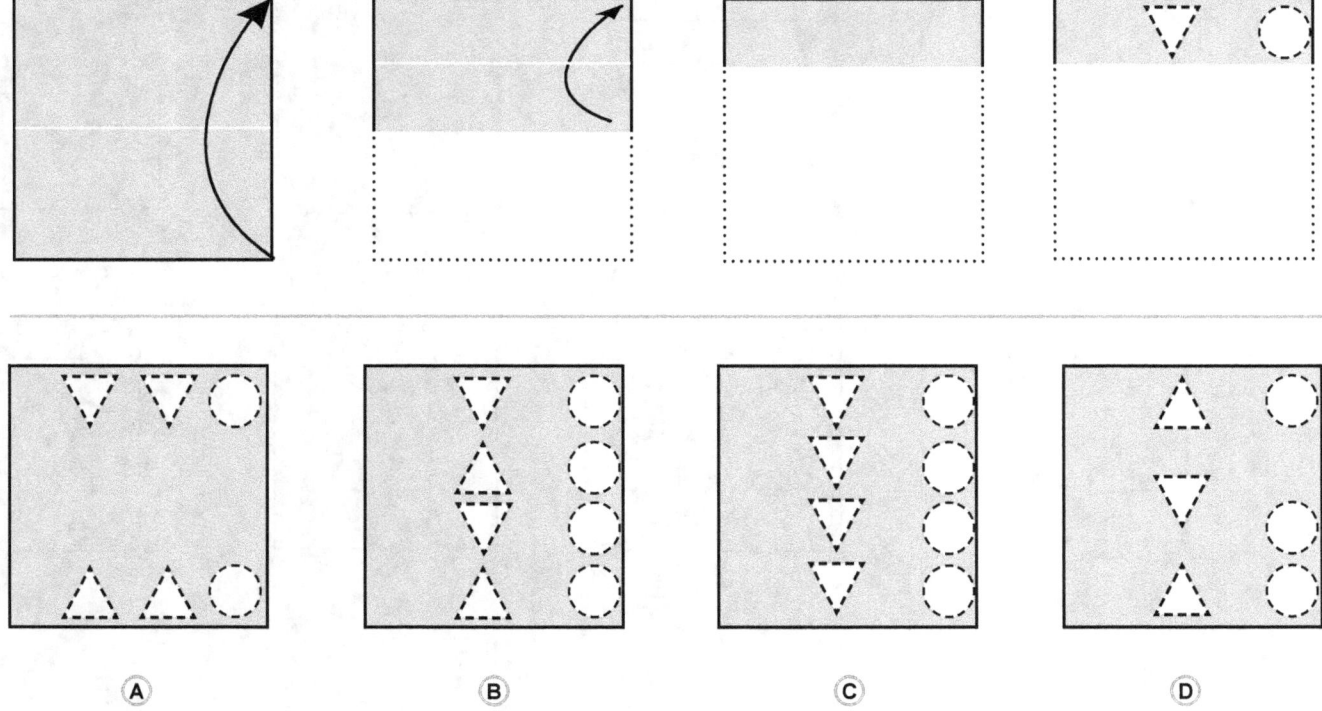

<table>
<tr><td>Ⓐ</td><td>Ⓑ</td><td>Ⓒ</td><td>Ⓓ</td></tr>
</table>

7.

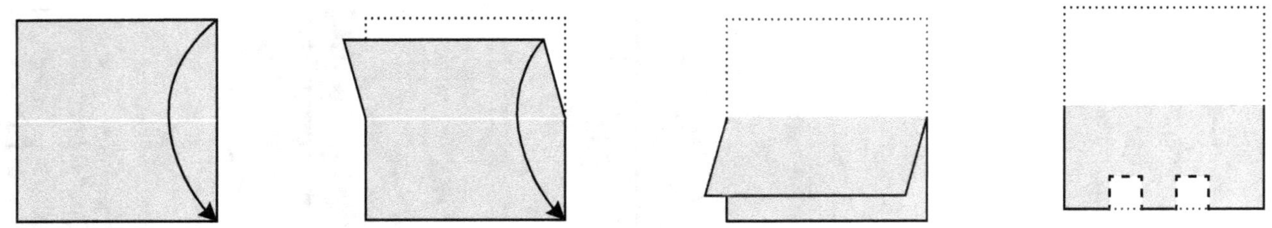

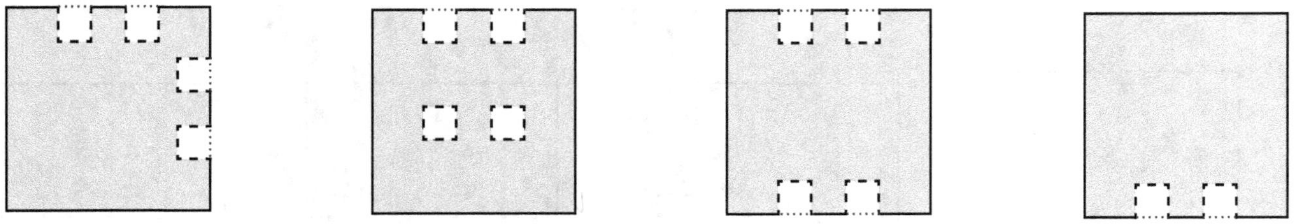

(A)   (B)   (C)   (D)

8.

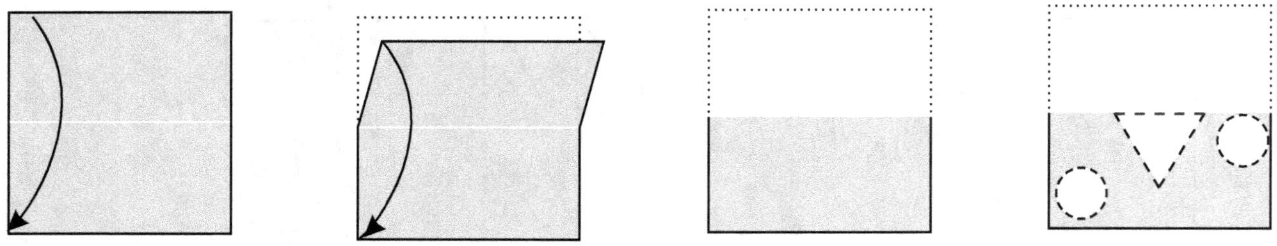

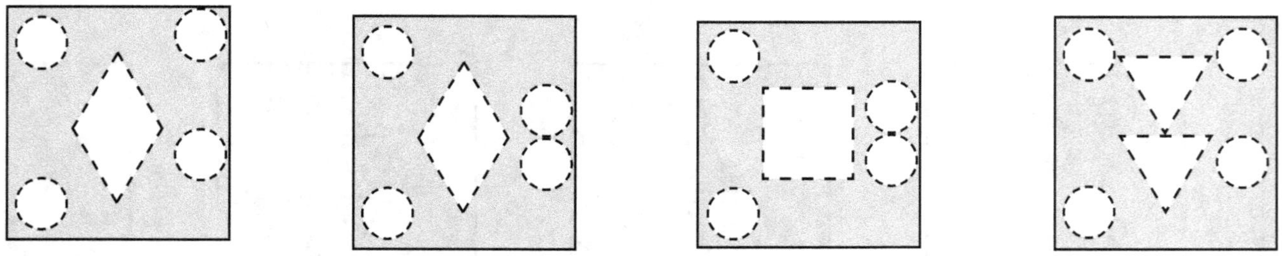

(A)   (B)   (C)   (D)

116

9.

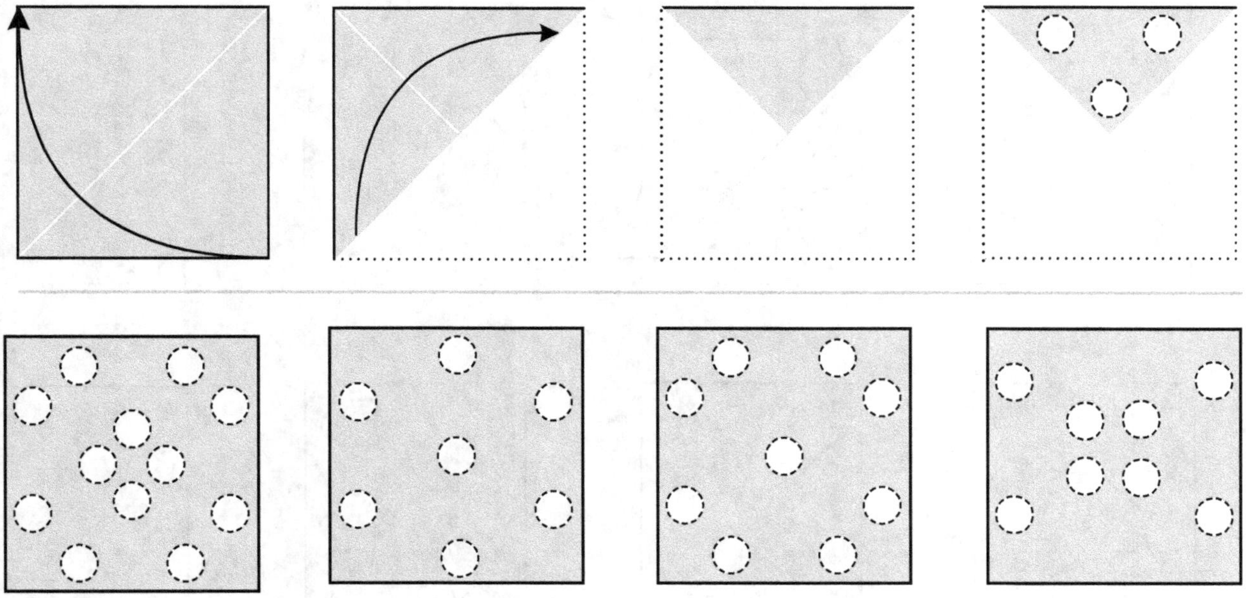

A   B   C   D

10.

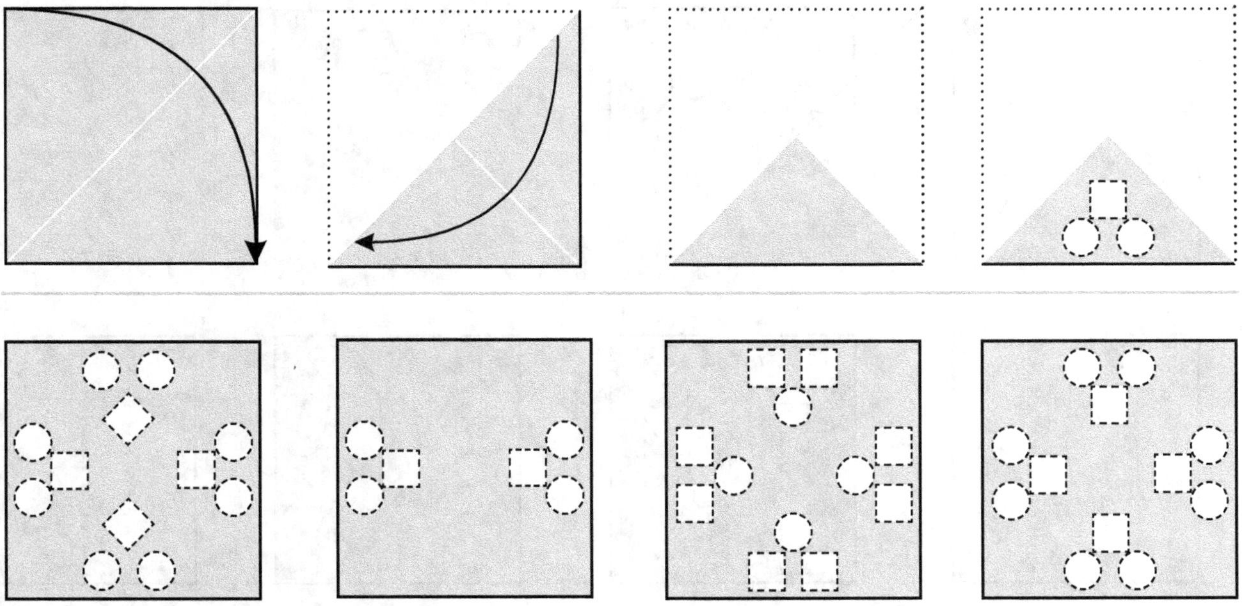

A   B   C   D

117

11.

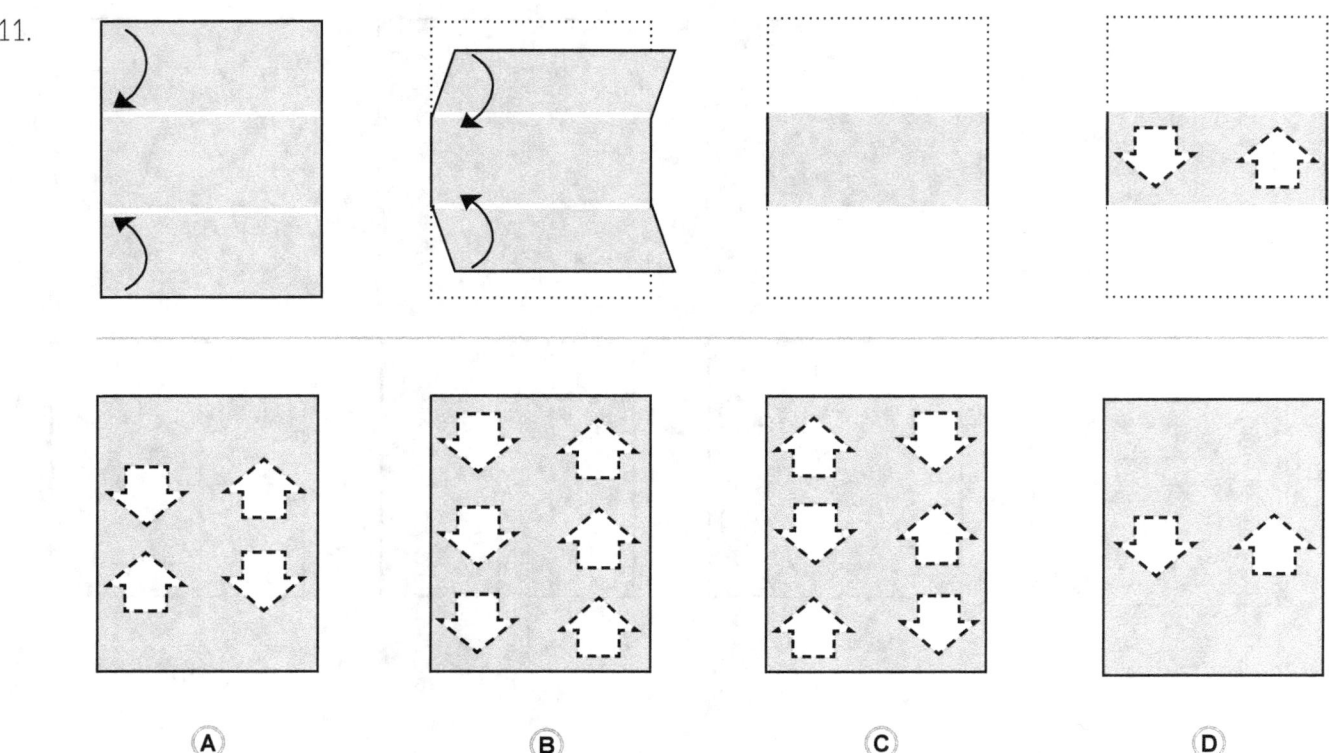

A   B   C   D

12.

A   B   C   D

13.

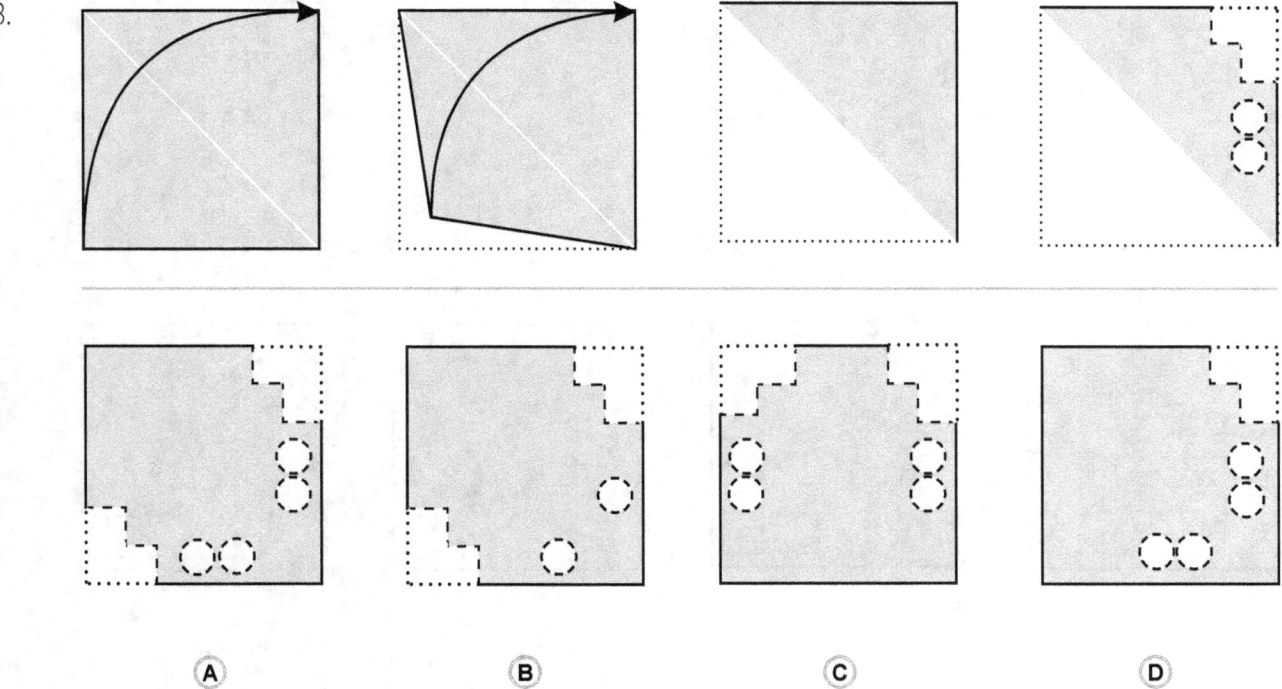

A B C D

14.

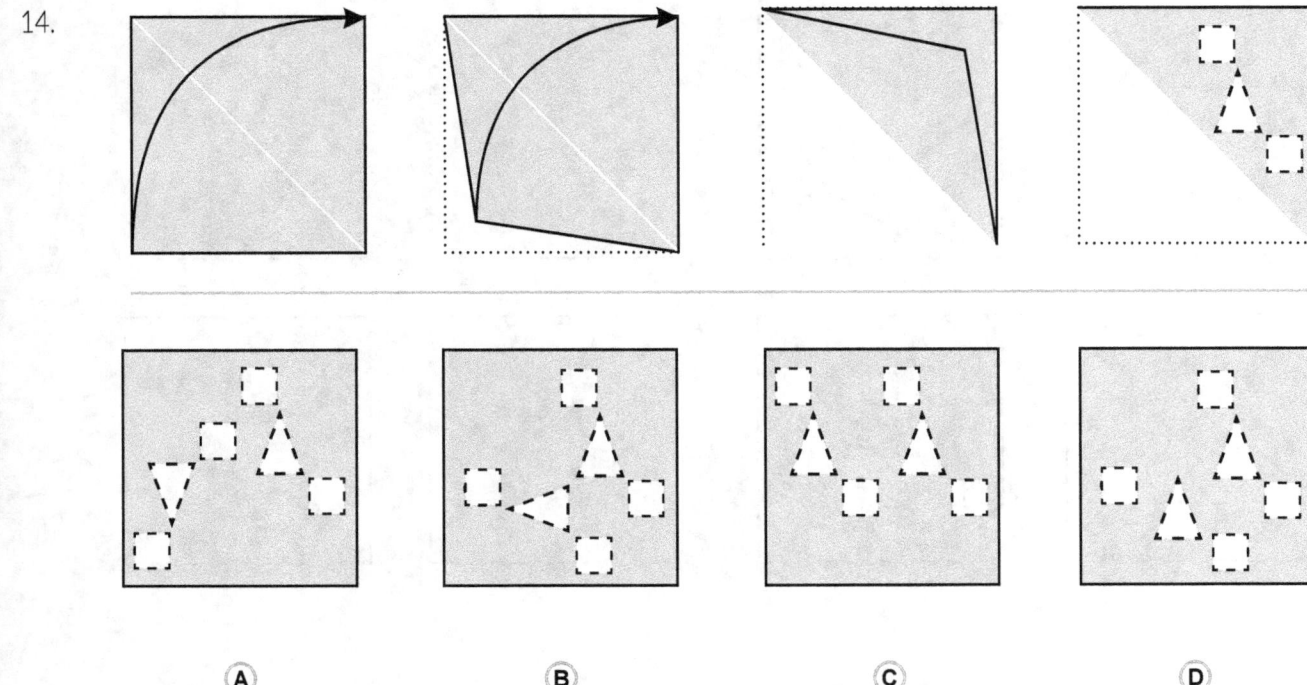

A B C D

15.

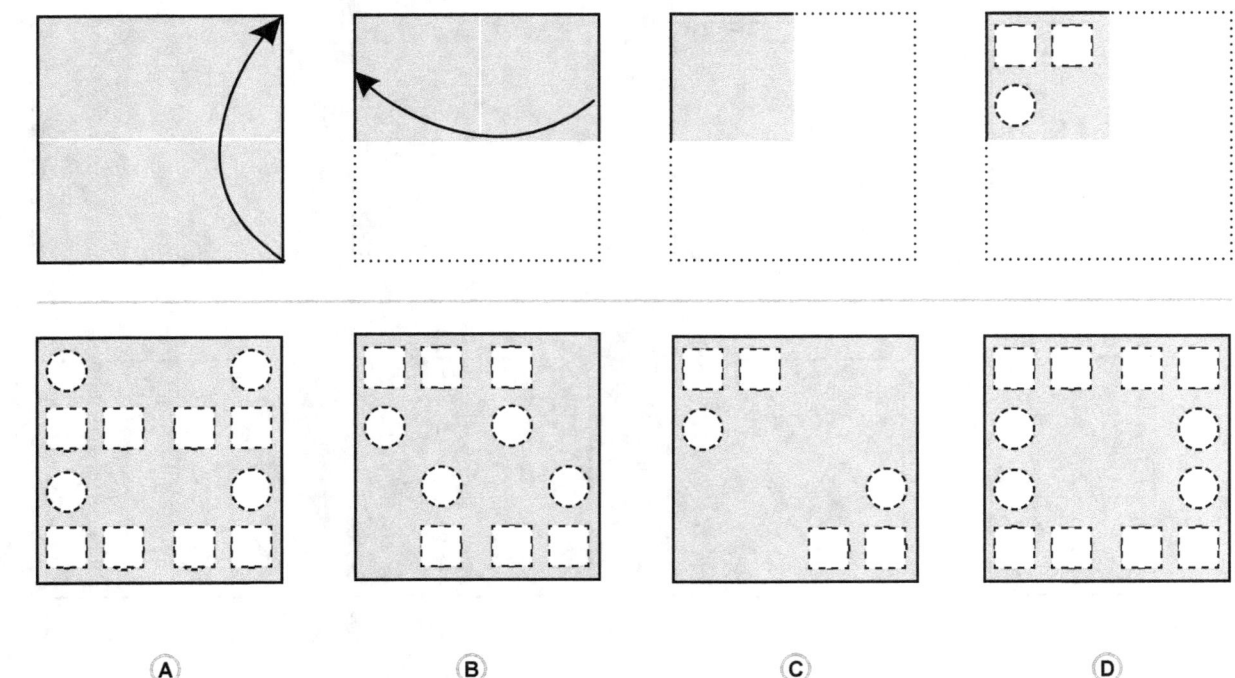

16.

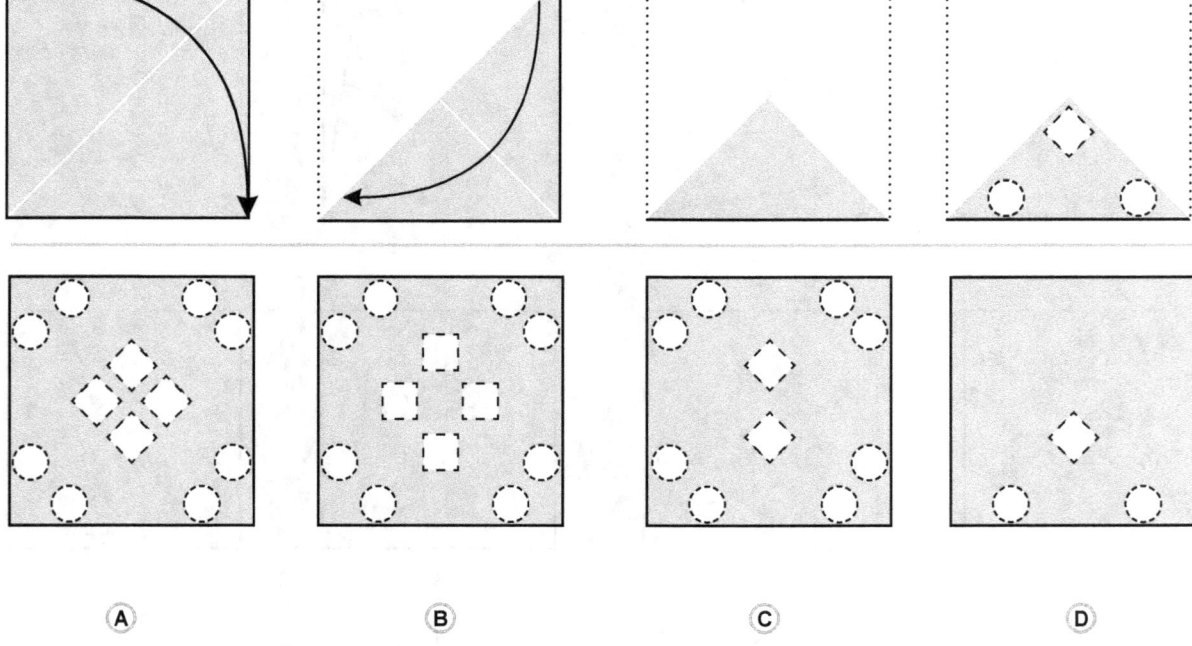

120

NUMBER ANALOGIES

Directions: The pictures in the top boxes go together in some way. One of the bottom boxes is empty.
Which answer choice goes with the picture in the bottom box in the same way the top pictures do?

1.

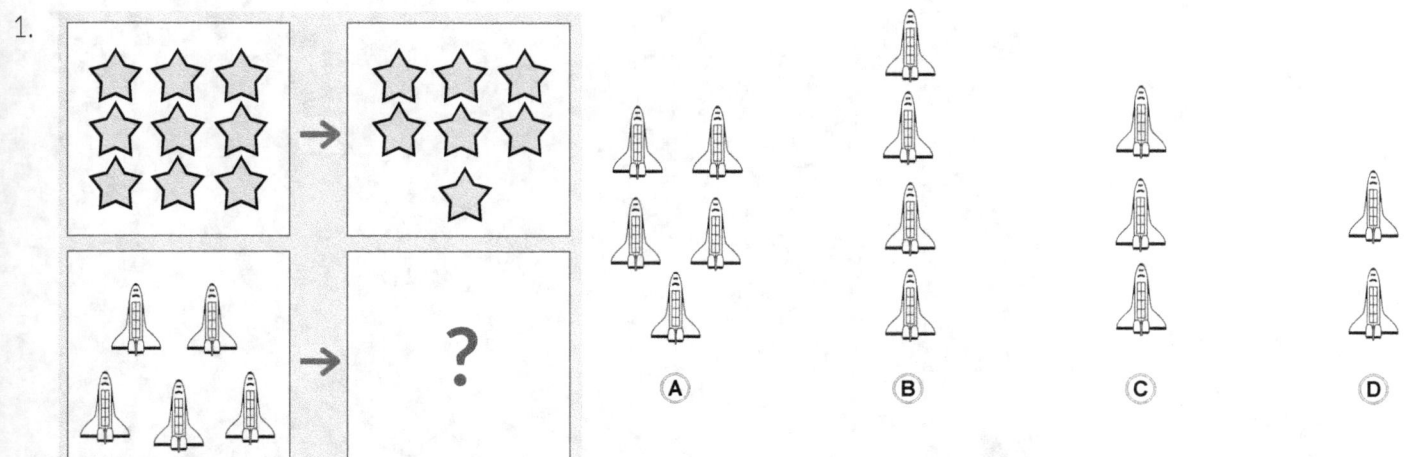

2.

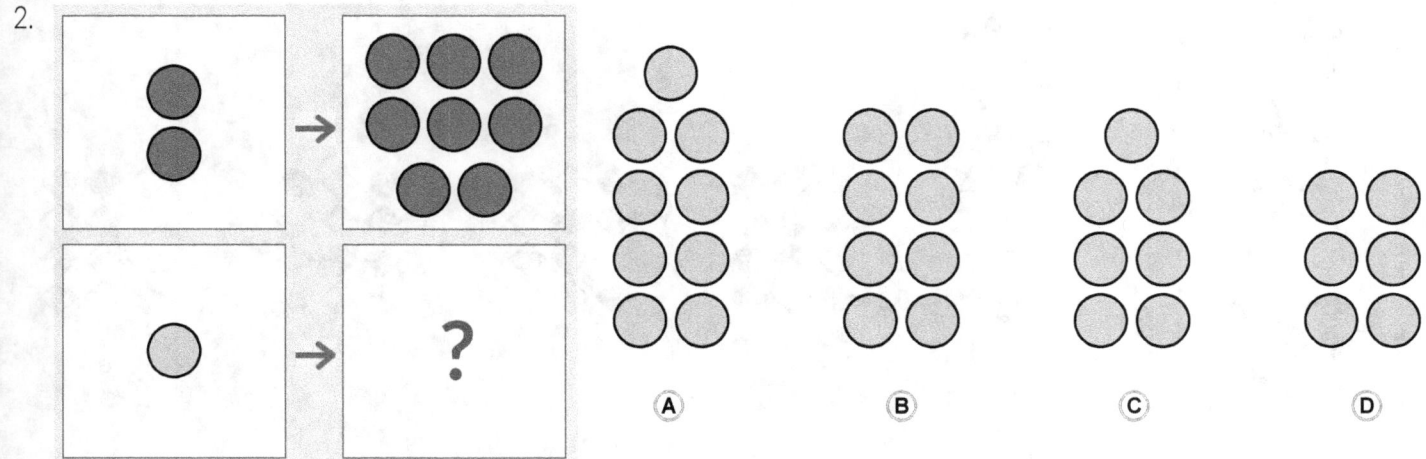

3.

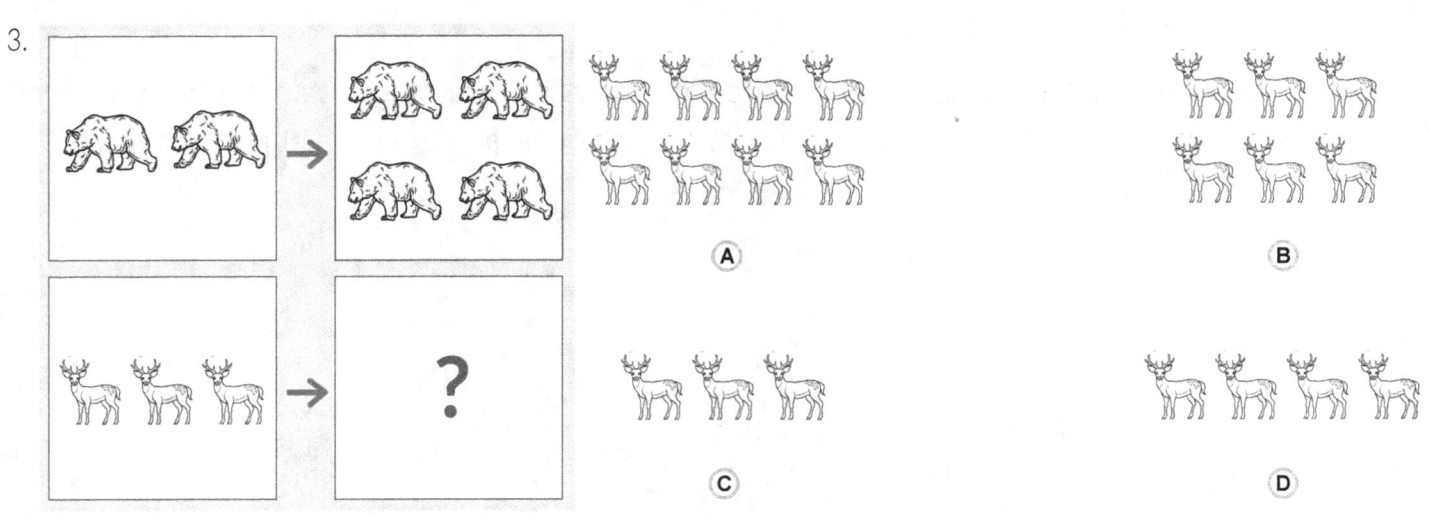

4.

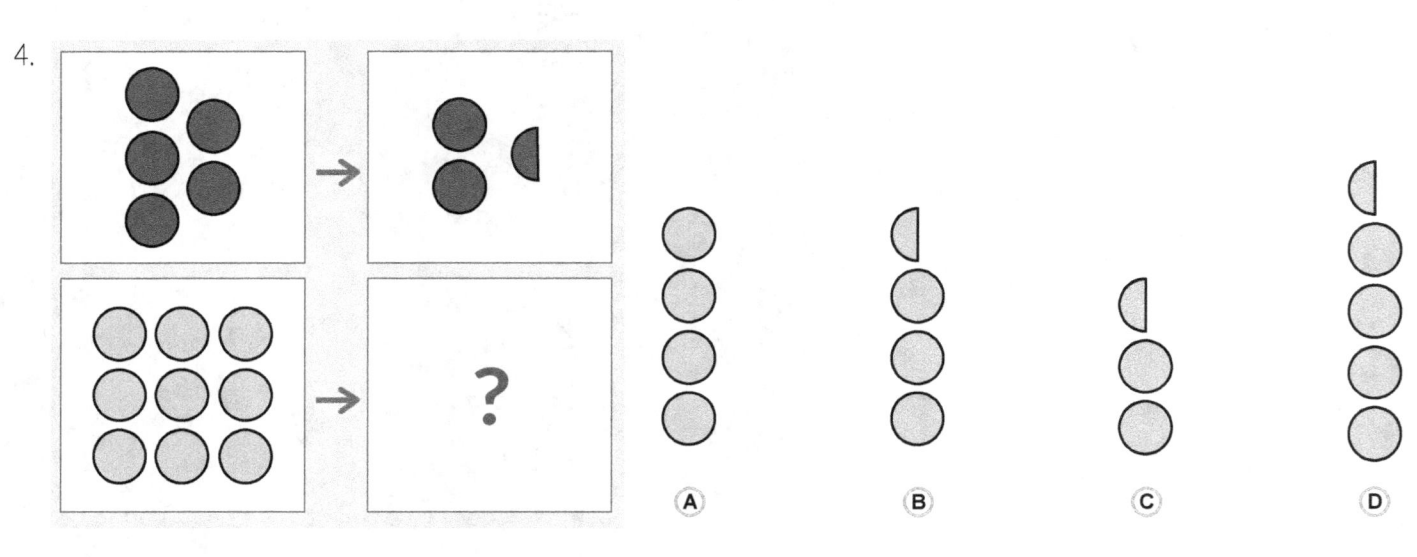

5.

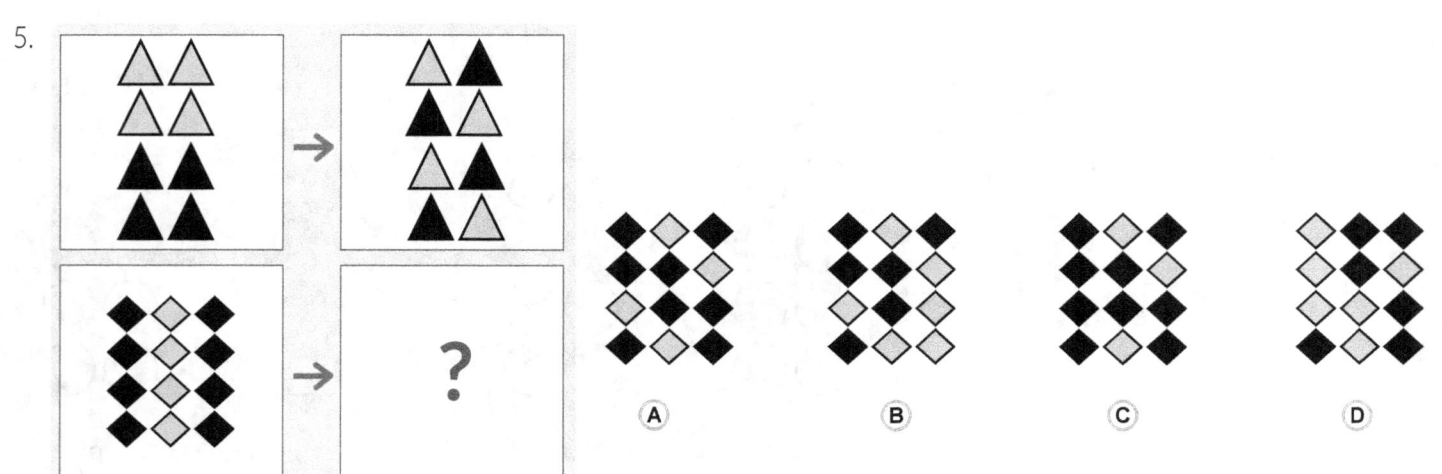

122

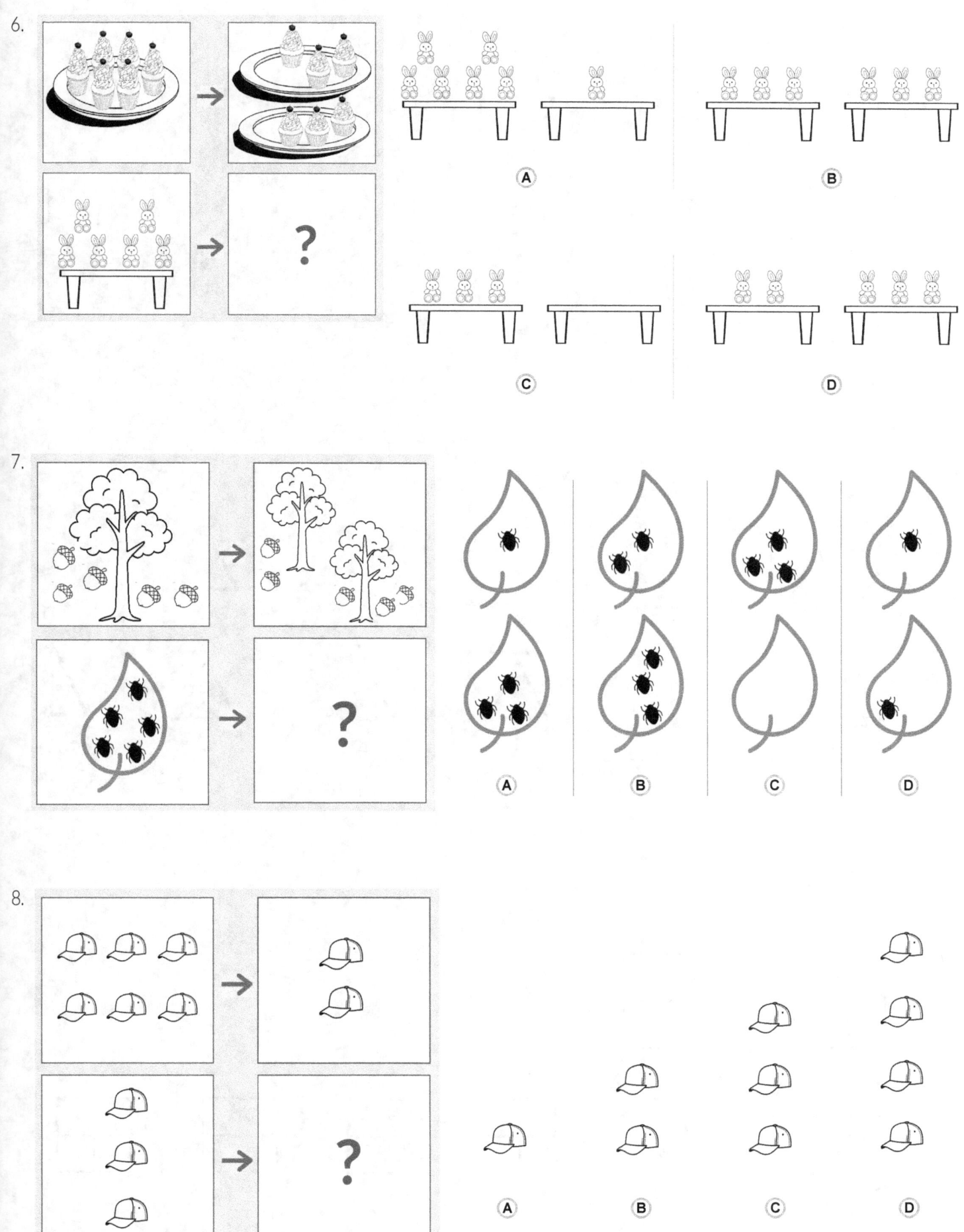

6.

7.

8.

9.

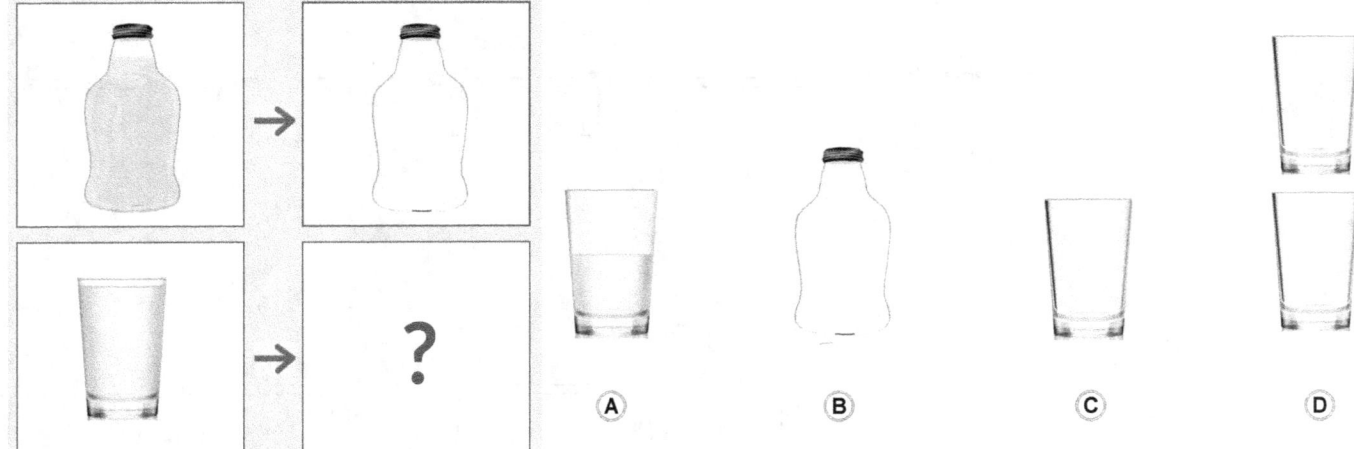

10.

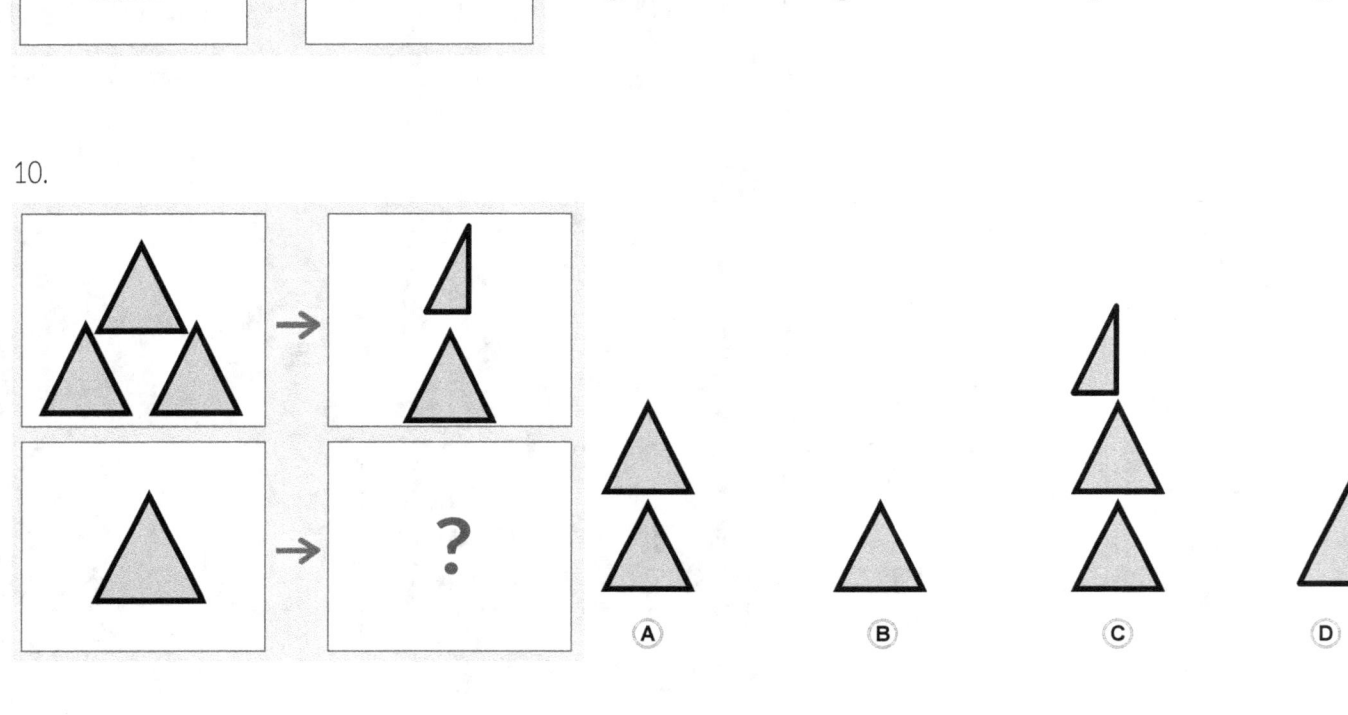

11.

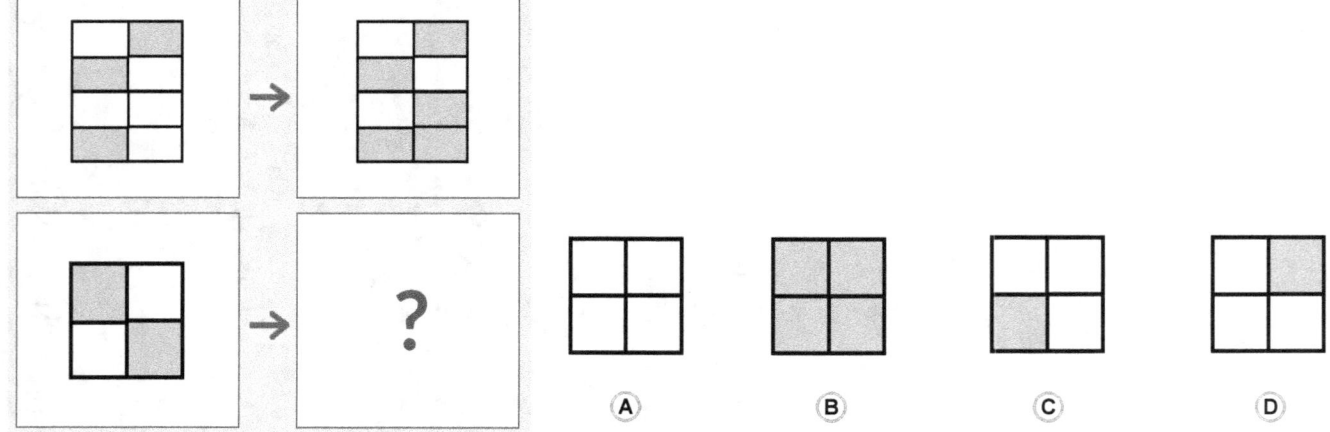

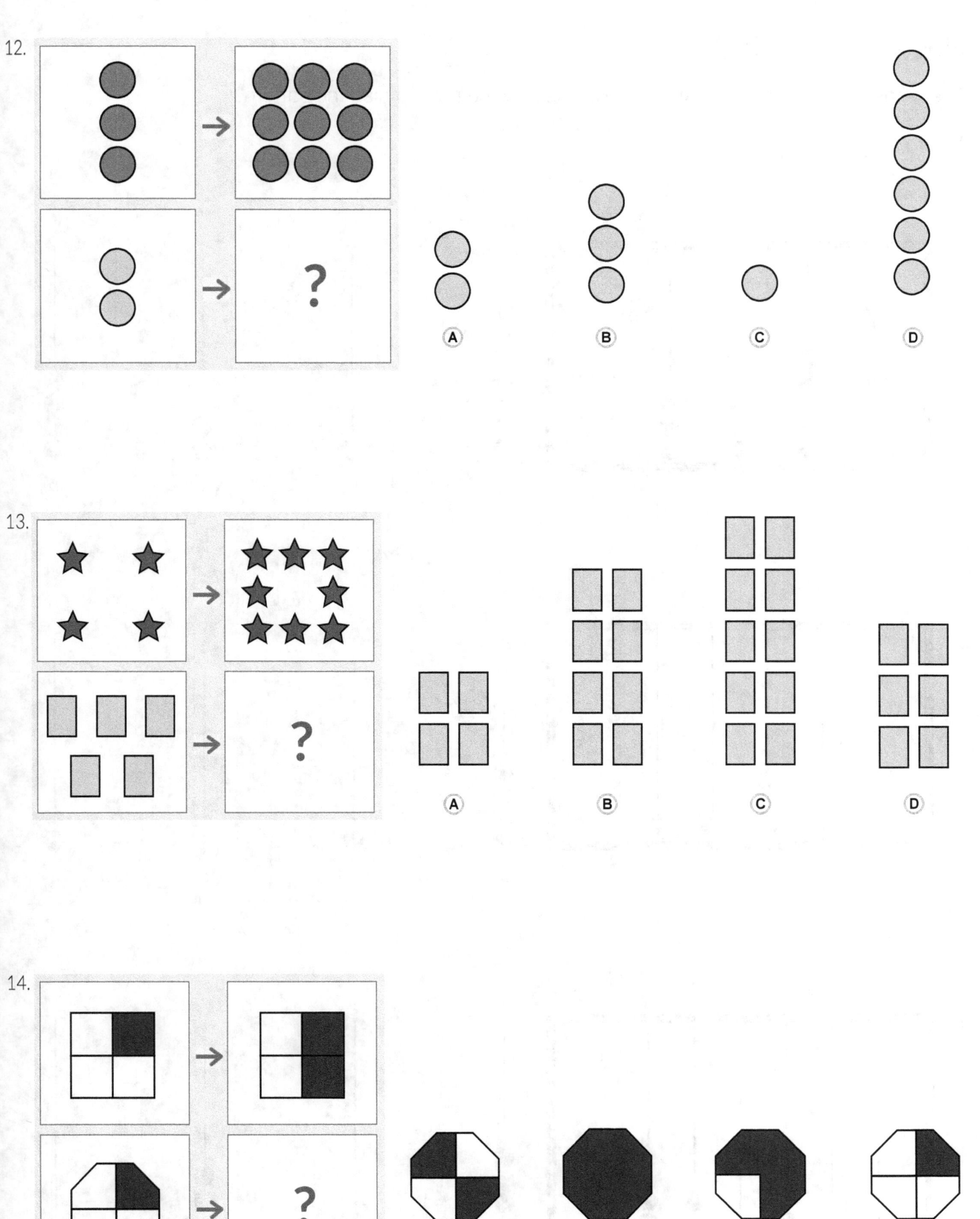

NUMBER SERIES

Directions: Which rod goes in the place of the missing rod to finish the pattern?

1.

    (A)   (B)   (C)   (D)

2.

    (A)   (B)   (C)   (D)

3.

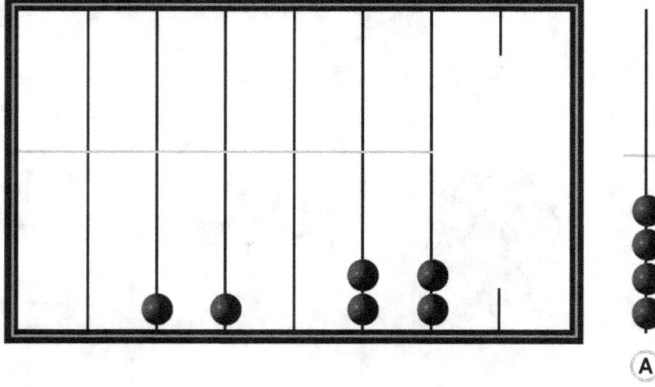

    (A)   (B)   (C)   (D)

4.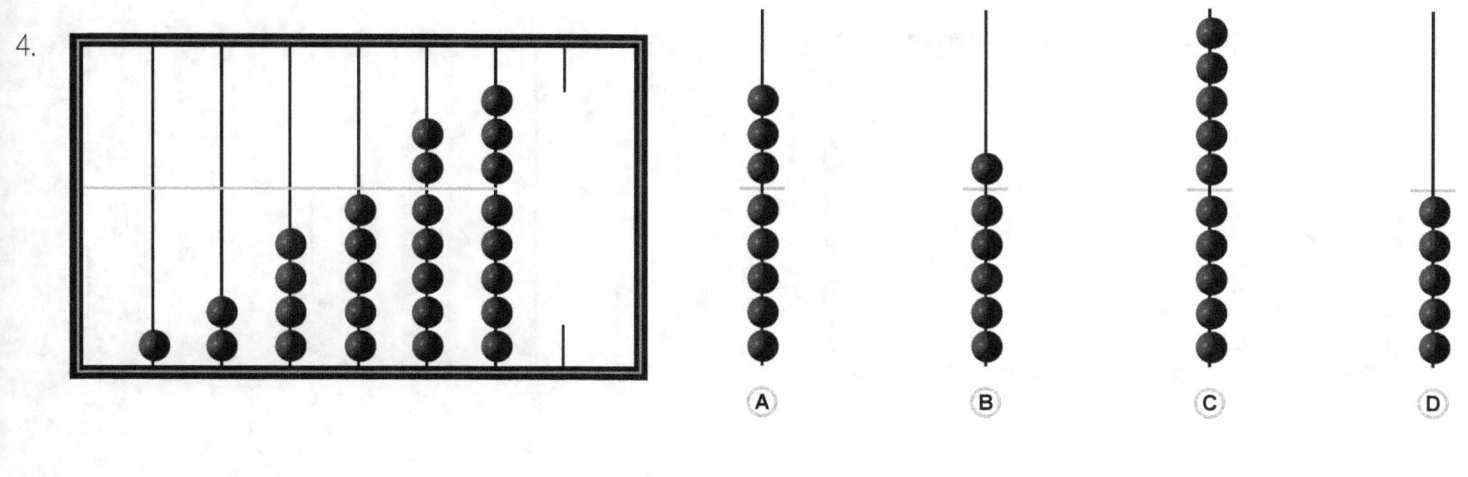

5.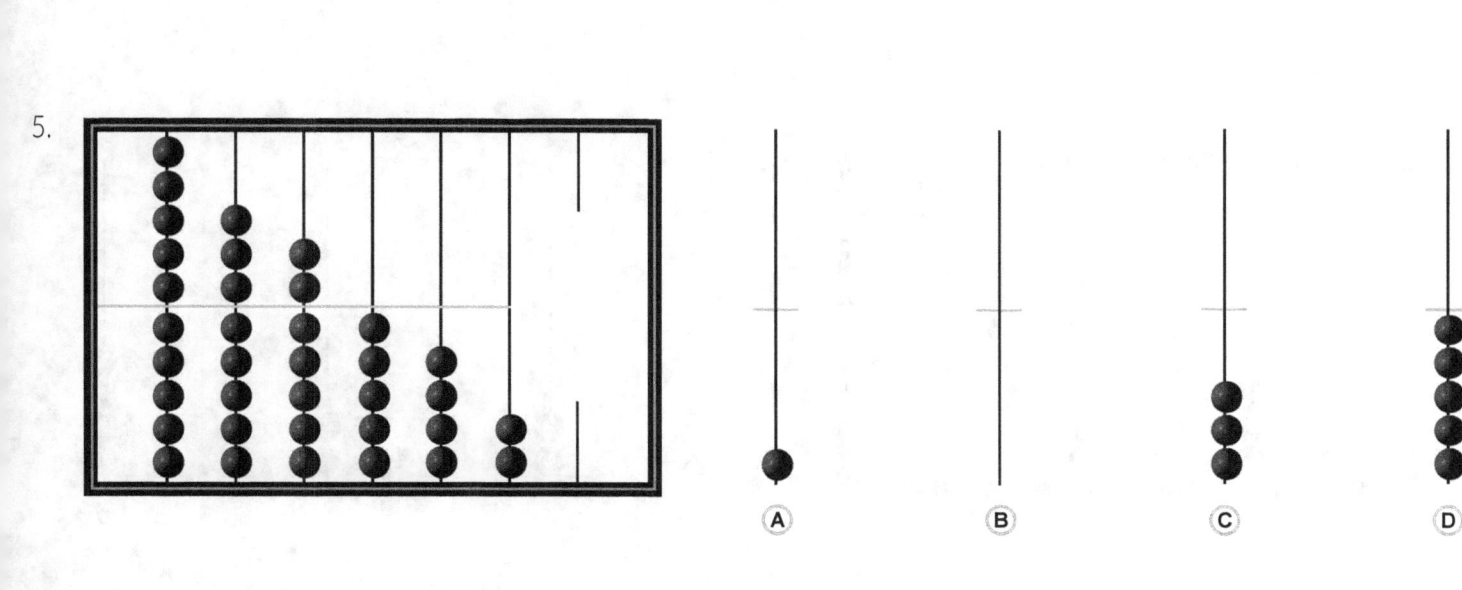

6.

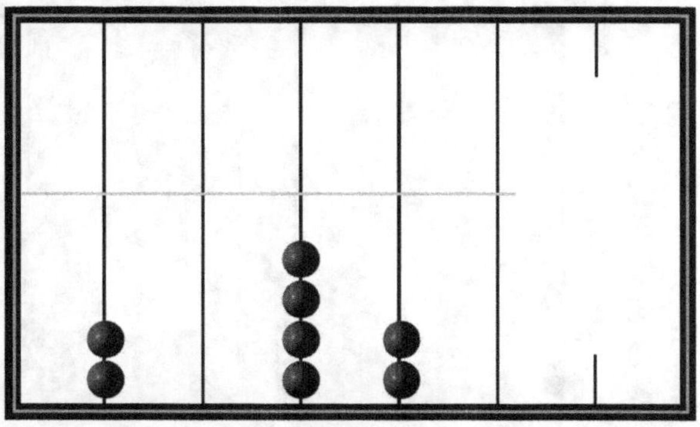

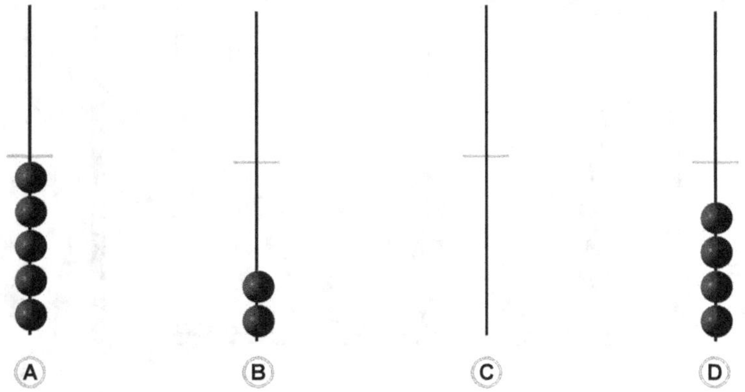

127

7.

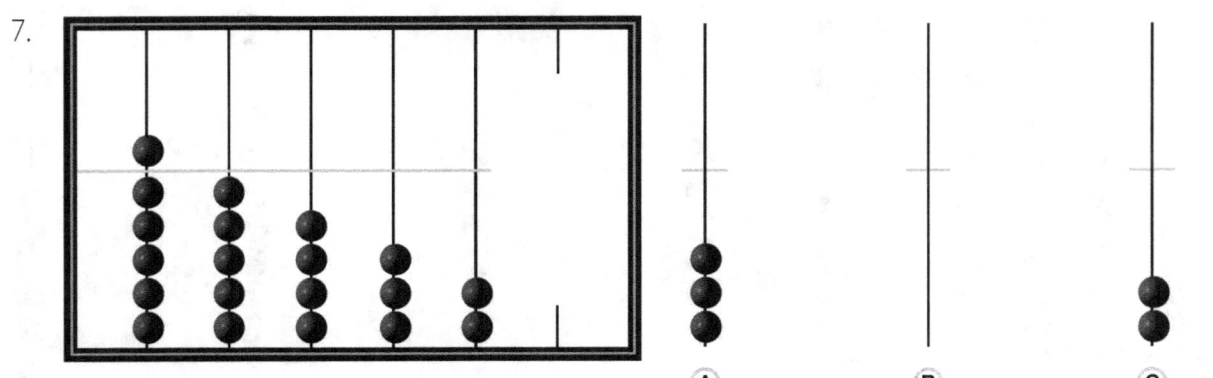

      Ⓐ   Ⓑ   Ⓒ   Ⓓ

8.

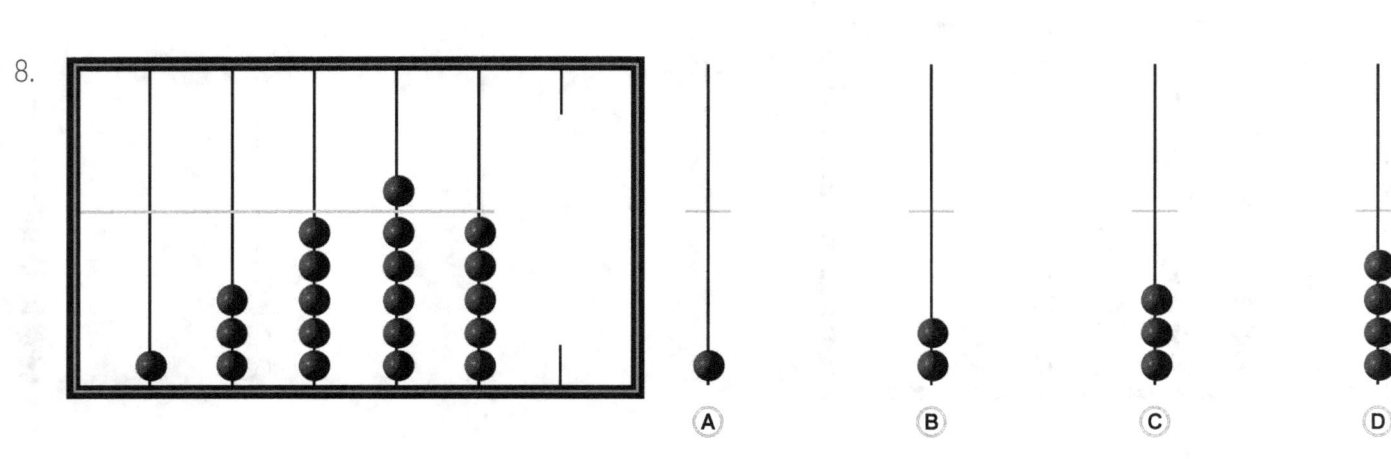

9.

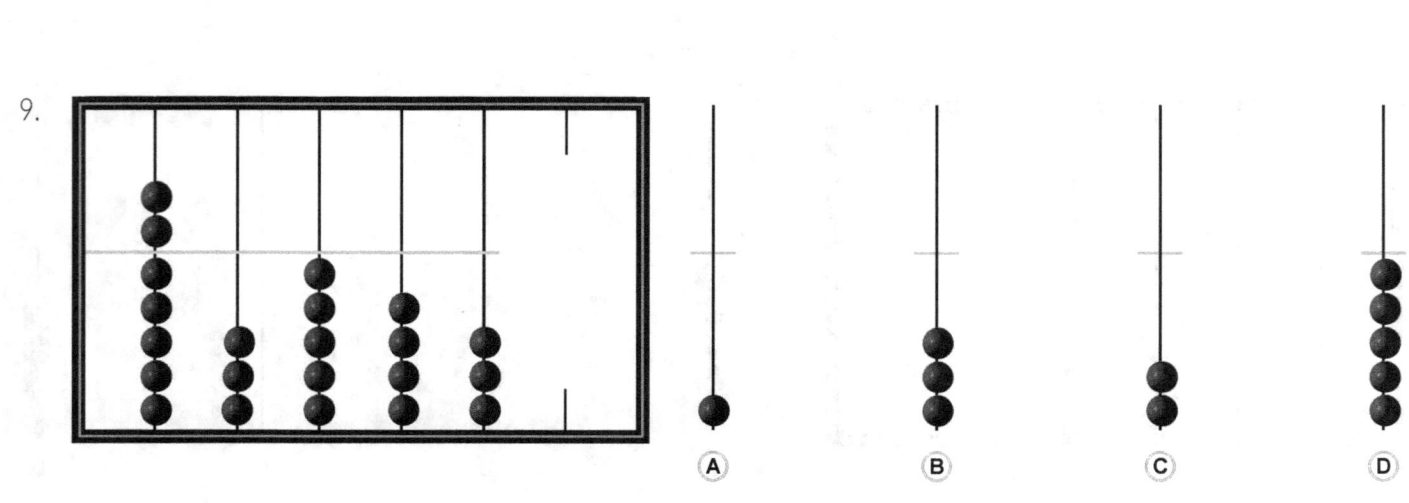

128

10.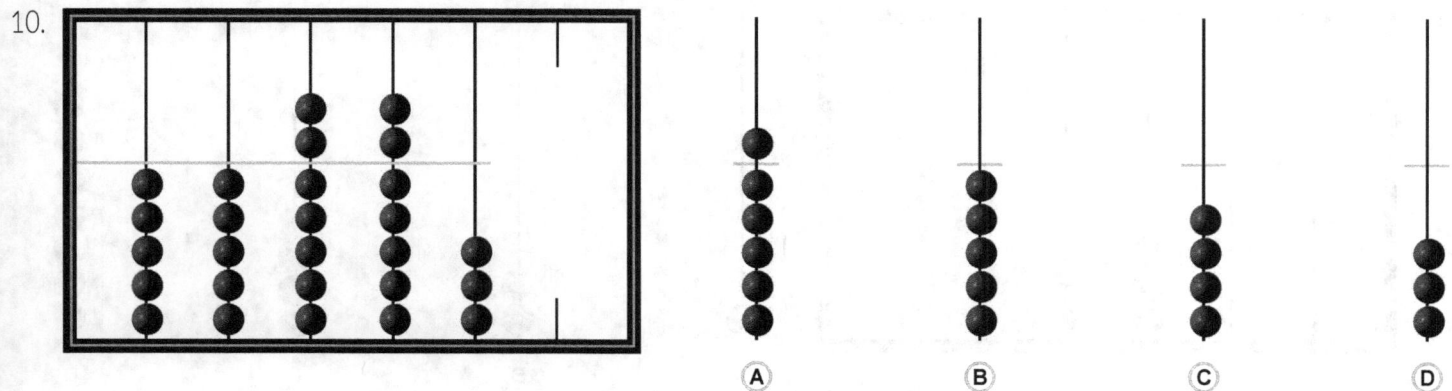

11.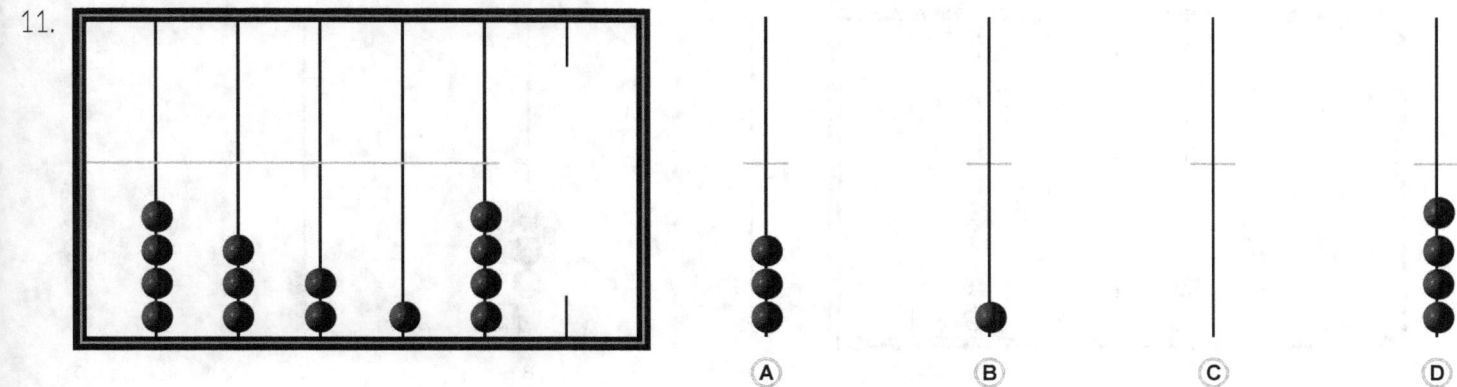

12.

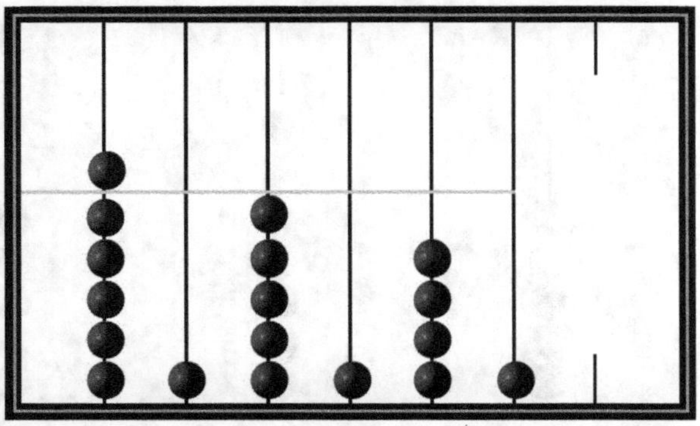

13.

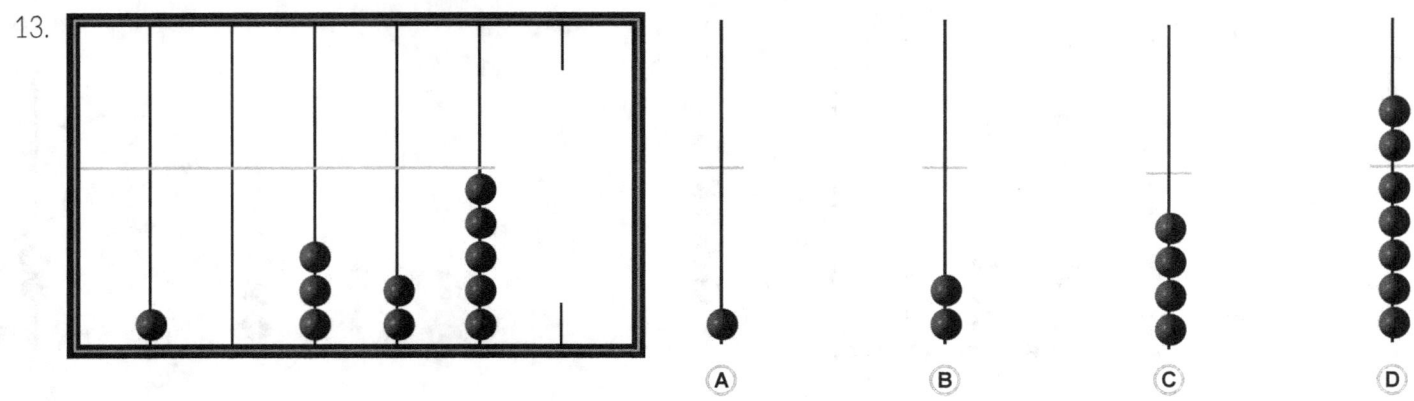

14.

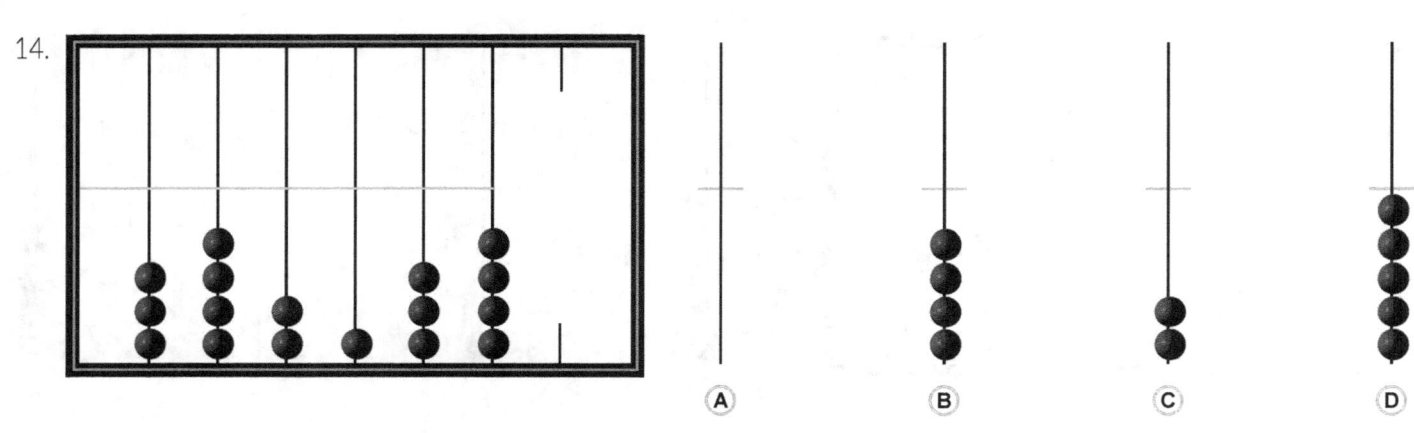

15.

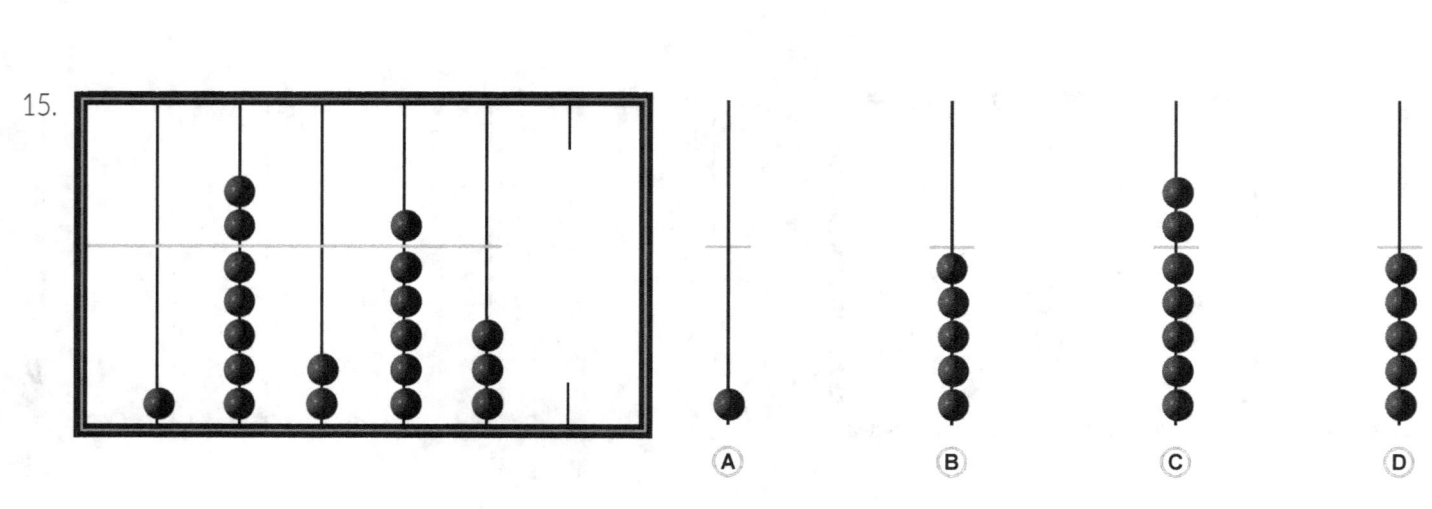

130

16.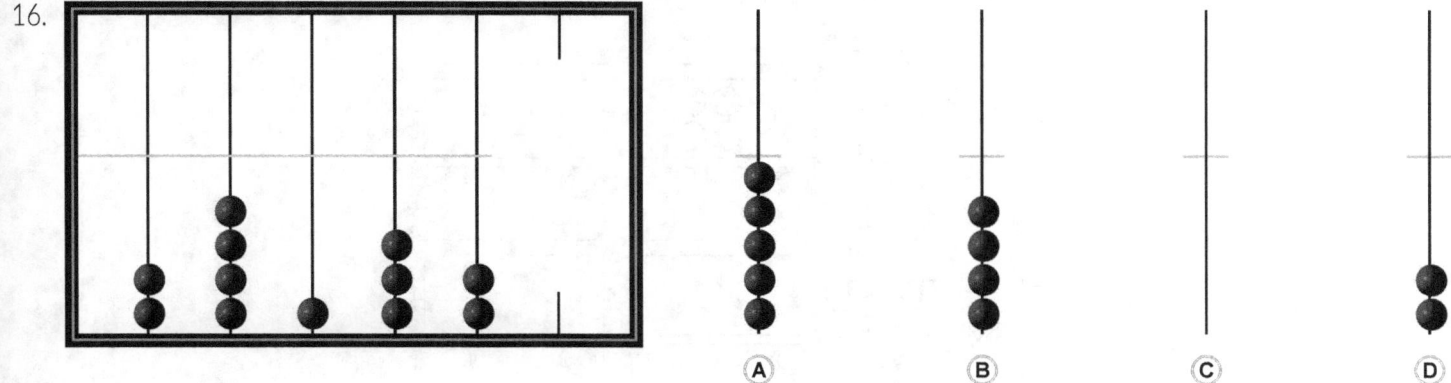

17.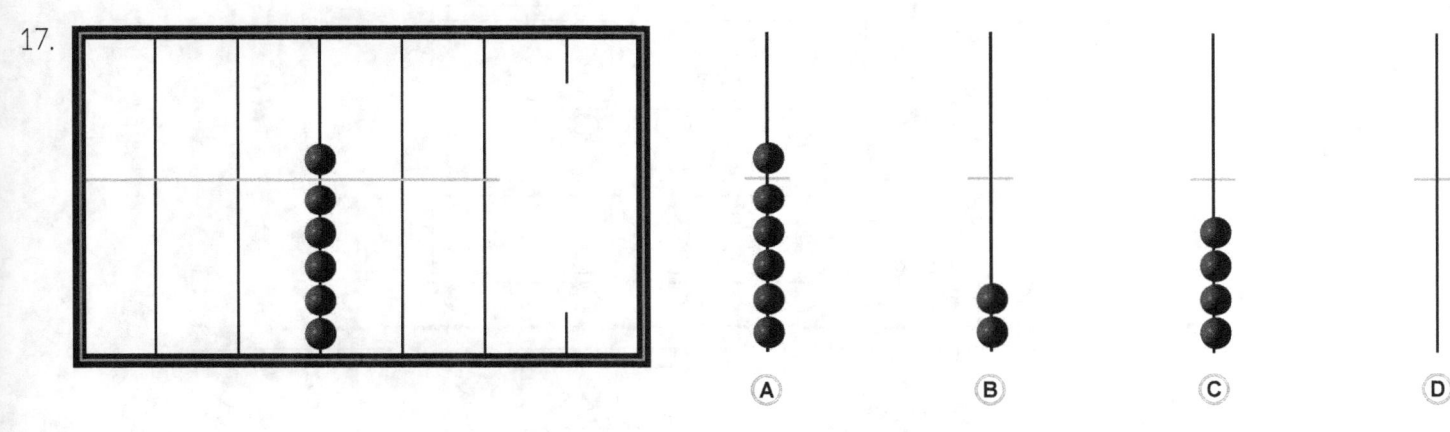

18.

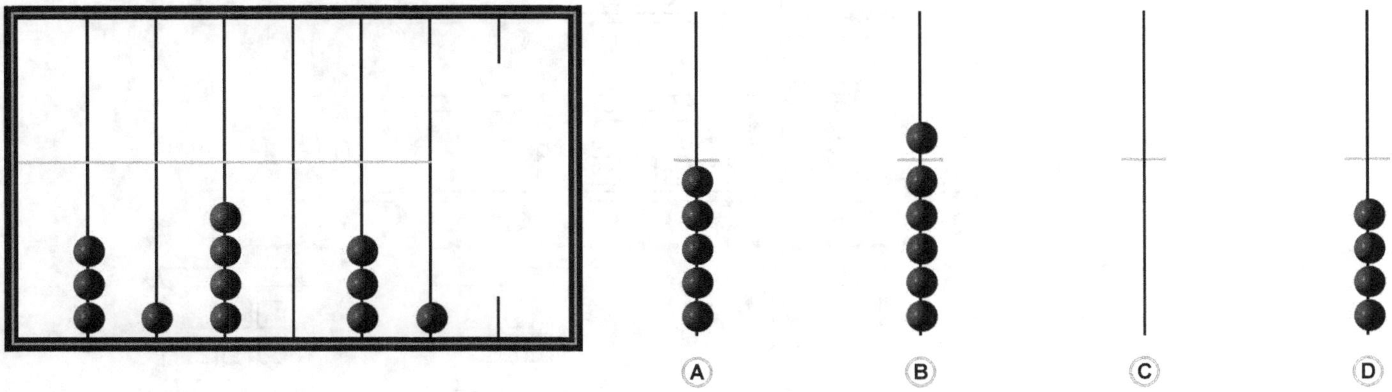

NUMBER PUZZLES   Which train car would make the top and bottom trains carry the same amount?

1

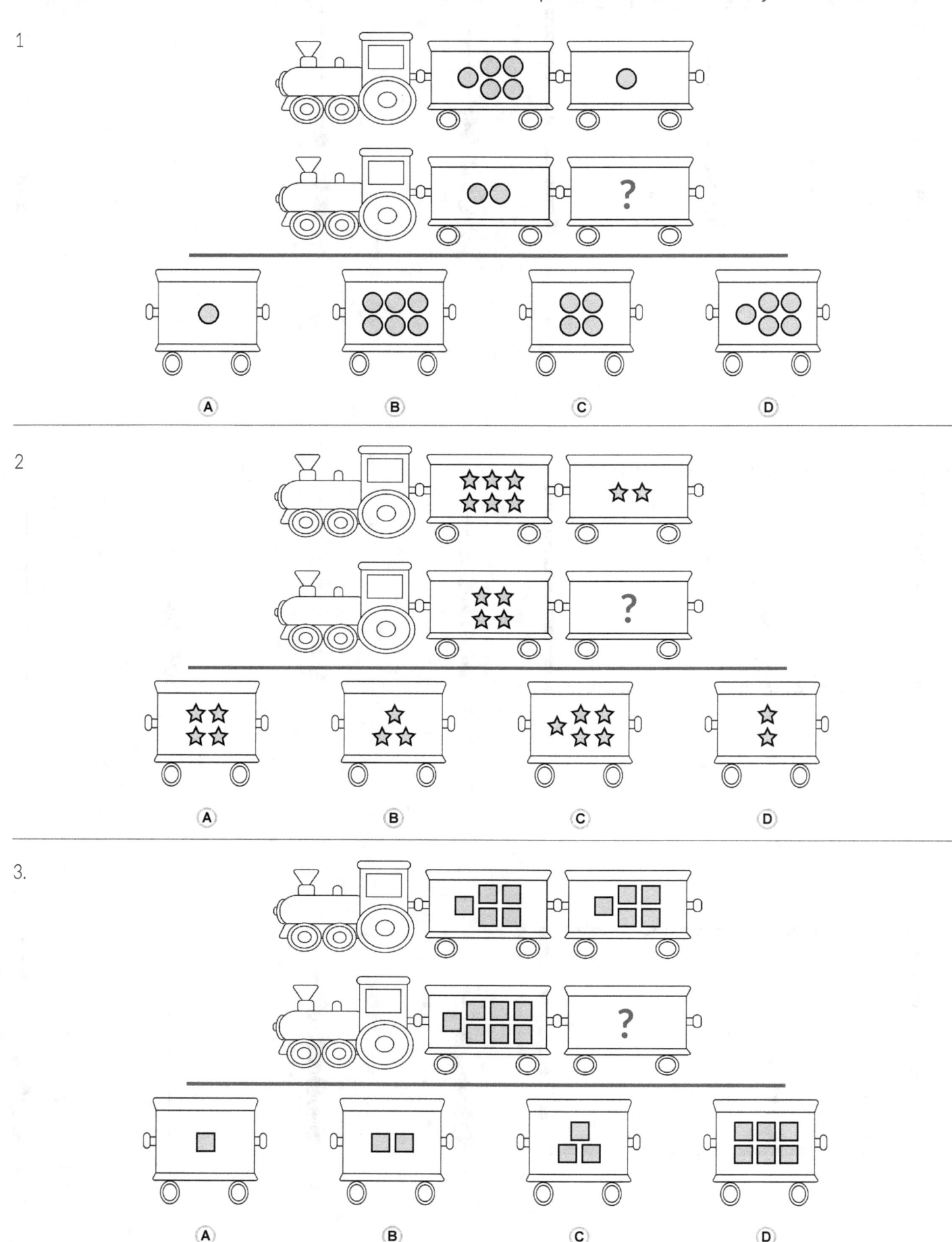

2

3.

4.

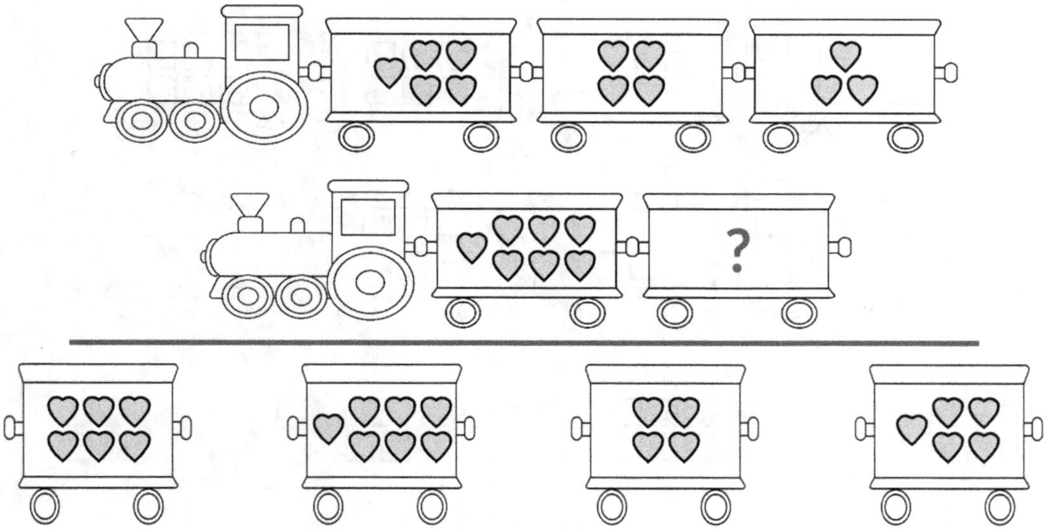

A	B	C	D

5.

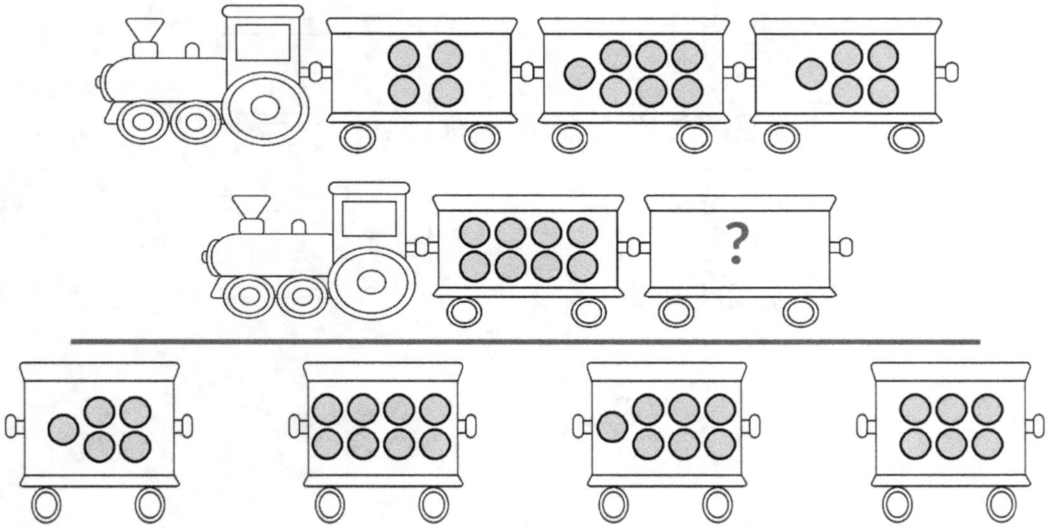

A	B	C	D

6.

A	B	C	D

7.

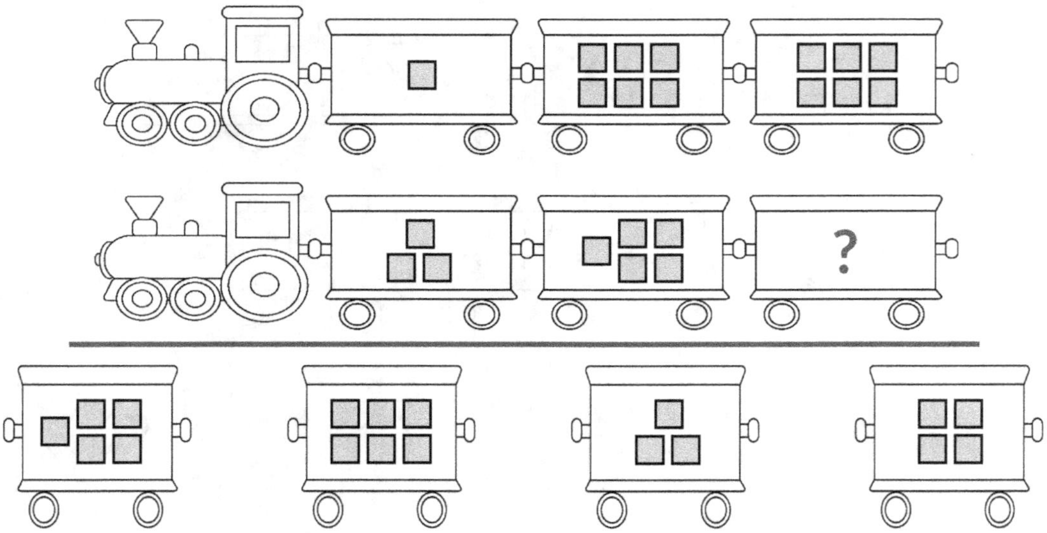

A   B   C   D

8.

A   B   C   D

9.

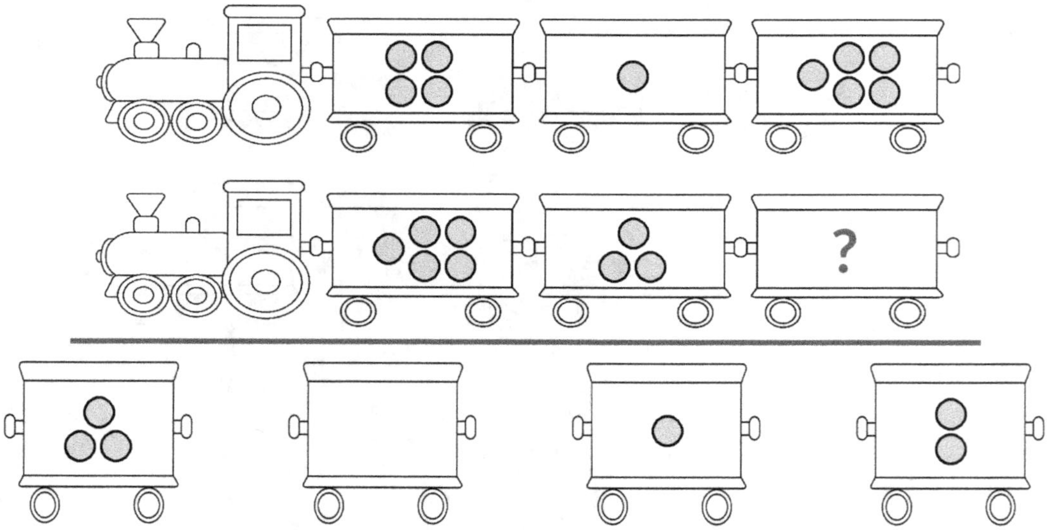

A   B   C   D

10.

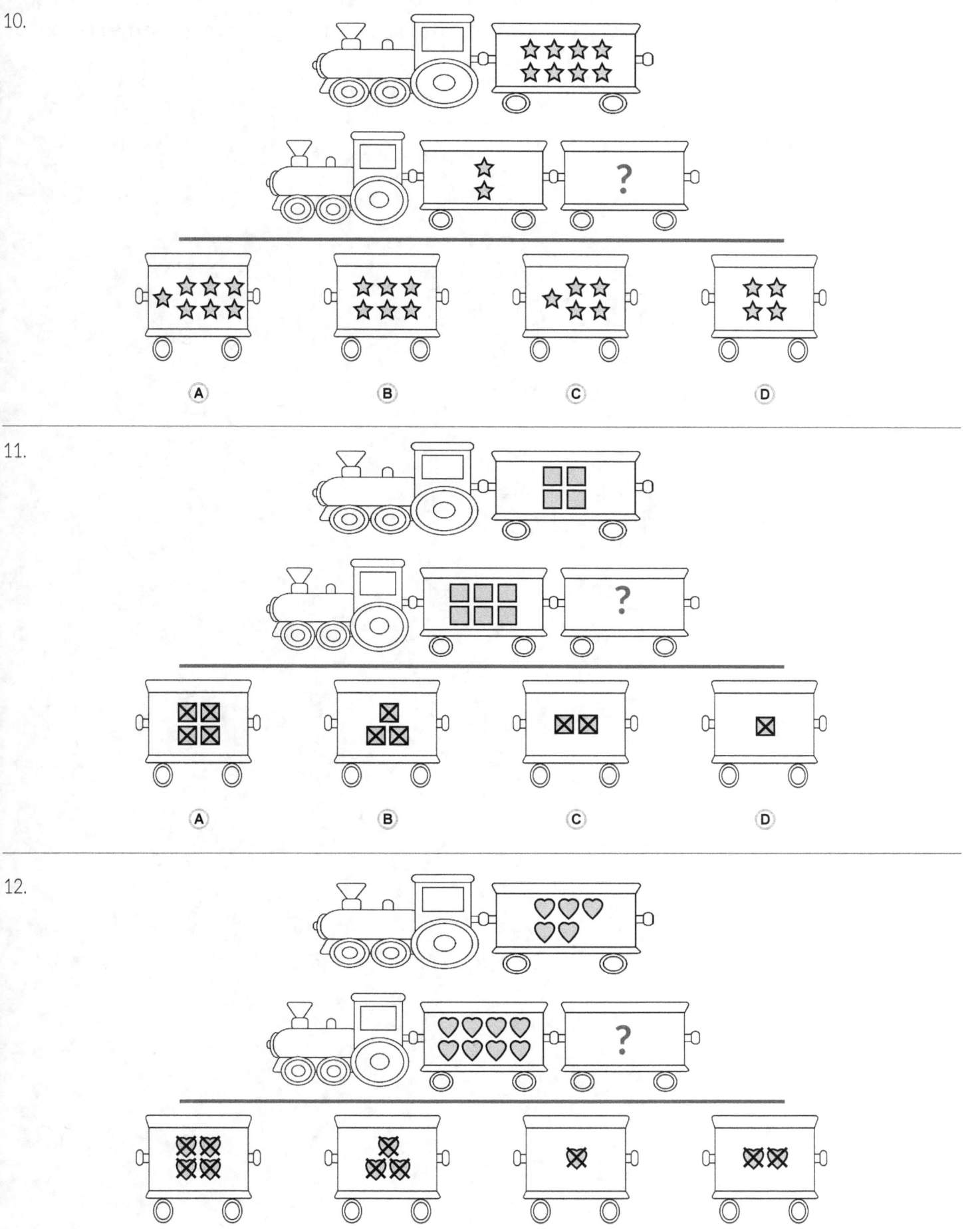

A   B   C   D

11.

A   B   C   D

12.

A   B   C   D

NUMBER PUZZLES

Which number would go in place of the box with the question mark so that both of the sides of the equal sign have the same amount?

1.

$3 = 18 - 10 - ?$

| 5 | 9 | 6 | 7 |
| A | B | C | D |

2.

$2 = 14 - 9 - ?$

| 0 | 1 | 3 | 5 |
| A | B | C | D |

3.

$8 = 19 - 4 - ?$

| 1 | 8 | 7 | 4 |
| A | B | C | D |

4.

$5 = 10 - 2 - ?$

| 5 | 8 | 1 | 3 |
| A | B | C | D |

5.

$2 = 17 - 9 - ?$

| 9 | 6 | 0 | 8 |
| A | B | C | D |

6.

$13 = 4 + 3 + ?$

| 7 | 5 | 6 | 12 |
| A | B | C | D |

7.

$9 = 15 + 4 - \boxed{?}$

10	8	9	11
Ⓐ	Ⓑ	Ⓒ	Ⓓ

8.

$8 = 19 - 4 - \boxed{?}$

1	9	12	7
Ⓐ	Ⓑ	Ⓒ	Ⓓ

9.

$10 = 18 - 7 - \boxed{?}$

1	3	11	0
Ⓐ	Ⓑ	Ⓒ	Ⓓ

10.

$4 = 15 - 4 - \boxed{?}$

8	7	2	11
Ⓐ	Ⓑ	Ⓒ	Ⓓ

11.

$12 = 1 + 4 + \boxed{?}$

6	7	8	9
Ⓐ	Ⓑ	Ⓒ	Ⓓ

12.

$2 = 17 - 8 - \boxed{?}$

8	9	7	11
Ⓐ	Ⓑ	Ⓒ	Ⓓ

13.

$8 = 12 - 10 + \boxed{?}$

7   2   9   6
(A)   (B)   (C)   (D)

14.

$3 = 18 - 4 - \boxed{?}$

14   2   11   4
(A)   (B)   (C)   (D)

15.

$7 = 14 - 11 + \boxed{?}$

4   2   5   6
(A)   (B)   (C)   (D)

16.

$3 = 19 - 8 - \boxed{?}$

0   2   6   8
(A)   (B)   (C)   (D)

CHALLENGE QUESTIONS

1.

$4 = 1 \times \boxed{?}$

0   1   4   3
(A)   (B)   (C)   (D)

2.

$5 = 1 \times \boxed{?}$

5   1   2   4
(A)   (B)   (C)   (D)

3.

| 6 | = | 2 | × | ? |

| 0 | 1 | 2 | 3 |
| A | B | C | D |

4.

| 8 | = | 2 | × | ? |

| 1 | 4 | 2 | 3 |
| A | B | C | D |

5.

| 0 | = | 4 | × | ? |

| 4 | 1 | 2 | 0 |
| A | B | C | D |

6.

| 10 | = | 2 | × | ? |

| 5 | 4 | 8 | 3 |
| A | B | C | D |

The Answer Keys begin on the next page.

ANSWER KEY FOR PRACTICE TEST 1 (WORKBOOK FORMAT)

Picture Analogies, Practice Test 1

1. C. The home of a fish is a fishbowl (man-made). The home of a bird is a bird cage (man-made).
2. C. A train travels on train tracks. A canoe travels on water.
3. D. The first picture is the animal/person. The second picture is their leg.
4. B. On top are objects found at the beach. On bottom are objects found at a playground.
5. B. You listen to music with your ears. You smell a flower with your nose.
6. D. You wear glasses for your eyes. You wear ear muffs for your ears.
7. A. A bat and an eagle fly in the air. A seahorse and a shark swim in the ocean.
8. B. A dog house is made by a person as a dog's home. A bird house is made by a person as a bird's home.
9. D. The first object is the open version of the second object (which is closed).
10. C. Up is the opposite of down. Happy is the opposite of sad.
11. B. There are 4 leaves on a 4-leaf clover. There are 2 eyes on a face.
12. A. A yacht and a canoe are used by people to travel on water. An airplane and a hot air balloon are used by people to travel in the air.
13. C. The objects on top are both open. The objects on bottom are both closed.
14. A. The first picture is the number of wheels that the object in the second picture has.
15. D. A globe and a tennis ball are both spherical. A log and a soda can are both cylindrical.
16. A. The number of circles shown on the dice equals the number of shape sides. A triangle has 3 sides. A square has 4 sides.

Picture Classification, Practice Test 1

1. C. tools
2. D. objects used for carrying things
3. A. homes
4. B. used for sports
5. A. things having to do with medical care or seen in a doctor's office
6. C. round objects
7. D. farm animals
8. C. things that are hot
9. C. pairs
10. D. things used to climb up or down

Picture Classification, Practice Test 1, continued

11. B. objects used to help you see better
12. A. cold things/cold places
13. A. used for telling time
14. B. things that have to do with 4 (4-leaf clover, quadruplets, and a shape with 4 sides)
15. A. used for holding liquid
16. C. things providing light

Sentence Completion, Practice Test 1

1. B. A duck can fly.
2. D. A carrot is a vegetable. Watermelon is a fruit.
3. A. A seahorse lives in the water.
4. C. A watering can is used to water a garden.
5. C. Scissors are used for cutting, not holding paper together.
6. A. A violin and piano are musical instruments.
7. C. Socks and mittens are things that come in pairs.
8. A. This choice shows wheat, which is used to make bread.
9. D.
10. A. A pizza would be the easiest to share. The other choices can't be easily shared.
11. B. A tree.
12. C. The other choices – a beehive and milk – are related to either bees or cows. A stove is not.
13. D. Wool comes from a sheep.
14. D. A farmer would use his/her eyes to see what they are picking. They would use their hands/arms to pick the corn. Choice D shows a nose, which would not be used.
15. B. Choices A and C are used to make objects that are close by (not far away) appear larger. A beaker is not used for seeing objects. Binoculars (choice B) are used for seeing objects that are far away.
16. A.

Figure Analogies, Practice Test 1

1. B. The top half changes from solid gray to filled with diagonal lines.
2. C. The diagonal lines inside the shape switch directions.
3. A. The shape gets bigger and turns gray.
4. A. The shape rotates 90 degrees clockwise.

Figure Analogies, Practice Test 1, continued

5. D. The shapes reverse their order. Or, the shapes "flip" to become a mirror image.
6. C. The shapes reverse their order and switch colors.
7. A. The shape groups switch colors.
8. D. The arrow "flips" to become a mirror image. It also changes color from white to gray.
9. D. Stars change to triangles. Triangles change to stars.
10. C. Gray becomes white. White becomes gray.
11. D. The shapes reverse their order.
12. C. The shape group "flips" to become a mirror image. Or, the shape group rotates 90 degrees clockwise.
13. A. The larger and smaller shapes switch their position and size.
14. C. The colors of the shapes switch from black to white & white to black.
15. B. The top and bottom arrows rotate 180 degrees.
16. C. The shapes switch their position and their color.

Figure Classification, Practice Test 1

1. D. The shapes are the same with a diagonal line going the same way.
2. B. The shapes are trapezoids.
3. B. The shapes have horizontal lines inside.
4. B. The shapes are: gray-white-gray.
5. A. The shapes are gray and white (in that order).
6. C. The shapes are: dotted-white-dotted.
7. D. One-fourth of the shape is gray and the rest is white.
8. D. A 4-sided shape in cut in half.
9. C. The same 2 smaller shapes are across from each other inside the square.
10. A. The large middle shape has a smaller version on top and on bottom.
11. B. Half of the rectangle is gray. Half is black.
12. B. There are 4 shapes (and only 4 shapes) in the group.
13. C. The shape has 4 sides.
14. B. There is 1 circle in the middle of the square.
15. B. The shape group has: 1 square, 1 small circle, and 1 small triangle.
16. D. As the shape group rotates, the gray line and star remain at the same spot (at the triangle's point).
17. A. The shape has 8 sides.

Paper Folding, Practice Test 1

1. B	2. A	3. D	4. B	5. C	6. D
7. A	8. B	9. D	10. C	11. D	12. A
13. A	14. C	15. B			

Number Analogies, Practice Test 1

1. C. Subtract 3.
2. C. Add 2.
3. D. Subtract 6.
4. A. Same.
5. B. Double.
6. A. Subtract 4.
7. D. Add 5.
8. C. Add 3.
9. A. Subtract 5.
10. A. Same.
11. B. Half.
12. C. Half.
13. D. Half.
14. C. Same (a shape divided in half).
15. D. Double.
16. B. There are 4 apples/cupcakes in the first box. There are the same number of apples/cupcakes in the second box, but they are split 2 and 2.
17. C. There are 4 seahorses/fish in the first box. There are the same number of seahorses/fish in the second box, but they are split 2 and 2.

Number Series, Practice Test 1

1. A. There are two of each number: 5 – 5 – 7 – 7 – 3 – 3.
2. B. Every other rod has zero: 6 - 0 - 4 - 0 - 2 - 0.
3. C. Each rod decreases by one: 6 – 5 – 4 – 3 – 2 - 1.
4. D. The pattern repeats: 2 – 2 – 5 – 2 – 2 – 5.
5. D. The pattern decreases then reverses: 6 – 4 - 2 – 0 – 2 – 4.
6. B. The pattern repeats: 5 – 2 – 3 – 5 – 2 – 3.

Number Series, Practice Test 1, continued

7. C. The pattern repeats: 5 – 0 – 4 – 5 – 0 – 4.

8. B. The pattern repeats: 2 – 0 – 1 – 2 – 0 – 1.

9. D. The number repeats three times: 1 – 1 – 1 – 4 – 4 – 4.

10. C. Each number repeats twice: 5 –5 – 4 – 4 – 3 – 3 – 2 – 2.

11. B. Each number increases by two: 0 – 2 – 4 – 6 – 8 – 10.

12. C. Every other number increases by 1: **1** – 4 – **2** – 5 – **3** – 6 – **4**.

13. A. Every other number increases by 1: **0** – 5 – **1** – 6 – **2** – 7.

14. D. The pattern repeats: 2 – 3 – 5 – 2 – 3 – 5.

15. D. The pattern repeats: 0 – 1 – 4 – 0 – 1 – 4.

16. B. Each number is repeated: 1 – 1 – 4 – 4 – 3 – 3.

Number Puzzles - Trains, Practice Test 1

	Train 1:	Train 2:
1. C.	5 + 2 = 7	3 + 4 = 7
2. B.	6 + 3 = 9	2 + 7 = 9
3. B.	6 + 2 = 8	8
4. D.	7	4 + 2 + 1 = 7
5. C.	3 + 1 + 4 = 8	5 + 3 = 8
6. D.	4 + 4 = 8	0 + 8 = 8
7. A.	5 + 0 = 5	1 + 4 = 5
8. A.	1 + 7 = 8	4 + 4 = 8
9. B.	3	5 – 2 = 3
10. D.	2	4 + 1 – 3 = 2
11. C.	6	4 + 3 – 1 = 6
12. A.	4	5 – 1 – 0 = 4
13. C.	2	7 – 3 – 2 = 2

Number Puzzles - Equations, Practice Test 1

1. C.	2. D.	3. C.	4. A.	5. C.
6. D.	7. A.	8. C.	9. B.	10. C.
11. D.	12. D.	13. D.	14. B.	15. C.

ANSWER KEY FOR PRACTICE TEST 2

Picture Analogies, Practice Test 2

1. B. On a bike, you use handlebars to steer. With a truck, you use a steering wheel.

2. A. You use a spoon to eat ice cream. You use a fork to eat the food shown in the bowl (salad).

3. C. A pie is similar to a cake. (They are both desserts.) A pear is similar to an apple. (They are both fruit that grows on a tree. They do not need to be cut open to eat. A watermelon is not correct because it must be cut open to eat.)

4. A. A monkey likes to eat bananas. A squirrel likes to eat acorns.

5. D. The first box shows the toy vehicle version of the vehicle in the second box (a train and a dump truck).

6. A. A telescope and binoculars are used to see objects that are far away. Also, a telescope is more powerful than binoculars. A microscope and a magnifying glass are used to see objects that are close by and used to make them appear larger. Also, a microscope is more powerful than a magnifying glass.

7. C. The objects in the first box are single versions of the objects in the second box. In the second box, they are shown together as a group.

8. D. The objects in the first box are the whole/entire version of the objects in the second box, which only show half.

9. B. The object in the first box is a pretend version of the object the second box (a toy tiger & a real tiger on top; a scarecrow & a real man on the bottom).

10. D. The object in the first box is an old-fashioned version of the object in the second box.

11. A. The foods in the top row are grown on vines (tomatoes and grapes). The foods on the bottom are grown in the ground (carrots and radishes).

12. A. On a woman's head, a crown is worn. On a woman's neck, a necklace is worn.

13. B. Six is the number of legs this bug has. Eight is the number of legs a spider has.

14. D. "N" is the letter that "nose" begins with. "F" is the letter that "foot" begins with.

15. B. A pan is found in a kitchen. A fish is found in a pond.

16. C. A kayak holds one passenger and travels on water, while a yacht holds many passengers. A unicycle holds one passenger and travels on land, while a bus holds many passengers.

17. D. A pine cone is on a pine tree. A feather is on a bird.

18. B. The first box shows the back view of the object. The second box shows the front view of the object.

Picture Classification, Practice Test 2

1. B. vegetables
2. A. tools used for cutting
3. B. objects worn on heads
4. A. objects that have nets
5. D. objects used for measurement
6. C. baked goods
7. C. reptiles
8. B. animal homes
9. D. mammals
10. A. words beginning with the letter "R" (ruler, raccoon, rooster, remote)
11. A. living things
12. D. different kinds of feet
13. A. things that have holes
14. B. objects used to hold things together
15. B. objects used for carrying things
16. C. objects made of metal

Sentence Completion, Practice Test 2

1. C. A microscope.
2. D. A shovel.
3. A. Snow.
4. C. An umbrella. (Rain is a type of precipitation.)
5. C. An octopus has 8 legs.
6. D. Dinosaurs are extinct (no longer living on Earth at all).
7. A. Bears hibernate (go into a long, deep sleep during the winter).
8. B. A calculator.
9. A. Carpenters use nails to build things.
10. B. A skateboard.
11. B. A frog and butterfly go through metamorphosis. (Metamorphosis is when something, like a caterpillar, changes into something completely different, like a butterfly.)
12. D. You must peel a banana, but not a pretzel. Also, A & B show drinks in their groups.
13. C. A horse and cow are mammals. A snake is a reptile.
14. B. A candle would still work without electricity. The others need electricity to work the right way because they need to be plugged in.
15. D. A train would travel the fastest between cities.
16. B. The other choices are used for measurement. A fork is used for eating.

Figure Analogies, Practice Test 2

1. B. The shapes switch their position and their color.
2. D. The shape group rotates 90 degrees clockwise and becomes white.
3. D. The larger and smaller shapes switch their position and size.
4. C. The larger and smaller 2 shapes switch their color/design. Also, the 2 smaller shapes change from aligning vertically to aligning horizontally.
5. C. The top and middle shapes switch position.
6. A. The top left and bottom right figures switch position.
7. D. From the left box to the right box, the top box gains a diamond. The bottom box loses a diamond.
8. D. The group of circles rotates 90 degrees clockwise and switches color from gray to white & white to gray.
9. C. Inside the shape group are 3 triangles. The colors of the triangles switch from white to black & from black to white.
10. D. The middle shape rotates 180 degrees.
11. D. The shapes reverse their order.
12. D. The order of the shapes change like this: the 1st and 2nd shapes change their order & the 3rd and 4th shapes change their order.
13. C. The circles change color from gray to black & black to gray. The smaller shape changes its position from being in the lower left to the upper right. It also changes from a crescent to a "pac-man" shape. It also changes its color from black to gray & gray to black.
14. C. The bottom shape becomes the top shape and gets smaller. The middle shape becomes the bottom shape and gets bigger. The top shape becomes the middle shape and gets bigger.
15. A. The shape group rotates 90 degrees clockwise
16. B. The shape group rotates 90 degrees clockwise. Or, you could say that the circles change designs like this: white becomes black, dots become white, black becomes gray, and gray becomes dots.
17. D. A shape with one less side appears in the second box. On top, a 6-sided shape becomes a 5-sided shape. On the bottom, a 4-sided shape becomes a 3-sided shape.

Figure Classification, Practice Test 2

1. D. The shape has diagonal lines going from lower left to upper right.
2. D. The shape group has 3 shapes pointing up and 1 shape pointing down.
3. C. The shapes have 4 sides.
4. A. The arrows either point up or down & have 1 point.
5. A. The shapes are divided equally in half.
6. C. Each shape group has 2 rectangles and 2 ovals. One of each is gray and white.

Figure Classification, Practice Test 2, continued

7. B. Half of the diamond is black. Half of the diamond is white.

8. A. Each shape group has a triangle in the middle.

9. C. There are 3 black diamonds in the shape group. Two are next to each other. The third one is in the next row (but not next to another black diamond).

10. D. The shape in the middle is surrounded by two shapes. These two shapes are exactly the same.

11. D. Each shape group has 1 pentagon, 1 heart, and 1 rectangle.

12. A. Each figure has 2 arrow points (and only 2 arrow points).

13. C. Each shape group has 2 shapes (squares or hearts) next to each other that are the same. Next to these shapes is another different shape.

14. D. The shape group rotates 90 degrees clockwise each time.

15. D. Half of the shape is white. Half of the shape is black.

16. D. The bottom shape is the same shape as the top shape, except that it has rotated 90 degrees clockwise.

17. A. The crosses have formed 3-of-a-kind (tic-tac-toe).

18. D. The shape group consists of: 2 gray circles, 1 dotted circle, and 1 circle with a black square inside.

Paper Folding, Practice Test 2

1. B	2. A	3. C	4. C	5. D	6. B
7. C	8. B	9. A	10. D	11. C	12. C
13. A	14. B	15. D	16. A		

Number Analogies, Practice Test 2

1. C. Subtract 2.

2. C. Add 6.

3. B. Double.

4. D. Half.

5. A. The second box has the same number of black/gray shapes as the first box.

6. B. The 6 objects (cupcakes/rabbits) are divided 3 and 3 in the second box.

7. B. The 5 objects (acorns/insects) are divided 2 and 3 in the second box.

8. A. Divide by 3.

Number Analogies, Practice Test 2, continued

9. C. The container goes from almost full to empty.

10. D. Half.

11. B. The number of gray sections in the shapes increases by 2.

12. D. Multiply by 3.

13. C. Double.

14. A. The number of black sections increases by 1.

Number Series, Practice Test 2

1. B. Every rod has 2 less beads.

2. A. The pattern is: 1-1-4-1-1-4.

3. D. The 2 rods that have beads are separated by a rod that has 0 beads: 0-1-1-0-2-2-0.

4. C. The pattern repeats: +1 bead, +2 beads, +1 bead, +2 beads.

5. A. The number of beads decreases in this pattern: subtract 2, subtract 1, subtract 2, subtract 1, etc.

6. D. The pattern repeats: 2-0-4, 2-0-4.

7. D. Each rod has 1 less bead than the previous rod.

8. C. The rods increase then decrease in this pattern: 1-3-5-6-5-3.

9. D. Every other rod (rods in the 1st, 3rd, and 5th place) has 2 beads removed. Then, every other rod (rods in the 2nd, 4th, and 6th place) has 1 bead added.

10. D. Every rod repeats once.

11. A. The pattern repeats: 4-3-2-1. After 4 beads will be 3 beads.

12. B. Every other rod (rods in the 1st, 3rd, and 5th place) has 1 bead removed. Then, every other rod (rods in the 2nd, 4th, and 6th place) has 1 bead.

13. C. Every other rod (rods in the 1st, 3rd, and 5th place) has 2 beads added. Then, every other rod (rods in the 2nd, 4th, and 6th place) has 2 beads added.

14. C. The pattern repeats: 3-4-2-1.

15. B. Every other rod (rods in the 1st, 3rd, and 5th place) has 1 bead added. Then, every other rod (rods in the 2nd, 4th, and 6th place) has 1 bead removed.

16. B. The pattern repeats: 2-4-1-3.

17. A. The pattern repeats: 0-0-6.

18. D. The pattern repeats: 3-1-4-0.

Number Puzzles - Trains, Practice Test 2

Train 1:
1. C.   5 + 1 = 6
2. A.   6 + 2 = 8
3. C.   5 + 5 = 10
4. D.   5 + 4 + 3 = 12
5. B.   4 + 7 + 5 = 16
6. C.   4 + 5 = 9
7. A.   1 + 6 + 6 = 13
8. B.   4 + 1 = 5
9. D.   4 + 1 + 5 = 10
10. B. 8
11. C. 4
12. B. 5

Train 2:
2 + 4 = 6
4 + 4 = 8
7 + 3 = 10
7 + 5 = 12
8 + 8 = 16
2 + 4 + 3 = 9
3 + 5 + 5 = 13
0 + 5 = 5
5 + 3 + 2 = 10
2 + 6 = 8
6 − 2 = 4
8 − 3 = 5

Number Puzzles - Equations, Practice Test 2

1. A.	2. C.	3. C.	4. D.	5. B.	6. C.
7. A.	8. D.	9. A.	10. B.	11. B.	12. C.
13. D.	14. C.	15. A.	16. D.		

Challenge Questions

1. C.	2. A.	3. D.	4. B.	5. D.	6. A.

Need more practice?

- Get **300+ <u>new</u> questions** per book!

- Check out more **Savant Test Prep**™ books on Amazon®.